D1196665

NOT A GAME

THE INCREDIBLE RISE AND UNTHINKABLE FALL OF ALLEN IVERSON

KENT BABB

ATRIA BOOKS
New York London Toronto Sydney New Delhi

ATRIA BOOKS
An Imprint of Simon & Schuster, Inc.
1230 Avenue of the Americas
New York, NY 10020

Copyright © 2015 by Kent Babb

All rights reserved, including the right to reproduce this book or portions thereof in any form whatsoever. For information, address Atria Books Subsidiary Rights Department, 1230 Avenue of the Americas, New York, NY 10020.

First Atria Books hardcover edition June 2015

ATRIA BOOKS and colophon are trademarks of Simon & Schuster, Inc.

For information about special discounts for bulk purchases, please contact Simon & Schuster Special Sales at 1-866-506-1949 or business@simonandschuster.com.

The Simon & Schuster Speakers Bureau can bring authors to your live event. For more information or to book an event, contact the Simon & Schuster Speakers Bureau at 1-866-248-3049 or visit our website at www.simonspeakers.com.

Interior design by Meryll Preposi

Manufactured in the United States of America

10 9 8 7 6 5 4 3 2 1

Library of Congress Cataloging-in-Publication Data is available.

ISBN 978-1-4767-3765-2
ISBN 978-1-4767-7898-3 (ebook)

For the young'uns who aren't supposed to make it

And, of course, for Whitney

PROLOGUE

Allen Iverson was thirsty the night before the test that would determine how often he saw his five children, but more than that he was restless.

His six-bedroom mansion in northwest Atlanta was a prison now: an empty, 7,800-square-foot jailhouse with one inmate, and Iverson could not stand the silence. It was late December 2012, and months earlier his estranged wife had moved out, renting an apartment in nearby Suwanee and taking the kids with her. She kept saying she wanted a divorce, but this was not the first time she had said that. Wasn't even the first time she had filed. Iverson told himself she would be back, because no matter how drunk or belligerent or violent he got, no matter the hour or condition he staggered home, Tawanna had always come back, filling these walls with life and sound—just the way Iverson liked it.

Now, though, it was silent. Uncomfortably so. Iverson had not played in the National Basketball Association in nearly three years, and his last game of any kind had been an exhibition in China two months earlier—a quick paycheck to keep the lights on and the creditors quiet. The house carried a second mortgage now, and in less than two months it would be foreclosed and later sold at auction. But for now, it was home, even if it no longer felt much like it. The previous day had been

Christmas, songs and voices filling the air, but now on this Wednesday evening, it was quiet again, and Iverson was stirring. Maybe he would go out for a while. He liked the bar at P.F. Chang's because it was familiar and close, five miles from his house, and there was valet parking and cold Corona.

One drink wouldn't hurt, would it? Just to take the edge off. Maybe two.

THE NEXT AFTERNOON, he walked toward the doctor's office near Hartsfield airport, assuming he had sobered up enough to beat the test. Iverson had more than a drink or two the night before, but it was four in the afternoon now, plenty of time for the alcohol to pass through his system. The problem was, Iverson had always underestimated his own metabolism, even before he was thirty-seven years old. His face was puffier now, his midsection and arms softer than they had been when he was named most valuable player of the NBA in 2001, when he led the Philadelphia 76ers to the NBA Finals and Iverson's determined play announced to the world that an athlete and man cannot be judged on appearance alone.

Back then, he could stay out until the wee hours, a friend helping him into his Atlantic City hotel room after a marathon night of gambling or Tawanna leading him up the stairs and into the bed, and still function well enough to make it to the arena in time to drop forty points, breaking some fool's ankles with his crossover dribble and then slashing toward the basket as he bounced off bodies almost twice his size. But he was pushing forty, and the years had been unkind. He drank more now, and the hangovers were less eager to loosen their grip. The booze made him edgy, more impatient and profane, and sometimes he would piss on the floor in front of the kids or, if Tawanna looked at him sideways, drag his high school sweetheart up the stairs by her hair or dig the toe of his Timberland into the top of her bare foot, grinding like he was putting out a cigarette. Sometimes he reminded her of his connections and how inexpensive it would be to have her killed; Iverson estimated her life was worth maybe $5,000.

She believed he was an alcoholic, and no manner of plea or threat would keep him home and sober. Tawanna spoke to his mother, Ann Iverson, begging her to talk sense into her son. She hounded Gary Moore, Iverson's childhood mentor and now his personal manager, asking him to say something because he might not listen to most people, Gary, but you know he'll listen to you. She cried and asked gently and, when that did not work, she showed her teeth and asked angrily, slinging a champagne bottle against the wall and threatening to take the kids and the rest of his money if he did not stop drinking and throwing their future away. He told her he could stop any time he wanted, but he would not be *told* to do anything; that was never the way to get Iverson to do anything. And so she did as she said, filing for divorce in 2010 before baiting Iverson into signing a lopsided postnuptial agreement before she moved back in one last time. She filed again in 2012 and hired a high-profile divorce attorney, telling him that she did not trust Iverson around their children. Not when they had been newborns, when he had blown off major events because he was too drunk—including the birth of his first son—and certainly not now that things had worsened. One of the court's first rulings was to order a substance abuse evaluation and gauge how severe the problem really was. The assessment by the substance abuse doctor, Michael Fishman, would go a long way in determining custody and visitation for the children.

The test was simple, and all Iverson had to do was not have alcohol in his system for one day. He had scheduled the appointment carefully, factoring in his hatred of mornings, and asked for a window late in the afternoon. Four o'clock it was, and now he entered the office and greeted the workers, two of whom could still smell alcohol on his breath from the night before. A while later, Fishman swabbed the inside of Iverson's mouth, and his saliva showed that even now, so many hours after that final drink, his blood-alcohol content was between .06 and .08, the latter number indicating that, according to Georgia law,

Iverson was still too drunk to even drive himself here. Then Iverson filled a cup with urine, and at 6 p.m., he still had enough booze in his system that the test showed his BAC was .05, suggesting to Fishman that on a most important day, with alcohol as the matter in question, Iverson had either gotten himself so shit-faced the night before that he was still drunk as afternoon turned to evening, or he had kept on drinking that afternoon.

Iverson's test results made Fishman's assessment easy, and when Iverson finally met with the case's guardian ad litem, a court-appointed investigator and mediator, at the Fulton County Superior Courthouse—he had blown off their first appointment and called at the last minute to reschedule the second—she noted that Iverson "smelled remarkably of alcohol." A different doctor had also smelled alcohol on Iverson's breath during yet another evaluation.

In February 2013, about six weeks after his substance abuse test, Dawn Smith, the guardian ad litem, took the witness stand. She had interviewed Iverson several times by now, and during her testimony she pointed out that a man whose penchant for dramatic plays at dramatic moments had made him one of America's most famous athletes was now wilting in his personal life—a time when, more than ever, he needed to be clutch. "People, in my experience, when you've got a guardian doing an investigation," Smith told the court, "they try to, you know, act their best, do their best job at parenting. So in the midst of this, he still wasn't able to step up despite the scrutiny."

DURING THE MONTHS that followed, friends and teammates from Iverson's life as a basketball icon tried to separate fact from fiction. How could he fall so far, so fast?

They read the reports in the newspapers and on gossip websites. Could Iverson really be *broke*, only a few years removed from a career that earned him more than $150 million in playing salary alone? Was it true that he and Tawanna, Iverson's high school sweetheart and that gentle soul they had come to know as the woman who had tamed the NBA's bad boy, really split up? Had his spending and gambling and drinking—especially the drinking—really gotten this far out of hand, that it seemed to now be on the verge of ruining Iverson's life? "Nobody can save Allen at this point except Allen," said Henry "Que" Gaskins, who in 1996 had been assigned by Reebok to help shepherd Iverson into adulthood and superstardom. "He's got to first admit that he needs to be saved. I don't even know that he feels like that's the case."

After the divorce was final, with the judge convinced enough of Iverson's instability that she granted Tawanna everything she had asked for, Iverson continued his desperate attempt to return to the NBA. He waited for the phone to ring day after day, assuming a franchise would come to its senses and bring back a former star who believed he still had something to offer. Iverson, for so long seen as an athlete who refused to accept his own limitations, was now nothing more than a sad and broken man unwilling to accept the truth—a truth many of those closest to Iverson had known and tried to ignore for years: Basketball had been the only thing holding Iverson's life together, and now basketball was gone. "God gave him this great gift," said Pat Croce, the former Sixers team president and the man who oversaw Iverson's selection as the NBA's top overall draft pick in 1996. "But you knew one day, He was going to take it away."

The days became weeks and then months, and the silence ate away at Iverson. The phone did not ring. Tawanna did not return. Friends did not come around. The divorce judge had decreed that Iverson avoid alcohol for a year, an attempt at returning a once-dazzling life to the rails. A life addicted to noise and stimulation had gone quiet, and so three or four nights a week he drove to Cumberland Mall in northwest Atlanta, parking on the shopping center's north side.

He walked past the fountain, through the revolving door at P.F. Chang's, and past the host's station. Along either side of the aisle were tables with families and laughing friends, and straight ahead was the crescent-shaped bar, where a pair of televisions were usually tuned to sports highlights. Comfort waited only a few strides away.

Sometimes diners recognized him, and Iverson occasionally smiled as a stranger snapped a photograph. Other times he wore a floppy hat and sunglasses, taking his normal seat and ordering the night's first Corona, his eyes finding highlights that no longer included him, tipping the clear glass bottle upward and trying like hell to hide from an unsympathetic world.

CHAPTER 1

STREET'S DISCIPLE

There he went, house to house, hoping he would find the little shit. It was Sunday evening, the sun setting in coastal Virginia, and Mike Bailey's patience was eroding by the second. He should have known better. No doubt about it now.

Nope, Coach, he's not here.

Sorry, Coach, you just missed him.

Bailey was the basketball coach at Bethel High School in Hampton, Virginia, a city on a peninsula that juts into the Atlantic Ocean, and after two decades he was familiar with the maze of teenage psychology. Now he was seething, played like a fool by a kid. *These* were the kinds of things that made him distrust Iverson, Bailey thought to himself, practicing what he would say when he finally found him. *This* was why the kid's word wasn't worth a damn.

Three days earlier, Iverson had asked to go home. Just one weekend, Coach. He wanted to see his mother and his friends. Bailey had gotten to know Iverson's delicate family situation, and he knew the kid had a chance to do something amazing. Two years earlier, the coach first watched the eighth-grade point guard on the junior varsity team. He was so fast, driving to the basket with such ease. The kid was a blur, and the other boys could not move fast enough to get in front of him or put a hand in his face, and *damn,* there he went again. Iverson would have a chance at a college scholarship, Bailey just knew it, a rare opportunity to lift himself and his family out of here. But there was so much work to be done, a total construction job, and the first time he had met Iverson they argued about school absences. Ten of them, the policy went, led to sports ineligibility. Bailey told Iverson he had missed seventy-six days of classes. Nah, Coach, the kid corrected proudly, it was only sixty-nine.

After Iverson's freshman year, Bailey had fallen for Iverson and his future enough that he and Janet, Bailey's wife, had gone all-in: paying for Iverson to attend summer school, allowing him to live with them, and walking the high-wire act of Iverson enrolled in a session in which one absence meant failure and sports ineligibility—a high-powered train coming off the tracks. Now, with Bailey kicking himself for allowing himself to become so enchanted, the kid was nowhere to be found.

He searched, one house and then the next, his eyes scanning the sidewalks and playgrounds and alleyways.

Yeah, Coach, we just saw him.

Bailey turned his car toward home, and the next morning he walked into the school and saw Iverson sitting in class. Later that day, he noticed Iverson walking alone.

"Come here," the coach demanded.

Iverson walked over, and Bailey pulled him into a dimly lit room, grabbing the kid by the throat.

"If you mess this thing up," Bailey said, "I'll kill you."

SHE MOVED INTO Hampton's Aberdeen district when she was still pregnant, fifteen years old, and a live wire. Look at her go, running through the neighborhood, which decades earlier had been part of resettlement legislation for some of the Virginia Peninsula's black residents, and now it was a kind of community within a community. The neighbors appreciated the quiet, but here she came, bursting from her grandmother's doorway yet again.

Her voice carried down the streets and through the windows, that round belly pulling up her basketball jersey. Ann Iverson kept running in the months after she celebrated her fifteenth birthday by going all the way with Allen Broughton, the boy she had met three years earlier in Hartford, Connecticut, the boy who seemed to never keep his distance from trouble, the boy Ann just could not resist. They had talked about it: first love, first kiss, first fuck—it all went together, didn't it, and so when she felt she was old enough, he would tap on her grandmother's back window at midnight of her birthday, and then they would go down to the basement.

Broughton had played basketball and earned the respect of men much older than him. Ann loved him, would fight for him, would do anything—and then he was just gone, not coming around anymore, even after the basketball trainer told Ann that her physical revealed she was two months pregnant. That would not stop her, though, from slamming doors and playing ball and bothering the neighbors. Then Ann's mama died, and her grandmother, Ethel Mitchell, moved the family to the Virginia coast, quieter environs, the old woman hoped, for a granddaughter known around the streets as "Juicy."

She went into labor in early June, and when her son came out she noticed the length of his arms. He was going to be a basketball player, she thought almost immediately, or at least that was what she would tell people she thought. She named him Allen after his daddy and her first love, but she would call him Bubba Chuck, combining two uncles' names.

Ann found stimulation even in Aberdeen, and other times she brought the party to Miss Ethel's house, the old woman trying to keep young Allen asleep or at least shielded from the ruckus in the other room. Bubba Chuck grew, and like his mother he liked to go fast, jumping on a ten-speed at four and five years old, roughhousing with his uncles Greg and Stevie in the backyard as Miss Ethel screamed for them to stop, for God's sake, y'all gonna break that boy in two!

"They would sling the hell out of his little ass up against the house or something," said Butch Harper, who lived next door. "He would take the hardest damn hit, and he'd pop right back up."

Ann worked evenings at the shipyard, taking on daytime jobs as a typist and a forklift driver. Miss Ethel was looking after the kids, Ann and her siblings included, and it was up to Ann to keep the lights on. She worked most times, and even when she was off, she was not home—another party to attend, even if the fun came back to Aberdeen or, later, their home in Newport News, a few miles northeast on the Peninsula. Often there was a man with her, Michael Freeman, who did mysterious things to make ends meet. Before they disappeared for the night or a few days, they put a ball in Bubba Chuck's hand and watched him go, and when he was nine Ann called Harper, her old neighbor, and begged him to waive the rule that kids had to live in Hampton to play in Hampton, where Harper oversaw the Deen Ball Sports league. Ann was so excited about it, telling the other mamas and daddies at work about how her son was so good, he was going to play in the NBA, just wait.

One of those people in earshot heard the commotion one day, the enthusiasm common but the details intriguing. Gary Moore was a coach for Harper, working with football players, and he liked what he was hearing. He wanted to take a look at this little dynamo, and so he put nine-year-old Bubba on the field with eleven- and twelve-year-olds, pushing the ball between his arms, and—*hot damn, look at him go!* "He was kicking so much ass, man, it was ridiculous," Harper would recall more than two decades later.

Moore vowed to Ann that he would do more than coach her son. He would look after him, protect him, shield him from the sharks that would forever circle him. He would see to it that he would be challenged and disciplined and sheltered. The way Moore looked at it, a kid with Bubba Chuck's gifts needed to be nurtured and strengthened, mentally and physically, built from the ground up like a house meant to stand for all time. My word, Moore told Ann, just picture what that finished product would look like, and she smiled and hooted and shook her head, thanking God for giving her this baby, this gift who would use those long arms to lift them all up and carry them toward a much better place.

THEY ROLLED THE balls out at the Aberdeen gym, and off Iverson went during warm-ups, toward the basket, draining long-range shots from the wing, flying past the kids trying to guard him. Then it was time for practice to start, and Bob Barefield announced they were going to spend the next hour working on drills. A few workouts to teach proper mechanics and footwork, and when Barefield started the lesson, there went Bubba Chuck walking out the door.

Basketball was fun, not work, and practice to him felt a hell of a lot like work. So no thanks, he told the coach, and if this was what it meant to play for the youth league, then they could keep the damn youth league. Barefield was stunned, but he tried to be patient as he monitored a kid who needed constant stimulation. Barefield talked Iverson into taking a leap of faith with him, and the kid obliged. But Iverson saw himself not only as an athlete but as a multitalented youngster with more than just his speed and jump shot to offer the world. He liked football better anyway, and besides, he was going to be an artist or a rapper. He met Rahsaan Langford, a kid from the east side of town. Everyone called him Ra. He could freestyle with the best of them, turning everyday thoughts and dusty old memories into a stream of rhymes, spitting them on stoops and street corners and playgrounds, the words lightning fast like Bubba Chuck was with the basketball. Maybe for the first time in Iverson's young life, he was jealous.

Ra was talented, the same as his new friend, and together they were going to make it out of Newport Bad Newz, they came to call it. Langford was quiet around strangers, but when he felt comfortable, he would brighten the room or the corner, keeping Iverson and the rest of their group laughing. And like Iverson, Langford and several other friends never wanted to go home. That was where Ann's parties were, where drinking and drug use packed the hours, and Iverson would develop a habit that would later come to haunt him: Rather than spend the nighttime hours sleeping, he would stay awake, finding fulfillment or entertainment in other ways. Sometimes Ann would ask Bubba Chuck to run an errand for the group, and off he would go, once knocking on the door of a drug house and walking in as a police surveillance unit watched from out front. One of the officers, a former athlete at Bethel, called up Dennis Kozlowski, the high school's football coach and athletic director, tipping him off that Iverson had entered a house filled with unsavory characters and had left with his hands full. The cops cut him a break, maybe the first time but hardly the last time an authority figure would look the other way, and Iverson walked home and delivered the package.

He spent his hours dreaming of a different kind of life and putting his imagination on paper—sometimes using whatever else was available when there was no paper within reach. Iverson once used the inside of his bedroom door as a canvas, sketching an image from above as Michael Jordan, his idol, glided through the air, the Chicago Bulls' star flying toward the basket and his jersey flapping like a flag in the wind. Other times he would grab a ball, the noise in the other rooms too much, and dribble it up the sidewalks. Occasionally there were other boys on the playground, even in the wee hours, and other nights he would stand there alone, taking shot after shot by himself.

Other times he and Ra and Eric "E" Jackson and Marlon Moore, the young men Iverson would later identify as his all-important "Day-one friends," would sit on a stoop or take a long walk. They were in it together, calling themselves "Cru Thik," born and raised on the hard streets of coastal Virginia, but by God they would not die here, young and unfulfilled and, worst of all, poor. They passed the hours and made a pact: If any of them ever made it big, whether it was through rap or sports or something else, the group would never dissolve.

If one made it out, then they all would.

• • •

IVERSON WAS IN ninth grade when Kozlowski's wide receivers coach entered his boss's office and closed the door. Iverson's school absences had already become a problem, basketball coach Bailey arguing with Iverson over the precise number of the dozens of times he had missed school. Now, even when he did make it to campus, he rarely arrived before eleven in the morning. Even early in the school year, he had missed the assistant coach's early morning history class nine times; one more, the coach told Kozlowski, and he would have no choice but to fail Iverson, making him ineligible to play for the Bruins. Hold on, Kozlowski told his assistant, he would get to the bottom of it.

He called Iverson into his office, getting quickly to the point: "Allen," the coach asked, "why the hell can't you get to school on time?"

The kid seemed to not even realize he had missed class so often, but he explained anyway. Ann and Freeman, the man she met at the shipyard and who had begun attracting attention for selling drugs, now had two younger daughters, Brandy and Iiesha, and after Ann moved out of Miss Ethel's house, there was often no one around to look after them. Kozlowski had heard things were occasionally bad at home; the lights occasionally shut off and, for a while, a broken pipe pushed so much raw sewage up through the floor that Iverson wore boots while moving from one room to the next. What his coaches had not realized was that Iverson making it to school at any hour was, many times, a small miracle. He collected enough pennies to call a taxi, then asked friends for a lift home to his house on Jordan Avenue, and other times he called a coach at four thirty in the morning and asked for a ride.

Even at age fifteen, he had grown used to waking up and being unable to find or awaken his mother, and if Brandy was to make it to school, it was up to him to get her there. But then if Iverson went to classes, who would watch Iiesha, who was born with a condition that afflicted her with seizures? Most mornings, Iverson saw Brandy onto the school bus and then sat with his baby sister until Ann came home, and only then would he wander to school himself.

Christ, Kozlowski thought, and depending on perspective this was either giving a young and talented kid a second chance because of unusual challenges or just another time Iverson was insulated from responsibility because of his skills on a football field and basketball court. Nevertheless, Kozlowski instructed one of Bethel's security workers, a former high-jumper on Kozlowski's track team, to take Kozlowski's car—the Buick Reliant wagon, the coach pointed out, with "KOZ" as the license plate—and each morning stop at Iverson's house, gathering the three children. He would then drop Brandy off at her school and bring Iverson and Iiesha to the high school, where the baby would spend the hours in the care of Bethel's home economics class.

Iverson felt at home when the games began, the fields and courts the one place no one worried about him, and sometimes spent nights with friends, an attempt to find peace after the sun went down. One of Iverson's mentors, a twenty-year-old former athlete named Tony Clark, allowed Iverson to stay with him some nights, imparting advice and wisdom into Iverson's young mind. But then Clark's girlfriend came over one night and stabbed Clark in the neck, Iverson running over and seeing his friend's blood running in the street. Iverson watched as another boy took a bullet as they sat together on a porch, and it was said that in one summer, eight of his friends were shot to death.

Many times Moore offered a spare room and a ride from here to there. Iverson came to trust Moore, who years earlier had played football for Kozlowski. He was already in his late thirties, older even than Ann Iverson, and Moore projected himself as wise and thoughtful, a fatherly aura that Iverson was immediately drawn to, and Moore was among those who believed greatness was in his protégé's destiny.

No matter the attempts at stability, Iverson moved around so often that he held precious the smallest reminders of comfort and peace. Before the family moved out of its house in Newport News, Iverson stared at the drawing he had done of Jordan, dreaming of someday controlling his own destiny, a gift that a professional athlete must surely take for granted. When they left the house, they gathered their meager belongings, packing them into trash bags and preparing for the next step—whatever it might look like. Iverson took a screwdriver to the hinge plate, pulling the door off its frame.

Iverson's biological father, Allen Broughton, was serving a prison term, the first of several—including one sentence in 1996 for stabbing an ex-girlfriend—and the first time Iverson met him, it was with guards watching. The boy asked his dad if there was any way he could help him get a new pair of sneakers, and Broughton told Iverson that there was no way, sending the boy home shattered. But Ann came up with an alternative plan: She used that month's rent money to buy her young son the shoes before a summer-league trip to Lawrence, Kansas, where one of the men who would stop to watch Iverson was a college coach named Larry Brown.

Ann maintained a relationship with Freeman, who attempted to be a father figure, but he also would spend most of the next two decades in prison, the investigations finally turning up enough evidence to convict him on drug charges. Iverson looked to Moore and his coaches as the stable men in his life, and when he and Bailey concluded their conversation about school absences, the basketball coach asked him a question whose answer was both revealing and heartbreaking, considering what Bailey had come to know about his young star: "What do you expect of me?" Bailey asked.

Iverson thought about it before answering: "Will you always be there for me?"

DURING SUMMERS, ANN Iverson trusted her son with Boo Williams, a former power forward at St. John's who now ran his own Amateur Athletic Union team. Alonzo Mourning had come and gone through Williams's system, moving on to Georgetown University and future stardom, and Iverson was his next project, a kid with so much talent and speed, and . . .

My God, Allen, do you ever *shut up?*

Fourteen hours. That was how long he talked, from Hampton to Memphis, teammate and future University of Maryland star Joe Smith going to sleep to pass the time in some way other than listening to Iverson's impressions and jokes and continual wisdom, but when he woke up, Iverson was still jabbering. He was going out to Tennessee, where the new arena was a damn pyramid—had they seen it?—and Iverson was going to help them christen that place. Watch how many points he scored, how easy it would be for him to get to the basket, how many shots in a row he would make, and anyway, did anybody want to bet? Just a buck or two, chump change, come on. Coaches learned early on that Iverson was an incentive-based organism: Ask him to do something, and he was just as likely to do it as tell you to go fuck yourself. But add five dollars to the equation or a pay-per-view movie in the hotel room or pizza instead of some bullshit boxed chicken, and now you had a damn machine, eager, ready to please.

He bet on free throws and bowling and late-night Monopoly marathons, Iverson always the banker to see to it nobody would steal, always the one with the fat stack of phony money when the night was finished. But he had won, goddammit, and that was what mattered. Could he not dunk at age thirteen, flying through the air and going above the rim on a regulation goal? "We don't play that YMCA shit," Harper said much later. Had Iverson not scored thirty points three games in a row at the AAU nationals in Winston-Salem, North Carolina—not just in each game but by halftime, propelling him to the top of the national recruiting rankings? "What he did will never be done," Williams would recall, "and I've been in this thirty-two years."

Iverson was going to show them in Memphis, too, he kept telling them, the teammates and coaches in that little van feeling trapped inside a cloud of Iverson's nonstop chatter. Damn, did the kid not sleep? Did his batteries never run low? Fuck nah, he replied, did Michael's? Did Mike's batteries ever run low? He hoped not, because he was ready to play Mike now, leave him in the dust.

Whatever, Williams told him. Michael Evans was a solid player:

Not just the best point guard in eastern Virginia but one of the best in America. Keep practicing, Allen, and maybe in a year or two you'll . . .

"I wasn't talking about no Michael Evans," Iverson crowed.

"Who are you talking about, then?"

"Shit, I'm talking about Michael *Jordan*!"

They rolled their eyes, and when they finally rolled into Memphis and that pyramid, Iverson and the Boo Williams under-sixteen team tore through the competition—well, most of it—and finished second. Iverson was named most valuable player, and that was great and all, but that meant it was time to go home: another fourteen hours of Iverson Radio, all the hits from today and yesterday, and commercials for tomorrow. That was some bullshit, he said early in the drive, talking about the second-place trophy, threatening to throw the damn thing out the window as they plowed down Interstate 40.

"Allen," somebody said, "will you shut up if we stop somewhere for dinner?"

He smiled, something in it for him now, and for a long time he did not say another word.

BAILEY TOOK HIS hand off Iverson's throat in that darkened back room, the kid's eyes finally returning to their normal size. Bailey came to understand his star player's challenges, or at least he tried to understand them, but he also made it clear he, Bailey, would not be played. More than that, he would not allow Iverson's questionable support system—and the destructive lessons and twisted sense of normalcy he had come to accept throughout his upbringing—to derail such a promising future.

Iverson saw toughness as strength, writing off those who took it easy on him as soft and a mark to take advantage of. The easier you took it on him, the harder he made life on you. So Bailey began taking inventory of all things Iverson, collecting intel from friendly teachers and monitoring Iverson's grades as they were posted. At the end of his freshman year, he took a D and would need to attend summer school. Iverson's mother, though, could not afford the tuition, and so Bailey made Iverson a deal: Live with Bailey and Janet, his wife, for those three weeks, sharpening his focus and completing his requirements, and the Baileys would pay for the summer session. Iverson liked an incentive, didn't he, so here it was, like it or not.

Iverson agreed, and the first four days had come and gone without incident. Then by Thursday evening, Iverson's mind began to wander. No matter the actions and intentions of those surrounding him, those who had known him and believed in him since the beginning would always be dear. And no one was more precious than Ann, no matter her own bad behavior, because she had always seen greatness in her son. Iverson wanted to spend the weekend at home, but Bailey balked at the idea.

"Allen," he had said, "we had a deal."

The kid smiled, though, showing a kind of charm that would later make him into an international icon and charismatic pitchman. Beneath the toughness was a sweetness inside, one that prevented those who cared deeply for him from ever writing him off, and Iverson kept chirping at his coach. He reminded Bailey that one of his coaching principles was trust—trusting teammates to do their jobs, developing on-court trust that assignments would be completed, trusting coaches to put players in the best possible positions.

"Why don't you trust *me*?" Iverson had asked.

The words ate at him, but Bailey held on, tired fingers gradually popping free of the ledge. Iverson was relentless. He caught his basketball coach walking around a corner. "Coach," the kid said. "Trust." He saw him in the kitchen and in hallways. "Trust," he said, again and again, and *fine,* Bailey said, agreeing to allow Iverson to spend the weekend with his family—but only if he was back by Sunday.

Then, of course, Sunday had come and gone, Iverson nowhere to be found and Bailey making his way through Hampton and having no luck. Then there he was, and Bailey snapped. "*I'll kill you,*" he said, reaching deep into Iverson's soul. For the next ten days, Iverson had perfect attendance at summer school. If Bailey spoke with Ann, she would align herself with the coach and not her son. No matter how she carried on, Ann rarely questioned the motives of those who made her son's future a priority. And she had taught her son pride: While Iverson lived with the Baileys, they noticed him rise early and ask to borrow an iron. He worked the shirt's creases and edges, draping it over his shoulders and turning to reveal a hole in the back. There was nothing he could do about the hole, he figured, but he refused to attend school with a wrinkled shirt. "Whatever he had," Mike Bailey recalled, "he valued tremendously."

Iverson and his coaches still clashed occasionally, a look into the future, and Bailey threw him off the varsity team three times before the storms passed and Bailey sent him back into the lineup. Kozlowski required that all players wear a suit on game day, and when he learned that Iverson owned no suit, Kozlowski spent five hundred dollars for his quarterback to be outfitted in a two-piece; by the next year, one of Ann's houseguests had stolen the suit from Iverson's closet, and Kozlowski bought him a replacement on the promise that Iverson would attend the Newport News *Daily Press*'s Athlete of the Year banquet on time. Iverson, with Moore as his chauffeur, arrived at seven fifteen for the six o'clock banquet.

The day before Virginia's Group AAA state championship football game during Iverson's junior year at Bethel, he organized something of a walkout. Kozlowski had called for a practice, and it was cold and snowy, and Iverson did not feel like practicing in such weather. Iverson, the Bruins' starting quarterback, approached Kozlowski. "Coach," he said, "everybody's sick. We shouldn't be out here."

It was a note Iverson would play many times throughout his NBA career, someone he cared about having come down with a mysterious and sudden illness. Then, a day or so later, it was gone and Iverson would return to practice, pulling on his green and gold. But this time Kozlowski swatted away his star player's excuse, moving forward with the walk-through, a half-speed tune-up scheduled to last an hour. *Punt team!* Kozlowski called, and Iverson took his place as the return man. The kick went up, and the coverage team ran toward him, positioning their feet to close down the avenues the quick Iverson usually tried to exploit. But as they approached Iverson, he just stood there. *One more time!* called Kozlowski, growing annoyed now. The punt went up, then downward, then into Iverson's arms, and he stood there again, refusing to return it. Kozlowski threatened to bench Iverson, going so far as to have the backup quarterback warm up and take a few snaps, but Iverson and Kozlowski both knew the old coach was not going to gamble away his chance to win a state championship to underscore a life lesson for his junior quarterback. In sports, the game results prevail, and years later, Kozlowski would show little regret for allowing Iverson to play, because on a wall near the bar in his home's trophy room was a plaque from the Bruins' 27–0 win against Lynchburg's E. C. Glass High School.

Iverson, naturally, scored one of Bethel's touchdowns on a punt return. When a local reporter pushed a microphone into his face afterward, Iverson tugged at his stocking cap and smiled. "I'm gonna go get one in basketball now," he said.

TAWANNA TURNER ASKED Kim Woodard if she could come over that night and meet the boy who played football with Kim's boyfriend, Tim Johnson. Was he the one on TV always running his mouth? Who did he think he was? Tawanna was hesitant to say it out loud, but she wanted to know.

In fact, she did not say much of anything out loud. Tawanna was quiet, and he was brash. She kept to herself, and he always seemed to have his crew close by. He was an athlete at Bethel High, and she was the manager for the girls' basketball team at Hampton's Kecoughtan High, fetching water and towels for the players, some of whom were Tawanna's friends. She was, as Iverson would later tease her for, a water girl. They could not have been more different. But they were both juniors. They were both sixteen. And opposites attract, don't they, and besides, here they were because they were friends with some of the same people, Kim and Tim, wasn't that funny?

Kecoughtan had a half day of school, and Kim set it all up. Tim asked Iverson to come over and meet the girl with the hoop earrings and the quiet way. What the hell, Iverson thought; beats going home for the night. They talked for a while, Iverson quiet now and Tawanna chattering, talking about how her daddy called her by her first two initials, "TD," like a touchdown, and insisting she had dated only one athlete before, and maybe she wanted to someday be a fashion designer or maybe an artist, leave this rat-hole town, and eventually Kim and Tim disappeared into the other room. Tawanna and Iverson talked for a little while longer, and then Iverson's hands started working, and then their pants were off, and anyway, it happened fast. When it was over, Iverson smiled at Tawanna, who smiled back. Would she come see him play sometime? Would she cheer for him even when Kecoughtan played Bethel? Could he call her his little water girl?

Iverson told Moore about her, the light-skinned girl from the other school. Moore listened as the puppy love unfolded, giving Iverson shit about it, but no, Gary, this was for real. Moore nodded and rolled his eyes, but then Iverson asked her to his junior prom, and when he stopped at Moore's house before picking her up, he was a wreck. Was his bow tie straight? How about these shoes, are they okay? How was his hair and his breath and his tuxedo, and no shit, was Moore sure these shoes worked? Moore put his fingers on the bow tie, adjusting it. He looked Iverson in the eyes, telling the kid that everything was working just fine. This, he told him, was a match made in heaven.

HIS BOYS SAT behind the bench at Bethel games, Langford and "E" and Marlon following him across town when the Bethel gymnasium could no longer accommodate the crowds. Kozlowski worked out an arrangement with Hampton University, which allowed the Bruins to play their home games at its 7,200-seat Convocation Center, though even before games against rival Hampton High, there were two thousand spectators turned away because entry would cause a fire hazard.

"Coach, we've got a problem," a police officer said to Kozlowski before a packed game, shortly before tip-off. Ann, in all her glory, and Iverson's two sisters were outside, raising hell because they could not get in. Kozlowski kicked three fans out so Ann and the girls could enter, and they soon took their place behind the Bruins' bench, too, the Bethel star's mother telling anyone within earshot that her baby was gonna get rich and buy her a red Jaguar one day. Iverson had emerged as a full-fledged star, named by the talent scout Bob Gibbons as the nation's top basketball prospect, sure to make his college choice among heavyweights Duke or Kentucky or Kansas or Maryland. But then again he loved football, too, and as a quarterback and defensive back, the recruiting analyst Tom Lemming suggested he and a New Orleans quarterback named Peyton Manning were the top two high school players in America.

The town spilled into the Convocation Center, most everyone trying to catch a glimpse of Virginia's newest favorite son. Moore, a Hampton University employee, pushed his way through the crowds, and Tawanna came to watch her new boyfriend, too—marveling then at how Iverson was more than just a talented player; he insisted on doing things his way. Iverson bickered with Bailey sometimes, usually if the coach tried to compel Iverson to pass the ball more often. "Coach, stop telling me how to play all the time!" Iverson shot toward Bailey during the game against Hampton High, and in exchange Bailey benched his star. The next game, Iverson refused to take a shot—nothing but passes. If Tony Rutland found him wide open near the wing, Iverson held the ball a moment and then passed it back. If he had a clear path through the lane, nope—he popped it to the outside, and the Bruins eventually trailed by twenty points. "Looking back," Bailey said, "probably today coaching somebody like Allen, I wouldn't say 'pass the ball.' "

In February 1992, Iverson and the Bruins were about to make good on Iverson's vow to win the Virginia basketball championship. Bailey, despite his occasional frustration, believed that Iverson had learned from his past mistakes; that the risk of him messing up his future was now mostly behind him. Nonetheless, the coach stayed on him, pushing Iverson and checking in on him. But now that Iverson was a junior, Bailey saw a talented youngster not just finding his way out but pushing through so many barriers that had been placed in front of him.

On a Thursday night, the evening before a game, Iverson was bored. Like usual, he did not feel like sleeping. A little before midnight he asked a few friends what they were in the mood for. One of them suggested they go bowling.

CHAPTER 2

THE WAY BACK

In February 2012, Gary Moore sent an email to Tawanna Iverson, the subject line's capital letters indicating its urgency: "THE BLUEPRINT FOR IVERSON RETURN." Moore's role as Iverson's manager, as much a paid friend and sounding board as anything, included making certain Iverson arrived at appointments on time and, years earlier, calling Larry Brown with an excuse when Iverson could not attend that morning's practice. This time, Moore had been instructed to sound the alarm, beginning Iverson's return to the NBA, where he was rich, famous, and coveted. That was where he belonged, not in the gymnasiums of Istanbul or the empty arenas of the NBA's Development League.

Moore had been honest with Iverson, out of shape and approaching age thirty-seven: It would not be easy. But he would try. In the email's body, he listed bullet points, and the first one stood out: "No more drinking!" He included a link to an article about the delicate strategy of finding an intervention leader, and a different email promised to Tawanna that he would get Iverson into Alcoholics Anonymous meetings, asking if she knew of any gatherings near their home in suburban Atlanta. Iverson had recently promised Tawanna that he would quit drinking, one of many agreed-upon ultimatums that Iverson eventually broke. The possibility of returning to the NBA and the adulation he had once known was further reason—an incentive he could not pass up.

Besides, Iverson needed the money. He still projected an image of wealth, spending thousands in a single night and traveling with an entourage, but the reality was far from it. Eleven months before Moore sent the email outlining Iverson's return path to the league, Iverson's five-bedroom, lakefront mansion in a Denver suburb had sunk into foreclosure—another cold reality about his financial situation.

Moore began calling his contacts in the NBA—coaches, scouts, executives, players—asking for an opportunity. He reached out to Tim Grover, the personal basketball coach who had prepared Michael Jordan for his return to basketball after a brief retirement to play baseball in 1993, and Grover had worked with stars like Kobe Bryant, Dwyane Wade, and Gilbert Arenas. Grover had reached out to Iverson months earlier but heard nothing; as usual, Iverson and his inner circle believed they were better equipped to handle his career. But now he was desperate, and Moore made the call—albeit with unusual demands.

Grover would need to travel from his headquarters in suburban Chicago to work with Iverson, Moore told him, whether that was in Atlanta or near Hampton. Grover had reservations about the arrangement: working with a player who had a strong reputation of avoiding or skipping workouts—to say nothing about what he had read about Iverson's financial and emotional state. But he agreed to take on the project, dropping a sample workout in the mail, and asked Iverson to begin working, a kind of test to measure his coachability. The real work would begin in a few weeks.

"My proposal," Grover said later, "was to come down there for a couple weeks, make an assessment, see where he's at, see how far we could push him, and be realistic about it and say: 'Hey, is this possible?' "

Grover spoke briefly with Iverson, asking him about his goals. He wanted to play again in the NBA, Iverson told the coach, and that was the long and short of it. "Saying all the right things," Grover said. The coach made no guarantees, underscoring the many factors that play into an NBA comeback, especially one in which the player is aging and likely out of shape. Nevertheless, he designed a custom workout plan to strengthen Iverson's legs and improve his conditioning. Sure enough, Iverson never bothered with the initial conditioning test or Grover's program, and a nondescript video of Iverson was as close as Grover actually got to his would-be pupil. A few weeks after agreeing to oversee Iverson's comeback attempt, Grover called Moore once again. "Allen needs somebody that, obviously, one, that he respects and somebody who can really dedicate the time," Grover would recall. "This isn't a one-hour, six-day-a-week process. This is literally—it's like going back into training camp, two-a-days and changing everything."

Anyway, Grover told Moore, the job of rebuilding Allen Iverson was just too big. He wished Moore luck, but he was out.

MOORE KEPT TRYING, hounding the Sixers and selling the idea that Iverson was a changed man. He was no longer interested in being the team's centerpiece; he was at a point in his life that he would mentor the team's youngsters. Secretly, Moore also lobbied the franchise for other roles for Iverson: something in the front office or as a kind of ambassador from the team to its fans. Philadelphia had traded Iverson in December 2006, ending more than a decade with the Sixers and leaving a sour taste in the organization's mouth. He had been a pain in the team's ass too often, seen at the time as a bad influence on the team's young players, and was late for important functions one time too many. But, at Moore's urging in late 2009, the Sixers were willing to bring Iverson back to Philadelphia. Now, after what had become yet another shit show a few months after his return, Moore had talked them into one last chance.

The team invited Iverson to the Wells Fargo Center in 2012 for a Sixers playoff game, handing him a replica jersey with guard Lou Williams's name stamped on the back. Someone put a basketball in his hands, and his job on this May evening was to walk the ball to referee Joey Crawford, the ceremonial start of the game. He waved to Sixers fans and then retreated to a luxury box, where he lobbied on national television for a roster spot somewhere—anywhere—in the NBA. "I want to play basketball so bad," he said, refusing to so much as utter the word *retire* and insisting that he did not believe his NBA career was finished.

Less than a year later, the Sixers held a bobblehead night for Iverson, distributing thousands of the dolls—basketball in the figure's hands, white sleeve on his right elbow, cornrows and a headband on its oversized head—as fans passed through the turnstiles. This was another opportunity for Iverson to prove himself reliable, a word that rarely applied to him throughout his career. Moore had arranged it, and he impressed upon Iverson that he needed to be on his best behavior. But Iverson did not see it that way. As always, he was going to be himself, and that sometimes meant arriving at his destination on his own schedule. In his own mind, he was still the star of the show, and the show would not start without him.

On this evening in late March, the game started at eight o'clock. About an hour before a ceremony, in which flames would shoot from canisters and a video would be aired of Iverson's most memorable highlights, employees began whispering to each other that Iverson might have missed his flight to Philadelphia. As fans made their way into the arena, tension had gripped the staff. Adam Aron, the Sixers' chief executive, smiled and made assurances that Iverson would be there. A woman scribbled in a rear corridor, passing the time nervously as Aaron McKie, a former Sixers player and one of Iverson's closest friends, walked past. What had she heard? McKie asked her, and the woman glanced up. Not much, she said, only that he is supposedly on his way. McKie knew the stories well, and he also knew that he was probably among the only ones not worried. "He's one of those guys, man, where you're wondering: 'Where is he?'" McKie said later. "And a cloud of smoke appears, and he'll come running out.

"That's the unfortunate part about that baggage that you get. It's just, that cloud follows you. Wherever he is, whatever he's doing, he's always going to be associated with that. If he has an appearance somewhere, there's always going to be anxiety behind it: Is he really going to show up? Is he going to show up on time?"

A few minutes before eight, a black SUV pulled into the players' parking lot, idling near an entrance. At seven fifty-nine, the doors opened, and Iverson stepped out of the passenger seat, shouting profanity and wrapping his arms around Aron before being whisked through a tunnel and onto the floor, Iverson walking in, to the Sixers' relief and annoyance, with only a few seconds to spare.

THE SIXERS OFFERED Iverson no contract and no job. In an interview with Comcast SportsNet reporter Dei Lynam, a friendly face in the occasionally unfriendly Philadelphia media, she asked what lay next. "I put it in God's hands," Iverson told her, and his voice cracked as he said it. "I've accomplished a lot in the NBA, and if the road ends here, then it does. You know what I mean? And I'm not bitter about it. I don't feel no type of way. I just understand that He helped me accomplish a lot of things in the NBA. I've done so many things that people thought that I couldn't do, and the NBA has been great to me.

"But at some point, it comes to an end. And regardless of however it comes—regardless if it's retirement, injury, or whatever—at some point, it comes to an end."

He paused for a moment, smiling. "Now, if I get a chance to play again," he said, "I would love the opportunity."

Iverson refused to give up on the possibility of returning to the NBA, returning peace and meaning to his life. Moore kept making calls, sending emails, working his connections. People around Iverson told him the ride was over, Bubba, time to move on. He would not hear of it, instructing Moore to keep trying. He turned down a contract to play for the Dallas Mavericks' Development League team, posting on Twitter that "it is not the route for me." As much as Iverson needed the money, he apparently felt his pride was more valuable. It did not hurt that Iverson was not alone in still seeing himself as a star: Moore, whose voice resonated loudest in Iverson's ears, did, too, urging his man to keep waiting for the right deal and the perfect situation.

Former teammates read the news reports, and Iverson's denial had a corrosive effect on the respect they once had for him. Determination was one thing, an Iverson hallmark, but many now believed he was relentlessly chasing a part of his life that was gone. "He just needs to accept it," former Sixers teammate Roshown McLeod said in spring 2013. "Now the league is all about potential, and his potential has passed, in the sense of he's not going to get any taller, he's not going to get any more athletic. It's actually going to deteriorate. That's an acceptance that he has to understand: His day has passed."

Others tried to understand Iverson's point of view, an attempt at convincing themselves why he continued reaching to scratch a distant itch. "Finding his last chapter of his career never happened," said George Karl, who coached Iverson with the Denver Nuggets. "I don't know whose fault that was. Some of it was probably his fault, but some of it probably was how the game reacted to him."

The wait continued, and Iverson's resolve began breaking down. When his eldest son was enrolled as a teenager in a private school in Pennsylvania, families were invited to several lectures and groups. Iverson skipped most of the sessions, and of those he attended, he usually said nothing, spacing out and allowing the other parents to ask questions and feed the conversation. Then during one of the final sessions, a group discussion with about ten other families, the speaker talked about success and what successful people like Donald Trump had done to achieve their goals. The words smacked

Iverson, who had once been one of those success stories but now felt as if part of his identity had been stripped away. To the surprise of everyone in the group, Tawanna would later testify, he spoke up: "What are you supposed to do when, you know, they don't want you anymore?"

CHAPTER 3

LANES NINE AND TEN

The phone rang after midnight on February 14, 1993, jarring Dennis Kozlowski from his sleep. A former athlete at Bethel High was standing at a phone in the police station, another of Kozlowski's informants, calling his old track and football coach.

Something had happened, Kozlowski heard the young man say as the groggy coach tried to shake the cobwebs from his mind. Something about a brawl at Circle Lanes, a bowling alley near the highway, and a chair thrown and an injury to a young woman's face. A man suffered a broken arm, a woman fractured a thumb; the scene was so violent that kids were hiding amid the bowling pins. Kozlowski heard his former player say something about white and black and that this could be only the beginning.

Then he heard the caller say something about the three young men in police custody, all of them black, including one they all know. "Coach," Kozlowski heard clearly. "They're going after Iverson."

ON THE PENINSULA, where the Chesapeake Bay meets the James River, they tell stories. They travel through the generations, and as the decades and centuries pass, cultures are born and reshaped. Opinions are formed, and biases and belief systems take hold.

The oldest of those stories is rooted in 1619, less than a decade after the town of Hampton was settled. A Dutch pirate ship called the *White Lion* sailed into the Gulf of Mexico and, after raiding a Portuguese slave ship, departed with more than thirty Angolan men and women. Now with their new cargo, the *White Lion* would return to an outpost on a horn of land where the river met the sea, in a British colony that would eventually be known as Virginia.

The ship docked at Point Comfort, and the Angolans disembarked onto the sand, their toes sinking into the soft grains—the first steps by Africans onto this new land and the birth of American slavery. Two of those passengers had been given new names, forced to abandon their own pasts, and the white men who instructed them up the hill and away from the waves called them Antonio and Isabella. When they were assigned to work on the plantation of Point Comfort's commander, William Tucker, they took on his last name.

Centuries later, one of Antonio and Isabella's direct descendants, a teacher named William Harper, stood in a classroom at Hampton's Bethel High and sometimes told stories like this one—and how certain historical facts began pulling a slingshot of racial tension that grew tighter as time passed.

The very soil Harper's students walked on so carelessly had occasionally been a battleground. Long after the Tuckers had children and grandchildren, Virginia was a slave state and a states' rights stronghold, becoming one of the leaders in southern defiance before the Civil War. White men in nearby Newport News lynched a black local in 1900, and though desegregation in the late 1960s had been intended to bring on equality, it led to the closures of black schools and a threatened way of life in African-American neighborhoods like Aberdeen. The bands of the slingshot had grown so tight that they were tense and cracking, ready to snap at any time.

As Harper taught, a teenage student named Allen Iverson, a basketball star with little interest in the stories or his teacher's lessons, sat in the rear of the class. He drew sometimes or daydreamed—whatever it took to drown the sound of the stories that had absolutely nothing to do with him.

BY EARLY AFTERNOON on Valentine's Day, rumors were swirling about what had happened the night before at Circle Lanes. Some said Iverson had initiated an argument with a table of young white men, and others were saying Iverson threw a chair that slashed Barbara Steele's face. Some of the opinions were following racial lines: African Americans believed Iverson was a target, arrested—along with three other young black men—only because he was recognizable. Many whites thought the hothead from Aberdeen, who talked and played with anger and rebelliousness—his televised vow to "go get" a state championship in basketball had ruffled feathers in the white community—had finally lost control.

But Kozlowski had a way of pulling honesty out of Iverson, and he wanted to hear his quarterback's side. In towns like Hampton, the football coach is also the area's best detective; former players feel loyal to the coach who trained and played and started them, and many times, the most valuable currency is information.

About a year earlier, the friend in the Newport News Police Department had called Kozlowski with the information about Iverson entering the known drug house and leaving with a package. The coach called Iverson into his office a day later, grilling the kid about why he went into a house like that and whether he was using drugs. Stunned by how much his coach knew, the boy confessed to leaving the house with his hands full.

"Did you do the drugs?" Kozlowski asked Iverson, and they stared at each other for a long time before the kid cracked.

"Coach, I don't do drugs," Kozlowski recalled Iverson telling him. "But my mother . . ."

Iverson told him that, on instructions from Ann, he had asked several friends to drive him to Newport News to bring back a taste of whatever his mother had wanted. What was he supposed to do?

"But Allen," the coach said, "you don't understand. The dream ends if you get caught."

Kozlowski was among the first shepherds of Iverson's future, navigating him through trouble time and again. He bought Iverson's suits and covered his tracks, playing peacemaker between Iverson and Mike Bailey, Bethel's basketball coach. One morning Kozlowski arrived to find two basketball players waiting for him, babbling something about how Bailey had thrown Iverson off the team—it wasn't the first time—because Iverson refused to execute Bailey's game plan. Bailey had benched his best player, who wanted to improvise and play as he had on playgrounds and in AAU tournaments, and in front of God and everybody, Iverson screamed back at his coach. Kozlowski again called Iverson to the athletic department, extracting the truth and later piling into the familiar Reliant wagon so the kid could apologize to Bailey in person.

This time was different, though; that stark possibility Kozlowski had dreaded was now really happening. Hours after he was released from police custody, Iverson again entered Kozlowski's office and closed the door. Just the two of them, Allen, same as always, and just like always, the truth is free and a lie will cost you.

Iverson detailed his version with the old coach. He and a friend, C. J. Ruffin, were hanging near the counter after bowling for a while with a group on lanes nine and ten. Iverson told Kozlowski that he heard a young white man, Steven Forrest, refer to him as a nigger; Iverson reacted, cursing at Forrest and getting in his face. But then, Iverson told his coach, as others were joining in, turning the confrontation into a brawl, Ruffin wrapped his arms around Iverson and hauled him outside to remove him from the situation. In a blur of people and lost tempers and thrown furniture, participants and onlookers identified Iverson and three other athletes: Melvin Stephens, Samuel Wynn, and Michael Simmons.

Iverson never broke eye contact or stammered, Kozlowski would remember for many years, and for some reason deep in his bones, one he wouldn't be able to explain even two decades later, the coach decided to believe him. "Well, look," Kozlowski said, "this is going to be a battle."

ANOTHER OF THE stories was passed down reluctantly, its teller biting hard on his pipe as the words pushed through and the man's children listened. Slavery had spread throughout the South and eventually split the nation, leading to the bloodiest war in American history. When tensions were highest and Union soldiers were passing through Richmond, Virginia, in 1865 a slave named James Wilder spent a night hiding in a grain silo, the idea of suffocation more appealing than what he feared would be done to him if he were caught.

Wilder was, like all American slaves, eventually freed. While he had been still legally considered a piece of property, Wilder had married a woman named Agnes, who taught her children—the couple would eventually have fourteen kids—and others on the plantation how to read. After the war, James built a house for his family, and one of the couple's children would become a doctor. Another son, Robert, who had been born free, started his own family, usually keeping secrets about what his parents had seen—but, when his ten children begged for stories about the hell their grandparents had endured, he indulged them, chewing his pipe as he shared the details.

The youngest of Robert's sons, Douglas, followed the tales and came to believe that if the son of a slave could become a doctor, then all manner of things could be possible. His mother, Beulah, made him learn a new word each day, pointing to the pages in her book of crossword puzzles and filling him with confidence. "You can do it all," she told him in the 1940s, in a full household in Richmond's Church Hill neighborhood.

Douglas kept learning words and reading, eventually discovering Aristotle and Ralph Waldo Emerson and Friedrich Nietzsche. His mother wanted him to become a minister, and so she pushed him to learn the art of public speaking. But he wanted to be a dentist. He left Church Hill to study chemistry at Virginia Union University, a black school during the days of segregation, and he later won a Bronze Star in the Korean War. He read about the *Brown v. Board of Education* case in Topeka, Kansas, a decision that marked the beginning of desegregation, inspiring Wilder to study law. He enrolled at Howard University in Washington, D.C., because the University of Virginia's law school would not admit him because of his skin color. He built a thriving law practice in Richmond, only miles from where his grandfather had once worn shackles and occasionally sneaked to a neighboring plantation to visit his wife and eldest three children, who were confined there. Then in 1969, L. Douglas Wilder won a seat in the Virginia state senate, and sixteen years later he became Virginia's lieutenant governor.

Wilder lived a life unconcerned with limits or tradition, because that was the way he had been taught. In January 1990, he made good on his hopeful mother's encouragement, standing with his hand on a Bible outside the Virginia state house, surrounded by a standing-room-only audience as he became the nation's first black governor. "From Capitol Hill to Church Hill," Wilder told the *Washington Post* a few months before the election, "it's a short distance to walk—but a mighty, mighty mountain to climb."

Three years into Wilder's term, his chief legal counsel, William "Mac" McFarlane, entered the governor's office. Each day they discussed the issues facing Virginia, some more pressing than others, and on this February day McFarlane had an urgent matter for the governor to consider. Three young men, all of them black, had been arrested in Hampton, and almost immediately a racial wedge not seen since those days of desegregation had begun pushing its way into the town. That slingshot, stretched taut for centuries now, had snapped.

Wilder leaned back in his chair and, as he had done so many years earlier, listened as the story unfolded.

• • •

HE WORE A double-breasted, light gray suit the day he stood in the courthouse, speaking softly and begging for forgiveness. "I did feel bad about what happened to the people in the bowling alley," Iverson said, seven months after the brawl. "I don't want that to happen to nobody."

In July 1993, Iverson, Samuel Wynn, and Michael Simmons appeared in Circuit Court Judge Nelson T. Overton's courtroom, listening as the one-word verdict bounced off the walls: *Guilty*, each of them, on three felony counts of maiming by mob. Melvin Stephens had previously been found guilty of assault and battery, a misdemeanor.

Iverson had testified that Forrest had called him the racial slur and that one of Forrest's friends hit Iverson with a chair; he then testified that, as he had told Kozlowski, he was pulled out of the bowling alley and into the parking lot. But Forrest, along with several other witnesses, described a different scene: Forrest said Iverson had been unprovoked when Iverson began swearing at him, shortly before one of Iverson's friends hit one of Forrest's friends with a chair. A bowling alley employee backed up Forrest's testimony, and Barbara Steele, who suffered a lacerated scalp when the thrown chair hit her, described Iverson striking one of her friends in the face, then turning toward Steele with a smirk.

Guilty, the judge said, that heavyset word piercing the air, gasps following a second later. Overton denied bond, saying later that he was concerned Iverson would skip future hearings. During the trial, prosecutor Colleen Killilea painted Iverson as a pampered, entitled athlete who had been conditioned to value sports more than real life. Just look, she said, at the 1.8 grade-point average during the first half of his junior year at Bethel High, compared with the 209 trophies and 62 plaques that mostly furnished his family's single-story, brick house in southern Hampton. Consider, she told the court, the favors Iverson's coaches had done for him—favors rarely afforded to other, lower-profile students. And, she added, the night Iverson had turned himself in to police for his role in the bowling alley incident he had been so shaken up, clearly, that he scored forty-two points a few hours later in a Bethel High basketball game.

Just look, she argued, at his history: A year earlier, Iverson had been convicted of reckless driving and driving without a license, then rearrested a second time for again driving without a license. He didn't bother showing up for his court appearance, and when he was sentenced to forty hours of community service at Hampton General Hospital, he completed it six months late. Killilea went on, describing the things that society holds in higher regard than civility and decorum: Nike paid for two round-trip airline tickets for Iverson to attend an All-American festival in Indianapolis, sent him to Virginia to attend his bowling alley trial, then sent him back to Indianapolis to showcase his otherworldly skills—giving the impression that a life-altering incident for so many was somehow less important than basketball.

The young men were convicted, and Hampton reacted. The city's African-American population largely believed Iverson had been merely an example, and about a hundred members of Hampton's black community raised money for a possible appeal. A newly formed activist group called SWIS—an acronym of the four defendants' initials—argued that the four youngsters were being railroaded, proof the Old South and its inequality were still alive and well.

Many whites hummed with satisfaction, believing the cocky youngster got what was coming to him and would finally have to accept life's realities after being shielded from them for so long. "People who normally speak to each other didn't speak," said Butch Harper, Ann Iverson's former neighbor and one of Iverson's youth coaches, "because of this little skinny-legged kid who was being carried around this city by the same people who later dropped him and stepped on him. That's how this city is: up one day and down the next."

In September 1993, Iverson made his way up a narrow staircase and walked back into Overton's courtroom. Protesters stood outside, chanting "No justice, no peace," and other inmates at Hampton's city jail shouted toward the demonstrators through windows: "Help us, too!" Inside, Ann Iverson held her daughters' hands and hoped for leniency for her only son—probation, perhaps. Iverson spoke his piece, the kind of apology he would become so adept at later, and then Overton delivered his sentence.

Five years, he said this time, a dagger that would send Iverson away until he was in his early twenties, effectively killing his chances of playing college basketball and realizing a dream shared by so many within Iverson's inner circle—whether they were supporters or enablers or both. In this moment, any dream of reaching the NBA and curbing the cycle of poverty in his family was locked in a guillotine, the blade dropping with Overton's words. Iverson stood there for a long time, saying nothing, before shackles were placed on his wrists and ankles, and then he was loaded into a van to begin his life's next, unexpected chapter.

Soon after, around two hundred supporters marched arm in arm in rows of four and five, starting at Queen Street Baptist Church and stopping at the courthouse in Hampton, singing "We Shall Overcome." They called the courthouse, the things it had seen and validated, a symbol of racial injustice. Several dozen attended a different rally organized by the Nation of Islam. Others had different ideas. Harper, the youth coach, took a call shortly after the sentencing, from a youngster who had grown up with Iverson. The young man said there was a group of them. The time had come for bold measures. They were heading out soon, the teenager told Harper, going to burn down the mayor's house.

IVERSON DISAPPEARED FIRST inside the Hampton City Jail, a three-story brick building whose windows looked onto a graveyard. After that he would begin his sentence at the Newport News City Farm, where he would dress in white and work in the bakery. "After all I've been through," Iverson said in a jailhouse interview with Tom Brokaw, "I know I'm an adult now." Supporters nodded, believing Iverson truly had grown up. Critics shook it off, believing the kid would never mature because he existed in an environment that would never force him to.

Regardless, a year earlier Iverson had been an impossible-to-miss talent, destined for nothing but stardom. Now, as he passed the time in this 190-inmate, minimum-security facility, others were wondering how this had gone so wrong—and what now lay ahead.

Kozlowski, the football coach and athletic director at Bethel, regretted that he had not been more forceful with Iverson during their meeting in Kozlowski's office the day after the brawl. He had asked Iverson if he wanted Gary Moore or himself to find an attorney. Iverson went with Moore, who selected his Hampton University coworker Herbert Kelly to represent Iverson. Kelly had once been a prominent defense attorney, but he was now seventy-three years old and had not tried a case in years. Kozlowski would spend the next two decades wrestling with his own remorse. "I think there would have been a totally different outcome of that whole scenario," he said, "had Allen said: 'Coach Koz, let me talk to *your* attorney.' "

Others suspected that Overton had his mind made up before the trial began that he would make an example of the youngsters involved in the brawl, and some even went so far as to suggest a conspiracy was afoot: that, after Iverson and Bethel had humiliated Newport News High, rival school officials, in an effort to make Iverson ineligible to play sports, had conspired to light the fuse on the incident. "The ones that had power that could bring some havoc on him, used that," said Bill Tose, a former childhood mentor of Iverson.

No matter how it happened, this was Iverson's updated reality: Kentucky stopped recruiting him, and Duke and most other top-tier programs backed away, too. Maryland, which for a long time was Iverson's dream school because his friend and former summer league teammate Joe Smith had signed to play for the Terrapins, expressed reluctance to be involved in any Iverson-related drama. "You have to look at how your program will be judged," Maryland coach Gary Williams told *USA Today* at the time. Moore would say later that Hampton University became Iverson's most realistic stop, assuming he was released in fewer than five years, and Iverson pondered completing his college-eligibility requirements at a prep school in Maine. His mother, Ann, racked her brain for options, asking friends if they thought it was worth driving to Washington, D.C., to pour her heart out to John Thompson, the legendary coach at Georgetown University and a man who had shifted so many wayward lives back on course.

Iverson's closest friends, those he had once promised to take with him if basketball pulled him out of the Peninsula's wastelands, drove to Newport News occasionally, offering support by standing vigil outside the prison fences. Their boy was at the city farm, and although locks separated them, they were here, too. At nights they kept attending Bethel High games, taking his uniform with them and sometimes draping it over a seat on the bench.

While inside, Iverson said and did all the right things, developing a relationship with Billy Payne, the warden of the prison farm, and doing as he was told in silence even when a white prison guard called him a nigger, an acquaintance would later say, instructing Iverson to sit the fuck down and shut the fuck up. It was an experience Iverson would rarely share with even those closest to him but one that would shape his attitude moving forward, particularly toward those who barked orders without bothering to explain their logic.

Otherwise, Iverson did what most prison inmates do: He waited, passing the time as best he could. He occupied his mind by writing letters, along with his attorneys: to Judge Overton, asking for the circuit to release the case to the state and reminding Overton of, attorney Tom Shuttleworth said, several procedural errors; to lawmakers, asking for them to take a closer look at Iverson's sentence; and to Governor Wilder, asking for compassion. As for Iverson's body, he worked his shift in the bakery and, for a short time each day, dribbled on the blacktop in the prison yard, shooting hoops alone, refusing to look toward the friends who had gathered on the other side of the fence.

WILDER LIKED TO sleep on decisions he believed would be controversial, such as intervening or not when a Virginia convict was entering his final hours on death row. Other times he was resolute, making his mind up quickly—even without much direction from his small, tight-knit cabinet inside the state capitol. "He would sometimes plow ahead," McFarlane, the governor's legal counsel, recalled, "and scare the hell out of you."

Wilder had honed his process years earlier, listening to a collection of facts, distilling them into a singular message, and then acting. It had taken him from poverty to providence, just as his mother predicted, all the way into the governor's mansion. Usually, Wilder and McFarlane met in the mornings, speaking about issues affecting Virginia and deciding the smartest, most prudent action. Wilder had received the letters from the Newport News City Farm, going on to personally research the facts of a complicated case. A city had torn itself apart through fears of racism and a case whose ambiguity had satisfied neither side. Always a student of history, Wilder could not help noticing that Iverson and his two codefendants had been convicted of maiming by mob, a law originally added to Virginia's books to protect the state's blacks from lynchings, usually at the hands of angry whites.

This time when McFarlane brought up the topic in December 1993, Wilder was well versed and had come to a decision. He would be leaving office in less than a month, and in one of his final acts as governor, he planned to right something he saw as wrong—providing a different ending to a story he predicted that Virginians, with so many dusty and transcendent stories already in the collection, would tell for years. Four months after Iverson entered the Newport News City Farm, Wilder granted him clemency, placing him on extended furlough on the condition he complete his high school equivalency, attend counseling, and not play organized sports until the following August, when he would be paroled. About two weeks later, Simmons and Wynn also were freed under similar conditions.

"The only thing I can tell you," McFarlane would recall much later, "is that the decision was made on what we thought was right. That's just flat-out it: what was right."

Not everyone agreed that Wilder's decision was appropriate; Killilea, the Hampton prosecutor, publicly wondered if Iverson's release had been yet another favor because of his basketball ability, and others whispered that a city and its social and judicial structures were broken—the wounds of a divisive summer still open and raw. Years later, Barefield said, many white residents resented Iverson's release and the defiant behavior that would come to define him, a continuing story like the old ones that still make their way through this region. "A lot of them people still haven't forgotten that," Barefield said more than two decades after the melee at Circle Lanes. "I work with guys on the job. They still hard on him. They're still hard on him now."

In late December 1993, Shuttleworth took a call and immediately drove to the prison farm, and when the door swung open, there stood a smiling Iverson. He had worn a suit on his way into jail, but upon his exit he wore green and gold sweats, Bethel's colors. Shuttleworth drove him down familiar streets, and Iverson waved to those who had waited for and supported him.

After the brief reunion, Iverson contacted Kozlowski to ask for a favor. He was no longer behind a locked door, but he didn't yet feel fully free. And so, for the first time but not the last, his old coach left his home in Poquoson, driving the fifteen minutes south and west, parking the Reliant in its usual space. Bethel High's new principal had banned Iverson from returning to school property, and Bailey had been fired for unclear reasons, though he would come to believe it was a result of continuing to publicly support Iverson after school officials instructed him to stay quiet. "Right or wrong," Bailey told the Newport News *Daily Press* in 1999, "I stood behind Allen."

Kozlowski, under similar orders, operated in secret. He found the key to the basketball gym anyway, opening it for Iverson, and for the next three hours the kid was a basketball player—nothing more or less—once again.

CHAPTER 4

BROKE

He whispered into the telephone in 2011, not knowing Tawanna was listening from around the corner. Iverson was asking Samuel Dalembert, a friend and former Sixers teammate, for money. Just a little help to get him through a tough time, Iverson told his friend, until his next signing bonus.

Iverson had for years accumulated wealth that, as a boy in Hampton, he could only dream of. Gone were the days of wearing boots to cross the sewage-soaked floor and bumming rides from coaches to practices. Distant were the memories of a kid whose mother paid the light bill and bought her only son clothes because drug dealers occasionally slipped her money. During the 2008–09 season, the Denver Nuggets and Detroit Pistons paid him nearly $21 million, the highest single-season salary of Iverson's career. But two years later, much of that—and most everything else in a vast, $155 million fortune in NBA salary alone—was mostly gone. Iverson's financial empire was collapsing under a mountain of growing debt and a refusal to abandon a lifestyle that, whether he accepted it or not, he could no longer afford.

Iverson was hardly the first to fall victim to a financial epidemic that, in the past two decades, came to afflict many former sports stars. Growing up in poverty and rampant want, young athletes were suddenly among the megarich, with seemingly bottomless bank accounts. The NFL star Michael Vick, a fellow product of Virginia's Tidewater region, was among many stars to file for bankruptcy. Others sold off championship rings and Heisman Trophies to make ends meet, because once the contracts were gone and the reality set in that these athletes possessed few real-world skills, there was nothing left but desperation. A combination of financially supporting family members and friends, a lack of knowledge about money management, and failed investments became a common and sad end to many of the athletes once among America's richest. Mike Tyson and Evander Holyfield, former world champion boxers who had experienced unfathomable paydays, squandered hundreds of millions in earnings. Vince Young, who led the University of Texas to a national championship and later signed a $26 million contract with the NFL's Tennessee Titans, blew it all in five years because he had a $5,000-a-week addiction to, of all places, the Cheesecake Factory. Iverson's weaknesses were chain restaurants and his "first-day friends," the crew from Hampton who had always believed in him. Not that he minded the jewelry and expensive clothes, but those were as much a statement of his climb as they were regular, high-dollar indulgences.

"Having nice things defines who you are, and the people you have hanging around, taking care of family, that's kind of a priority for us," said Roshown McLeod, who came from a similar background and eventually played and partied with Iverson as a member of the Sixers in 2001. "As an athlete, playing in the NBA, you feel a little bit invincible. It's almost a god complex, where you can't be touched."

By 2011, NBA teams were no longer calling Iverson with contract offers, forcing him to wait for an annual $800,000 payment from Reebok, part of his lifetime contract with the shoe manufacturer. But not long after the payment hit each year, it was gone, in part because Tawanna needed to pay bills on their homes, including a $4.5 million gated estate in northwest Atlanta that Iverson had spared no expense in customizing. Among the features of the house were nearly ten thousand square feet, a sprawling bar and a gourmet kitchen, and rain gutters made from pure copper.

Now, with creditors calling, his wife threatening divorce, and Iverson's representatives repeatedly striking out on a new NBA contract, the walls were closing in.

ON APRIL 14, 2011, Tawanna entered Regal Collection, a jewelry store in Atlanta's upscale Buckhead district, and unveiled much of her jewelry collection. Four rings, including her diamond eternity band, hit the store's showcase, along with an 8.47-carat diamond baguette, a 5.27-carat radiant-cut loose yellow diamond, and a diamond choker necklace that Iverson had given her as a gift. Seven sets of earrings and eight watches also were among the forty-two pieces, all of which Tawanna asked the store to sell on consignment.

She left with a $40,000 deposit and the hope that thousands more would follow, depending on which items sold and when. She had already visited a pawnshop to unload more jewelry and several furs, trying to get a tourniquet on the way her husband's extravagant spending was affecting her family. Already they faced significant debt and the monthly expenses her family had grown accustomed to. By then Tawanna had moved out of the family home in northwest Atlanta, taking the children with her. And it wasn't as if her own tastes had suddenly grown conservative; she too had become addicted to spending and the highest-end luxuries, and she had leased a seven-bedroom, twelve-bathroom house in Suwanee, Georgia, complete with limestone columns, reclaimed barn wood floors, multiple verandas—and a monthly rent of $5,700.

This had become their new normal, the modesty of coastal Virginia now buried under years of riches and revised expectations. Material items such as cars and jewelry had become the couple's obsession. Paying for it, at least when Iverson was doing the shopping, was another story. Iverson, who early in his NBA career defaulted on payments for the Mercedes-Benz he dreamed of shortly after the draft, often did not remember to pay for things, used to accepting valuable gifts or others taking care of his bills. He later faced a judgment for $895,000 in jewelry that he just didn't pay for, and a court opted to garnish his wages. He moved money around, giving the impression that his accounts were empty and there was no money to seize. He first transferred money to an account he didn't think was being monitored, and when he received his annual payment from Reebok and was paid for two exhibition appearances in China in 2012, Tawanna would testify, Iverson instructed the payments go into an account in Gary Moore's name.

Tawanna had become versed in the habit of transferring dollars, too, usually to pay for household expenses and paying down the thousands on her American Express card. Two months after visiting Regal Collection, she made two transfers from savings into their joint Bank of America account—one each of $60,000 and $20,000—to cover July's bills. A few days after the transfers hit, Iverson walked into Forever Diamonds and spent $20,000, part of a day of spending that included a stop at a liquor store and a hat boutique, four $200 withdrawals from a cash machine, and the first of three consecutive days at a Ruth's Chris steakhouse. A week earlier Iverson had withdrawn $10,000 in cash, and a few days later removed a combined $7,000 in two separate stops at the ATM.

Once Tawanna's payments for two of the kids' private school tuition had cleared, along with the family's $15,178 mortgage payment, Iverson's shopping spree through Buckhead left too little in the account to pay the remaining bills. Tawanna's rent check bounced, and so did her payment to Georgia Power, which as a result decreed that it would no longer accept Tawanna's personal checks. To pay the family's monthly electric bill, she would now have to send a money order or cashier's check.

Clever accounting had by then become common for Tawanna, whom, despite no schooling in finance or money management, Iverson had put in charge of the family's expenses nearly a decade earlier.

She handled all of Iverson's finances, including after they had separated, and paid insurance on fourteen cars—five of which belonged to Iverson, two to herself, and the rest to various friends and family members whom Iverson supported. In all, upward of $12,000 per month in car insurance was billed to Tawanna's AmEx. She covered a $25,000 gambling debt Iverson never got around to paying to Caesars Palace, $50,000 to reimburse the family's personal assistant for various expenses, and tens of thousands each month to pay Iverson's security detail and the family's household staff, some of whom were full-time employees. Tawanna often maintained a defensive posture in case of surprises: $300,000 in attorney fees from a 2002 incident in which Iverson chased Tawanna around Philadelphia with a pistol in his waistband; $260,000 more to settle a judgment after one of Iverson's security guards in 2005 battered a man at a nightclub in Washington, D.C., leaving him with a concussion, a perforated eardrum, and a damaged right eye; more attorney fees when Iverson was named in lawsuits while he played for the Detroit Pistons and then for a team in Turkey. Iverson's fortune had, since he entered the NBA in 1996, suffered a million cuts of varying depth, just like these—a blend of financial assistance for friends and family, investments that never got off the ground, and just plain irresponsibility—and now his accounts were hemorrhaging. No one had bothered to teach Iverson how to manage money, and he simply never considered his fortune would run out. But even part of his nest egg, the game-used memorabilia he had wisely hoarded, had gone to waste: Many of the treasures had been sold at auction after Iverson forgot to pay the storage bill.

In another panic-induced move to bring in cash to cover the essentials, the couple unloaded a home near Denver for a $400,000 loss, and in August 2011, Tawanna worried that she couldn't afford school supplies for the kids. She sold more jewelry—more expensive possessions dropped at a fraction of their original costs—and a 2011 Range Rover that had been set aside as a gift for their daughter Tiaura, a reward for earning her driver's license. It was, Tawanna came to believe under the new standards she and Iverson had set for themselves, the only way to survive.

THEY SAID GOODBYE to Tawanna's personal assistant and household staff, and Moore stopped receiving regular payments for his management services. To keep their heads above water, Iverson pondered a book deal and played in the two exhibition basketball games in China. Tawanna briefly considered moving to Miami to appear on the reality show *Basketball Wives,* and they inched toward financial windfalls deep into the future: Iverson's NBA pension, which wouldn't kick in until he turned forty-five, and a decade later, the remainder of a trust fund Reebok had earmarked in a final draft of Iverson's lifetime contract: $32 million that, for better or worse, would not become available until his fifty-fifth birthday.

But it did no good to look so far ahead, especially with the challenges now facing them. Unable to afford paid help for the first time in years, Tawanna learned to curb her own expenses after a new life of excess, cosmetic surgery, and luxuries. She moved her mother from Virginia to Atlanta to assist with household responsibilities. Tawanna, who had never worked, wondered what lay ahead—she dreamed of doing something innocent and peaceful, such as writing children's books or opening a business that hosts parties for kids. For a long time Iverson refused to acknowledge that his earning power had disappeared, at least in the way he had once known it. He told himself a team would call, and then he would be back to making millions.

Tawanna and Iverson might have been imagining equally unlikely possibilities, but Iverson was alone in refusing to acknowledge the facts: He was in his late thirties and possessed diminishing ability; worse, he was seen throughout the league as a high-maintenance player just as likely to tear a locker room apart as improve its chances of winning a championship. Iverson also would not take a realistic look at his own value, not just hoping for a major contract but *expecting* it. And if no team was willing to pay for a former league most valuable player and superstar—even one beyond his career's twilight—then he would just sit home a while longer and stare at his phone, even as his bank accounts were beaten to a pulp.

Moore and others had advised him years earlier to save money and plan for the future, but Iverson would not hear of it—at least not yet. Like so many bankrupt athletes before and after him, Iverson had appearances to keep up, because the only thing worse than *being* broke was everyone *knowing* you're broke. So he kept partying, kept traveling, kept picking up the dinner or bar tab when a group went out, even as the anxiety intensified. Had executives just forgotten that he was an icon, only a decade or so after he led the Sixers to the NBA Finals? Now the same refusal to accept perceived realities that had pushed an undersized guard from Hampton to the NBA mountaintop was also draining his finances.

"Sometimes we don't want to accept the fact that with truth comes consequences," Moore said. "I just don't think that he ever really grasped the fact that that existed. And maybe he never really accepted that fact because so many times, he didn't have to."

Iverson waited and waited, his spending almost becoming the last thing to go in his NBA career, even as his dream home in suburban Atlanta sat on the real estate market for months. Its slashed sticker prices and opulent details attracted no buyer. It had been refinanced and now carried two mortgages, the second issued from the builder after no bank would lend Iverson money. In February 2013, with Iverson no longer able to cover the monthly payments, the property was foreclosed and he moved into a hotel in Charlotte, North Carolina, spending months there because he had no place else to go.

His bravado was gone, turned into full-on panic, and with the divorce wheels turning, he emptied the remaining $12,000 from a Wells Fargo account, along with the balance of another account he and Tawanna had access to. When she asked for money to pay bills, Iverson told his estranged wife that he had none. During a divorce hearing in 2012, Iverson estimated that his monthly expenses were nearly $360,000 and his monthly income was about a fifth of that. At one point he stood, turning toward Tawanna, and pulled out his pants pockets. "I don't even have money for a cheeseburger!" he shouted in her direction, at which point she opened her wallet, removed the cash, and handed him $61.

CHAPTER 5

THE HILLTOP

A change was necessary, and the big man sent word out into the street: *Bring me the gangster. Bring him here.*

In the late 1980s, John Thompson began hearing unsettling things about the people his players were associating with. One person, really, and that man liked basketball and he liked hanging around basketball players. The man liked Georgetown, and he wore gray and blue Hoyas gear, and he talked about the stars that Thompson had once coached, including those who won the 1985 national championship. Rayful Edmond III had grown up with John Turner, a Georgetown player, later following the careers of Patrick Ewing and Eric "Sleepy" Floyd. Now Edmond had a way into the program, developing a relationship with young star Alonzo Mourning.

Edmond grew closer with Turner and Mourning and sometimes invited them to Chapter III, a nightclub in the southeast part of Washington, D.C., which was then known as the murder capital of the world—and Edmond, the city's drug lord, was its king. He oversaw the city's cocaine trade, distributing at its height some 440 pounds a week and pulling in as much as $100 million annually; his organization was linked to more than thirty deaths, including one in 1988, when a woman was killed at Chapter III, not far from where Edmond sometimes sat with Mourning and Turner.

Edmond, once a skilled playground basketball player himself, had come to know many of the city's best athletes—the same ones Thompson often recruited to Georgetown, the players who some said couldn't get into any other college, who could not be controlled or disciplined, who played on the same courts as young men who would grow into kingpins and take orders from no one.

Federal agents warned the players to keep their distance from Edmond, and Georgetown's president, Rev. Timothy Healy, called the association "stupid." Mourning and Turner did not listen, and Edmond was unfazed. This was his city; he designed his own social circle, not federal agents or Georgetown's president. Thompson, who himself had become a man on those playgrounds in the District, understood his players' attraction. When you grow up on the streets, seeing the things you see and adjusting to this perverse normality, you stick by the crew that was always there. But these were his players, and if it took a war with the city's most dangerous man to save them, then so be it.

And so Thompson spread the word: He wanted a meeting with Edmond, and soon the coach's wishes circulated, through the clubs and onto the corners, and there Edmond was, waiting outside Thompson's office at McDonough Gymnasium. When Edmond walked in, there Thompson was, all six-foot-ten of him, 270 pounds, and size-sixteen shoe. His thundering voice, famously laced with profanity, boomed toward the gangster, telling Edmond about how he came to be hired at Georgetown at age twenty-nine, using fear and confrontation to build a program and intimidate opponents. He had survived all manner of indiscretion, including when someone climbed into the rafters at McDonough, unfurling a bedsheet with "Thompson the nigger flop must go" written on it. He talked about giving opportunities to kids who barely knew the meaning of the word, teaching them to fight for themselves on and off the court, taking pride in how the university was referred to casually as "the Hilltop," because it sat overlooking the Potomac River and most of D.C. And he talked about defending his program from warlords and pissants, and how he had never let anyone undermine it, and he would be goddamned if he'd sit here and let Rayful fucking Edmond be the man who brought down his empire.

Thompson told him to stay away from his players, or else there would be consequences. Then Edmond left, just the latest person to wilt under Thompson's enormity, and did exactly as he had been told.

ANN IVERSON HEARD stories like that one, the whispers of Thompson's reputation making their way to Hampton. The coach invested in his players, protecting them and building them. He didn't give up on a young man if he made a mistake, and by God he demanded loyalty and hard work in return.

She read the legends, feeling the flare of goose bumps and hope when Thompson's bigger message dawned on her. He had designed a long-term plan for Dikembe Mutombo, the seven-foot-two future NBA star from the central African nation then known as Zaire, allowing the big man to spend his first year at Georgetown simply learning English, his fifth language, and improving his understanding of the American game. Thompson removed the pressure, watching as the young man blossomed, but because of this, when Mutombo was ready, the coach would expect perfection. Mutombo missed one class early in his career and arrived at basketball practice later that same day to find a one-way airline ticket to Africa sitting in his locker. Thompson told the young man that he was sending him back to his father, where he could join Mobutu Sese Seko's army. Mutombo tried to explain: He had awakened with a toothache, and he missed the class to visit the dentist and have the tooth removed. Thompson didn't care.

"He told me I should have scheduled time around school to take care of my tooth," Mutombo would tell the *Washington Post* in 2007. "It was chaos in my life. I thought it was the end of my education. I told the advisers: 'Why is he doing this?' One day I miss. Can you imagine?" Thompson gave the kid one more chance, and Mutombo never missed another class.

Thompson was perfect, Ann thought to herself as Iverson sat confined at the Newport News City Farm. She had visited her son in October 1993, looking into his eyes and hearing his voice describe how he was passing the time. The warden was nice, he told her, and he was studying so that he could enroll in school, whenever he was released, and return the train to the tracks. He had thought about playing basketball at a small college or, considering it was the only school that had not backed off its recruitment, staying home at Hampton University. Now eighteen years old, he signed over power of attorney to his mother, allowing her to make life-altering decisions on his behalf—a move that would cause problems later—and her first decision was to get him the hell out of Hampton, away from the life and the bias that she believed had sent him to this house of cages in the first place. Her son needed Thompson, and more than that, he needed Thompson's discipline and structure. So after returning home, she called Boo Williams, who had coached her son on the AAU circuit and knew Thompson through Mourning, and Butch Harper, her old neighbor and one of Iverson's earliest mentors. Ann wanted a meeting with the Georgetown coach, and, considering the concern she felt about the direction of young Allen's life, she would ask Thompson to save him.

Word reached them that Thompson would accept the meeting, interested in hearing from the young mother—Ann was still in her mid-thirties when Iverson was in prison—and learning more about the compelling kid now sitting in a cell. Thompson believed in second chances, sure, but this would be a big one. In December the group piled into a car in Hampton, Ann and Williams and Harper, along with Harper's sister and Iverson's friend Jamil Blackmon, and drove toward Washington. They discussed the plan as they passed through Richmond, where at the time Governor L. Douglas Wilder was contemplating an order that would free Iverson, into the District of Columbia, and finally parked outside McDonough Gymnasium, the Hoyas' cozy and historic practice facility and the offices that had, at one time or another, hosted legends and gangsters.

Thompson invited several aides to the meeting, and Ann's convoy sat and began talking. Williams and Harper discussed Iverson's potential as a basketball player, and Harper's sister, Pat Covas, a teacher at Bethel High, assured Thompson that Iverson would devote himself to becoming academically eligible and making it so Thompson would never need to worry about his academics. Then Ann, wiping tears, asked the others to leave the room. She wanted to speak one-on-one with Thompson, a mother speaking to a father, explaining the way Iverson had grown up and that she was desperate for the cycle in her family of want and poverty to end. When it was just the two of them, Ann broke down, pleading with the coach to help her son; give him one of those second chances he had offered Mourning and Mutombo. Thompson nodded, offering no promises.

But Ann's visit was effective. Thompson made up his mind. "She asked me to help her son," the *Washington Post* quoted the coach as saying in June 1996. "I saw the love of a mother who was afraid for the life of her child."

SUE LAMBIOTTE ARRIVED occasionally with her books and pencils, lugging them through the fences and past the chains at the minimum-security prison on the banks of the Warwick River.

She had known Iverson since he was twelve, already showing athletic talent and a general dislike of school. Her husband, Art, had briefly coached Iverson, the fresh scars from a tortured youth already visible. Once, Art Lambiotte said, he asked a friend where he could find young Allen. There were no guarantees he would be at his mother's home in Aberdeen, and the friend told Art that his best bet was to drive the streets between the hours of two and four in the morning, and chances were he would find the kid wandering from house to house, restless and alone during another of Ann's parties.

Sue wanted to pull the kid in close, show him how to do simple things, how to work out problems, how to understand. It was what she had done for years. She and Art had moved to Poquoson, a waterfront community on the outskirts of Hampton, in 1987. She opened a Kumon learning center to help youngsters sharpen their math and reading skills, and in her downtime she tutored students on how to improve their Scholastic Aptitude Test (SAT) scores. “Everywhere she went,” Art Lambiotte said, “she created ripples. Because being the new kid on the block, they would give her the slower kids, and she would put those kids together, and next thing you know, her kids were outshining all the other kids.”

Then she couldn’t help hearing a few years later, as the downtown uproar reached the suburbs, that four young men from Hampton had gone bowling the night before Valentine’s Day, a brawl breaking out between some white boys who lived in Poquoson, along with the response and so-called justice that followed.

Now here she was, sitting with the kid she had come to know during simpler times, now at the fringe of manhood and passing the days and weeks in prison, the outlook and uniforms colorless and drab. She enrolled him in Kumon, tutoring him and trying to keep Iverson from falling further behind during the summer of 1993. She learned that it wasn’t school itself that Iverson hated; it was its slowness, a slow current that could wash away no daydreams. He had trouble sitting still, a mind and body that needed constant stimulation, and she found ways to keep him engaged. Sue asked him to draw for her sometimes, and she saw the lifelike sketches that sometimes were laced with, as she would describe later to the *New York Times*, “piercing social statements.” She found that he responded well to sociology lessons and was fascinated by how people from different places and economic backgrounds coexisted, or tried to, and it wasn’t lost on either of them that here sat a black youngster from Hampton and a white, middle-aged woman from Poquoson exchanging stories and hopes, and if you stop and think about it, maybe they were not so different.

Iverson was released that December, a few weeks after his mother had taken a ride and emptied her emotions in the office of John Thompson. Unable to play organized basketball, according to Wilder's order, Iverson enrolled in Richard M. Milburn High, an expensive alternative school in Virginia Beach for dropouts or those considering dropping out. According to Larry Platt's 2003 Iverson biography *Only the Strong Survive*, Bill Cosby, Michael Jordan, and Spike Lee were among those who contributed to Iverson's tuition costs.

Thompson drove to the coast that spring, formally offering Iverson a scholarship and talking about the future. Thompson, along with top assistant coach Craig Esherick and academic coordinator Mary Fenlon, had talked Georgetown's president, Rev. Leo O'Donovan, into signing off on bringing Iverson to the school. Thompson said nothing to Iverson about the incident at Circle Lanes or the trial and sentencing, saying later that he wanted Iverson to know that he was interested only in the future. But, he said to Iverson, so long as they were being honest with each other, he was not interested in having jackasses on his basketball team. Thompson told Iverson in that deep cadence of his that if someone put forth a tiny bit of effort, it was not difficult to make Iverson seem like a jackass. Is that what he was? Was it? If not, Thompson said, issuing the first of many challenges to his new project, Iverson should get his ass eligible and on up to D.C. so they could get to work. "We're not a program for problem people," Thompson would say in 1995 when asked about Iverson.

Iverson kept working with Sue, sometimes at her home, six hours a day, five days a week. She taught the classes she had been certified for, and for the others Sue brought in friends with the patience and skills to reach past Iverson's defenses. She demanded not just completion of her work but enthusiasm. *Fake it, Allen,* she would tell him, *for me.* His friends and classmates had graduated from Bethel, wearing caps and gowns and celebrating as they walked across the stage, a memory their families could enjoy. He had missed out on this. What else was he willing to miss out on because of things he could control?

She was hard on him, even with such a soft spot for the kid. It was common for her to come home and, over dinner with her husband and two children, tell them about the breakthrough they achieved or approached, the kid who moved so fast on the basketball court finally slowing down enough to let his studies sink in. She told them about the time Iverson watched a friend, sitting on steps inches from him, get shot down when he was eight; about foraging for food and clothing, along with the late nights and rusted pipes he endured at home; and he told Sue about his mother, who wanted so much for him but, no matter how much she wanted it, so often could not get out of her own way.

They kept working. Sue insisted that Iverson stay focused. She split her lessons into fifteen-minute, easy-to-digest blocks, promising a reward—he always did respond to incentives—if he completed his assignments. She would allow him to express himself through art if he first expressed his thoughts within a term paper. He took the SAT in June 1994 and, a month later, the American College Testing (ACT) assessment. He knew the scores he needed to enroll at Georgetown—a 700 or better on the SAT or at least a 17 on the ACT—and afterward, he and Sue crossed their fingers. Unable to play organized basketball until that August, he stayed sharp and blew off steam in pickup games, inviting local stars to Bethel High—the school's athletic director, Dennis Kozlowski, kept opening the gym doors for Iverson and watching as spectators filtered inside—and against college players at Hampton University and Langley Air Force Base. Tawanna watched sometimes, and eventually they headed off together to hold hands or watch a movie.

Iverson passed his final two courses, psychology and United States government, and his final exam results arrived. He had done it. Iverson would be eligible to play college basketball. He stood and hugged Sue, who had pushed and pulled the results out of Iverson, never swayed by his obstacles or his excuses, and he would not forget what she had done for him. But she was not yet finished. On a summer night in 1994, two or three dozen Lambiotte family friends, fellow teachers, and a few members of Iverson's family pulled into the Moore Building parking lot in Poquoson, where Sue had opened her Kumon center years earlier.

Backstage, Iverson slipped into a graduation gown and slid on his cap. The ceremony started more than a half hour late because Ann Iverson felt it was important to make a McDonald's run, but anyway, when they were all seated, Iverson was introduced. He was the only graduate. They called him the valedictorian. "I know I didn't always make it easy," he said into the microphone, "but I want all y'all to know how much this here means to me." He walked across the makeshift stage, wrapping his hand around his diploma, and the look on his face would stay with Sue and her husband for years. "Grinning," Art Lambiotte would recall two decades later, "from ear to ear."

JEROME WILLIAMS WALKED into McDonough, eager to lay eyes on the kid who could seemingly do it all. Allen Iverson must be eight feet tall and made of polished marble, the way the stories had traveled. Williams was Georgetown's other big-name recruit in 1994, a six-foot-nine power forward who had become a star at Magruder High in nearby Rockville, Maryland, and spent his first two college seasons in Pennsylvania at Montgomery County Community College.

So where was he? Where was this beast who could do it all and had topped every recruiting ranking, who could make every shot, who had beaten a felony rap the hard way?

Williams spotted a skinny kid in the stands. Maybe he knew where he could find his new teammate. "Hey," Williams called toward the young man, who must have been a high school student who wandered over to the Georgetown campus. "Have you seen Allen Iverson?"

The kid smiled. "You mean me?" he said.

Iverson had arrived to the Hilltop amid fanfare rarely seen, even at one of the nation's premier college basketball schools. The expectations were that he was going to take the Hoyas back to the Final Four and, maybe more impressive, make Thompson put a bigger emphasis on speed and guard play. For years the coach had won games in the low post, bringing in quick and agile big men like Mourning, Mutombo, Ewing, and now Williams. Point guards had, in particular, become mostly an afterthought in Thompson's universe, but now with Iverson, maybe that would all change. Iverson was granted parole in late July 1994, just in time for him to participate in the Kenner League at Georgetown, a summer league in which high school, college, and professional players compete against each other in a three-day event. The tournament's director, Eddie Saah, noticed Iverson before the opening game and ran outside to fetch him a jersey, and when the game began and Iverson hit a three-pointer, Saah shouted into the microphone—"Allen Iverson!"—and felt an immediate buzz in the crowd. Iverson scored forty points that night, dazzling the maybe eight hundred people in the crowd. The next day, three thousand were on hand, leaving an impression on Williams. "The whole ghetto came out to watch," he said, and on the final day, four thousand were packed into the 2,400-seat McDonough Gymnasium. Eight rows back was Mutombo, trying to catch a glimpse of his alma mater's future.

Iverson scored ninety-nine points in three games, leading his squad, the Tombs, to the tournament championship, and soon everyone wanted to know about the new kid's limits, assuming he had any. "He doesn't get tired," an exhausted Morgan State University player said after guarding Iverson during the tournament.

Thompson assigned all first-year players to the treadmill, testing their conditioning. It was especially important for a player like Iverson, who had not played a regulation game in more than a year, since winning the state championship, as he controversially had promised, as a junior at Bethel. So on you go, kid, and he began by jogging. Then the belt started moving faster, the incline growing, and soon he was sprinting. A well-conditioned player could usually last ten or so minutes on the treadmill, one of Thompson's many equalizers to whatever otherworldly talent the player thought he possessed. Williams lasted maybe twelve minutes. After nearly twenty minutes, Iverson still going, they geared the machine down, figuring that was good enough. Iverson hopped off, smiling at Williams and barely breathing hard. "Superhuman," Williams would say later.

Thompson liked to assign laps after a marathon practice if his team had struggled through a session, sloppy passes and stupid shots that "Big Coach" would not abide, whether here or in a game. They ran, their legs weak and their lungs screaming, and there Iverson would go, cruising past his teammates as they fell onto the floor, and laughing as he passed. The coach assigned Iverson to room with Don Reid, the team captain and one of the Hoyas' seniors. Reid had hosted Iverson on his official visit to Georgetown shortly after Thompson had extended his scholarship offer and the noise of the previous year was beginning to fade.

They walked the campus, Iverson coming off to Reid as a man thankful for his opportunity and eager to return to the hardwood. Iverson asked questions and talked about what lay ahead, leaving out anecdotes from his youth and his time in jail, saying only that many people back home had turned their backs on him—but not everyone. There were people from his childhood who had always stuck by him, Ra and "E" and Jamil and Andre "Arnie" Steele, and the previous eighteen months had been no different, and influences like the Lambiottes had helped him get this far. Iverson, his mind wandering now, wondered aloud if he thought Thompson would allow him to play football, too, and sure, Reid told him, knowing how the coach would react; go ahead and ask. "I don't think you can write it in a magazine, what he [Thompson] said," Iverson would tell *GQ* magazine in 2007. "I didn't think about playing football no more after that." He would tell friends later, though, that on his walk to McDonough, he would pass Georgetown's football stadium and feel a lump in his throat, regretful that a part of his life—and maybe his best sport—was behind him.

When Iverson arrived on campus, he moved his things into a bedroom in Village A, a student townhouse community whose upper levels overlooked the Potomac and nearby Rosslyn, Virginia. Most upperclassmen entered a lottery for space here, but basketball players were guaranteed residence, and soon after Iverson moved in, his roommates marveled at the determination of the kid—and, if they were honest about it, his weirdness. Iverson fractured his ankle during a practice, and after visiting the trainer, he was fitted into a walking boot, shaking and tiptoeing around the apartment as he tried to get used to it. Finally he kicked off the boot, telling his roommates that his Timberlands worked better anyway, and sure enough, Iverson went outside, running around campus, and they never heard about the bad ankle again.

They came to learn that the freshman grew bored easily, and he hated silence, playing his new Notorious B.I.G. album, *Ready to Die*, quoting the lyrics from "Big Poppa" so often that his roommates sneaked it out of the disc player and threw it away.

The back of the club, sippin' Moët
Is where you'll find me
The back of the club, mackin' hoes
My crew's behind me

Iverson naturally bought another one, playing the songs again and again, and soon that CD was gone, too. He decorated the walls with posters of rappers who had inspired him and now lived a life he hoped to someday experience. He talked loudly and screamed jokes and blasted music, the lyrics to his new favorite song, "Juicy," addictive to the self-anointed "baddest guard to ever play at Georgetown."

And my whole crew is loungin'
Celebratin' every day, no more public housin'
Thinkin' back on my one-room shack
Now my mom pimps a AC with minks on her back

His roommates just shook their heads, eventually coming to associate Iverson with nonstop chatter and noise. "You could hear him coming from a block away. He was echoing all over," Reid said, and eventually they convinced him to move out of his bedroom and stay on the couch downstairs, so he could stay up as late as he liked. When they headed off to bed, Reid said, Iverson, still wide-eyed and craving entertainment, found his way to the apartment of some students from India, watching television and telling stories with new friends who liked to stay up just as late.

Sometimes in search of late-night fun, he found his way to parties, where he indulged his new taste for alcohol. His teammates watched as he pounded beers, the little man thinking he could drink like a power forward, apparently, and then he would walk over to Jerome Williams, lean an elbow on the big man's shoulder, and tell his teammate he loved him. "Things he would never say," Williams recalled with a laugh.

During one of those nights before his freshman season began, Iverson walked into a tattoo parlor. Thompson had a strict no-tattoo policy, but Iverson was determined. A few hours earlier, Iverson and Jamil Blackmon, his old friend from the Peninsula who had taken in Iverson's family during a particularly difficult patch and was later in the room during Ann's meeting with Thompson, had been folding laundry and brainstorming. Iverson wanted a nickname like all the summer-league greats: Earl "the Pearl" Monroe, Frank "Shake 'n' Bake" Streety, Rafer "Skip to My Lou" Alston. What would Iverson's name be? Then it had dawned on Blackmon: The NBA, approaching the end of the Magic Johnson, Larry Bird, and Michael Jordan eras, faced nothing but questions. Blackmon blurted out his suggestion, and Iverson loved it.

Hearing the nickname echoing in his mind, Iverson sat in the tattoo chair and pointed at his left arm, where his shoulder met his biceps. He wanted his new handle to ride with him forever, to define him, to speak for him. The needle vibrated and pierced Iverson's skin, forming nine letters in Old English type, and when the artist was finished, Iverson saw it for the first time: THE ANSWER.

BE ON TIME, he told them. No. Five minutes early. Cut your hair. Lose those earrings, and what is that, a gold chain? If you want to step on this court and wear this jersey, it stays home. Or you do. Your choice.

Road trip this week, so wear a suit. Don't have one? Then you're a bum. "A man that's in college that doesn't have a suit has no projection for his future," Thompson told reporters during Iverson's freshman year. "Don't tell me the poverty story. You can go to Goodwill and get a suit."

Class papers are to be turned in before arriving at the airport, not after. So what if it's Connecticut or Syracuse on the schedule? You won't be playing anyway unless that paper is finished, so why is it your concern who we're playing? And, Iverson, just what in the fuck is that on your arm?

Iverson was restless and loud at Village A, performing his impressions of Martin Lawrence and Eddie Murphy, but when Thompson was around, he was all business. He listened to his coach's words, smiling and nodding, and the big man softened and walked over to put his arm around the kid, saying a few encouraging words—the closest thing Iverson would ever have to a father. "Just watching him," Iverson said of Thompson years later, "and how he conducted himself, and how he handled himself in every situation. Just paying attention to how he went about his life—it was so easy to listen to the advice that he always gave me, because you could see the success that he had. Not being a basketball coach, the success that he had in life, and the respect that he had of so many other people."

As Thompson had done for Mutombo, he tried to take pressure off his nineteen-year-old point guard. He wouldn't allow reporters to interview him, and the coach told few people outside his inner circle that Iverson was even on campus. Thompson called him a "child," and came to feel responsible for Ann Iverson's boy, because that was the job she had asked him to take. He pondered changing Iverson's position to shooting guard, easing the burden of leading the team. On opening night, it was Williams—all six-foot-nine of him—starting at point guard so that Iverson would not have to run the offense in his first contest as a college player.

Thompson's protective nature was publicly visible during that game, an exhibition against Fort Hood, when the visiting team's center threw a forearm into Iverson. Thompson ran onto the court, screaming at the young man, "Don't hurt my boy!" before officials restrained him. Not that everything was perfect for Iverson: He would be remembered almost as much for his turnovers as his dazzling fast breaks and bolts through the lane, tallying eight miscues against Arkansas. But no matter: The secret was out, and not long after the season began, even President Bill Clinton, a Georgetown alumnus, entered the locker room to meet the kid everyone was talking about.

Thompson, the strict disciplinarian who did things his way, offered Iverson unprecedented freedom, the meticulous and detail-oriented coach so often telling the kid to run out there and just make something happen. He even looked the other way on that damn tattoo. Iverson argued with teammates when games or practices turned heated, and even if Thompson admonished Iverson, he secretly had fallen in love with the kid's passion. "He's an extremely argumentative person," the coach told the *Washington Post* during Iverson's freshman season. "But the kids love him."

Georgetown games became reunions, and Iverson took to inviting old friends and loved ones to watch him play. The Lambiottes drove from Poquoson to Washington more than once, Iverson leaving tickets at will-call as one of many ways he tried to repay a perceived debt. And his mother, who was responsible for so much of this, sat in the stands often, wearing a Georgetown jersey with MS. IVERSON on the back and holding a sign that read: "Mommy loves you."

During an NCAA tournament game at Richmond Coliseum, Ann arrived late, a habit her son would apparently come by honestly. She sat in the stands and cheered when Iverson made basket after basket, finishing with thirty-one points against Mississippi Valley State. She watched as her son interacted with Thompson. The seed of an idea was now in full blossom. "I made the decision that I wanted Allen to go to Georgetown. I chose John. John wasn't recruiting him. I came to John," Ann Iverson was quoted as saying by the *Washington Post*. "And I think if you lift up John's arm, you'll see Allen underneath. Allen has matured so much. He's a little man now. When I sent him to John he was a boy."

Later that same night, Ann noticed Governor Wilder watching her son, the young man he had freed, and she crossed the two sections to greet and thank him, wrapping the Virginia governor in a hug.

INDEED, IVERSON FELT like a man. He was not even twenty, but a lifetime of expectations surrounded him, and his confidence had grown. Iverson had lost trust in humanity, perhaps, and certainly became slower to believe in strangers, particularly those who had grown up under different circumstances. So he grew closer with his inner circle: the friends from Hampton who had looked after him; the family members who always believed; Tawanna, the young woman who had followed him from game to game, making him feel like the most important man in the world.

They were the ones who understood him, never questioned him, would always support him. And so he spent much of his downtime back on the Peninsula, checking in on his young sister Iiesha, who had been born nine days late, had suffered complications during birth, and as a toddler now occasionally had seizures. Iverson liked being there, making sure they were all okay, even if he was missing some of the socializing back in Washington.

This was as important as basketball, he came to believe in his tender moments, and early in 1994, midway through his first season at Georgetown, Iverson decided that he wanted to start his own family. He had dreams, and not all of them centered on basketball. He wanted a big, jubilant, happy family, and looking back on his own hard road as a youngster, among his goals was for his children to have both parents to watch and guide them, to care for and love them, to give them a life without the want or worry he had come to know. Yes, he said during one of those visits home, he was ready now to be a father.

He shared his wishes with Tawanna, who was also nineteen. She told him that she was ready, too.

CHAPTER 6

FAMILY MAN

Good morning, Miss Iverson," Iverson's divorce attorney, Melanie Fenwick Thompson, began on the morning of January 16, 2013.

"Good morning," Tawanna replied.

It was time to discuss their children, whom Iverson insisted he adored. Years earlier he had declared that he wanted all of his children to grow up in an environment different than the one he had experienced. He wrote a sociology paper during Sue Lambiotte's tutoring sessions, imagining a civilization in which women handled most responsibilities, with men only in charge of providing sustenance—the rest of the time open to bond with and love the children. Among his goals was for each of his children to have the same mother and father. Tiaura came first, when Iverson and Tawanna were each nineteen, her father a rising star at Georgetown but still so much ahead, and then three years later, Allen II—they would call him "Deuce"—was born. Then came Messiah, Isaiah, and Dream.

Actually being there for each of the kids' births, though, was apparently less important to Iverson than the goal of having the family.

"You mentioned in your testimony yesterday that he was not there for her birth, for Tiaura's birth?" Thompson asked.

"Yes, that's correct," Tawanna replied.

When she went into labor in December 1994, Iverson was nowhere to be found. At first he had been excited by the idea of having a child, but then his enthusiasm seemed to dissolve. Teammates and friends warned him after Tawanna had become pregnant that having a baby out of wedlock might jeopardize his future, fueling a perception that Iverson's focus was divided—with basketball, sure, but also with his past problems, a tenuous family life, and now a child.

Iverson would tell Tawanna, irate that he had missed Tiaura's birth, that Georgetown coach John Thompson required that players remain on campus throughout December. But this made no sense: Classes were suspended for the holidays, and years later, several of Iverson's former college teammates said Thompson never had such a rule. Regardless of his reasons, Tawanna would testify later that Iverson did not meet baby Tiaura until two weeks after her birth.

Three years later, Iverson, by then a young NBA player who was showing early signs of personal problems, was "very intoxicated," Tawanna would remember, when she went into labor with Deuce. Iverson was so drunk, according to court testimony, that he was unable to drive her to the hospital; one of Iverson's uncles instead drove her.

Iverson blew off future ultrasounds and refused to change diapers. Before their youngest child, Dream, was born in 2008, Iverson came home at four o'clock in the morning from a night of partying in Denver; three hours later, Tawanna's water broke, and she was unable to wake him. She instead called a personal assistant, Candis Rosier, who drove the expectant mother to the hospital; when Iverson awoke and found his way to the delivery room, he passed the hours on his phone, complaining to friends that he had no idea how long he would have to be there. "She's not even pushing yet," Tawanna would remember him grousing.

"He did not hold my hand, rub my back," Tawanna told Fenwick Thompson. "He just said he didn't care. He was just concerned with it being over with."

• • •

TAWANNA SAW THE video taken on Deuce's phone in 2012 of a man she did not recognize flipping a butterfly knife and showing her fifteen-year-old how to use a Taser. A photograph showed the same man with Dream, who at the time was four years old, sitting on his lap.

Iverson had taken his children on a weekend excursion to the Great Wolf Lodge, a family hotel and water park in Williamsburg, Virginia, that prefers its guests be in their rooms by a reasonable hour. But each night Iverson went to get drunk with friends, grown men whom Tawanna didn't know, leaving Iverson's twenty-one-year-old goddaughter in charge. After midnight one evening, Tiaura sent her mother the contents of Deuce's phone: the knife and the instructions about the Taser, several adults staying in the room, and children sleeping only in swimsuits because Iverson would not make time to use the on-site laundry.

Tawanna, who had spent the weekend traveling to Pennsylvania and Atlanta, exchanged her car for her more spacious truck at the airport, needing to fit the children in the vehicle. She sped toward the hotel in Williamsburg, seething that Iverson had done it again.

Three years earlier, the family planned a trip to Disney World. Iverson had promised this would be a family vacation, and he and Tawanna made plans to spend time with their five children—away from basketball and the couple's problems, beyond the glare of the media spotlight, out of earshot of the distractions of real life. They would take a private plane and, for a few days, live like royalty.

Instead, shortly after landing in Orlando, Iverson called a friend who lived nearby and together they went to the bars each of the four nights. During the day Tawanna took the children to the park, where they took in the rides, spent time by the pool, and ate meals together. Iverson, each day sleeping and nursing hangovers, complained that central Florida was simply too hot, and so he rarely left the room. On the final night, Iverson vowed that he would join his family for dinner, and then they would take a boat to watch fireworks over the resort. Then he came in late, long after his family had been seated, embarrassing Tawanna by allowing the children to run around the restaurant. Rather than go on the fireworks cruise, Iverson convinced Tawanna to return to the hotel so that he could spend time with the kids at the pool. Instead he met with the same friend and watched basketball before returning to the bars.

The next morning, Tawanna rose at five to drive a friend of Tiaura's to the airport. Iverson was still out with his friend, and when she returned he was passed out in the room. Hours later, with Iverson still unresponsive as the hotel's checkout time approached, Tawanna packed the kids' clothes and toys and arranged for her mother to take the children to a movie before the family's flight home. Tawanna, meanwhile, helped Iverson into a hired van and sat there with him, the driver, and their luggage. The hours passed and the car idled, Iverson lying on the floor with a leg draped onto a seat. Tawanna was afraid to leave because she thought the driver might take photographs of Iverson—bad publicity he did not need after an especially tumultuous time in his career.

As she sped now toward the Great Wolf Lodge, Tawanna was furious. It was one thing for Iverson to break promises and ignore his children; it was another to endanger them. She arrived, charging through a lobby empty except for maintenance workers and employees, and burst into the room. It was messy, and at two in the morning the adults were gone and the five children still awake. "And he was nowhere," she would say in court testimony later.

She gathered their belongings and her children and loaded them into her truck. Tawanna drove to her mother's home as the kids slept, and after four that morning, Iverson found his way there, too. He rang the doorbell repeatedly and screamed insults at Tawanna through the door, waking three of the children as Tawanna dialed 911. When the police arrived, Iverson still screaming that his wife was a prostitute and her mother a bitch, the officer attempted to calm Iverson, reminding the basketball star that he was intoxicated and making a scene. "You don't know me!" screamed Iverson, who denied he was drunk. "Sir, you are obviously intoxicated. Let's go away," the policeman said, according to courtroom testimony based on the cruiser's dashboard camera. Iverson refused to leave; eventually the officer left.

Iverson kept shouting, kept ringing the doorbell, kept declaring that Tawanna had screwed every man in the neighborhood, even as nine-year-old Isaiah peeked through a rectangular window to a disturbing view of his father's ugliest side.

AS HIS CHILDREN grew, Iverson did not bother getting to know them on more than a superficial level. He instructed Tawanna to make decisions about their futures, and he made little effort to involve himself in extracurricular activities or the selection of his kids' schools. Tawanna searched the Internet for answers to some of her family's most important decisions and, wherever Iverson happened to be playing, solicited advice from her husband's teammates or their wives. "I was responsible for everybody's everything," Tawanna said.

Iverson never took Isaiah to karate or chess, did not bother attending his kids' birthday parties or playdates, and never spoke with teachers or coaches. Three times when he was asked to pick up Dream from her private school, Iverson was at least an hour late, leading to late fees of $255 per hour and a warning that if the tardiness continued, Dream could be removed from the school. Iverson did not even show an interest when Deuce, his eldest son, entered the family business, playing basketball for his schools' teams. Iverson never took him to practices or attended games; Tawanna shuttled the boy to and from his games until middle school, with his world-famous basketball player father never sitting in the stands. When Deuce enrolled in the private school in Pennsylvania, Iverson skipped the final two days, including a private session with only Deuce and the family. On another occasion, he had promised one morning to take one of his children to see a specialist; Iverson apparently changed his mind, opting instead to go back to sleep.

In August 2012, when Tawanna asked him to pick the kids up from school on a Wednesday and then drop them off the following morning, Iverson sent her a text message saying he had no idea which schools they attended. "1st all I don't know where MY! Kids go 2 school as crazy as a man that's been take care of them all their lives may sound but it is what is so u or 1 of your ppl have 2 meet me somewhere with them."

He occasionally played with them, rolling on the floor as his laughing children crawled around their famous father, but he broke promises and used them as pawns during his separation with Tawanna. He once threatened to spill details about childhood problems two of his kids had dealt with for years, saying he would contact the gossip website TMZ with the information. "Our kids will have 2 deal with & I hate It but I tried!" he texted Tawanna in March 2012.

He demeaned one of his sons, Tawanna told the court. Iverson, she said, told the boy that he was weaker than his father because, although this was the very thing Iverson had once hoped for, he had grown up in far more comfortable circumstances than the ones endured by his dad. "You ain't no real nigga," Tawanna recalled Iverson saying. "You a white boy, you preppy, you rich boy."

Testifying in January 2013, Tawanna described how she tried to get her husband into therapy and attempted to get him help for his drinking. He would not hear of it, even when she threatened to keep the children away. "Only since the divorce has been filed that I've been so serious about him getting help," she said on the witness stand.

"I understand," the attorney said. "Now, why weren't you serious prior to the divorce?"

"I always thought that my kids needed their father," Tawanna said. "And what I've learned is that they don't need him if he's going to be that destructive in their lives."

CHAPTER 7

CROSSOVER

Iverson wandered into a Mercedes-Benz dealership two months before his twenty-first birthday, assuring himself that he was there just to look. His sophomore season at Georgetown had ended a few days earlier, and the draw of the S600 coupe had pulled him off campus, over the Potomac River, and into Arlington, Virginia, where the high-end cars cruised almost hourly off the dealership lot.

He was browsing, and the salesman spotted him. A beauty, isn't it, with the fine lines and the gleaming black paint? Hear the hum of that six-liter, V-12 engine? Have a seat in it, the man told the basketball star. Notice the heated leather seats and the voice-activated cellular telephone. Not only that, but it's a steal, the salesman went on, preowned and available for the low, low price of $107,000.

Iverson climbed out, and the salesman did what good salesmen do: He kept the conversation going, kept asking questions, kept reeling information out of the young man. Iverson *would* most likely be turning pro soon, he told the man, and maybe he could afford the car then. But now? It just wasn't happening. Well, that's okay, the man continued; if you've made up your mind, and with the NBA draft approaching in only eight weeks, then what difference would two months make, especially between a pair of new friends?

But, Iverson said, he had not even discussed his options with his coach, John Thompson. He had not told *anyone* that he'd made a decision, indicating his preference only in a letter to Michael Freeman, his mother's longtime boyfriend. Thompson had coached the Hoyas for a quarter century now, and no player had ever chosen to leave school without exhausting his four-year eligibility. Patrick Ewing, Dikembe Mutombo, Alonzo Mourning—all of them eventually entered the draft, but none had left school early. It simply wasn't done back then. Who could even say how Thompson would react to such a suggestion? Most everyone around Iverson had advised him to stay in school for at least one more season; get another year's worth of experience, television exposure, and mentorship, and *then* make the biggest leap of his life.

Standing amid the high-performance vehicles in the Mercedes-Benz showroom, the salesman sweetened the offer: Just take the car, shake hands on it but hand over no money, and after your NBA contract is signed, come on back to Arlington to settle up. Iverson smiled and climbed back in. He eased the powerful car back onto North Glebe Road, pointing its nose and the famous tristar logo back toward Washington. Iverson had perhaps unwittingly just made his decision: Accepting such a favor, no matter his intentions to pay later, would void his amateur status. There would be difficult terrain yet to navigate, but at least now he could travel in style. "I only wanted to test-drive it," Iverson would say later.

***GO AGAIN,* IVERSON** said, shaking his head. *One more time.*

Dean Berry, a walk-on teammate at Georgetown, shrugged and nodded, bringing the ball back toward the half-court line before Iverson's sophomore season. Georgetown's practice was finished for the day, another attempt at finding something the kid could not do, and so followed the daily sprints and closing address from Thompson. But even after all that, Iverson did not want basketball to be finished for the day, to head back to that quiet-ass Village A apartment, and so he begged teammates to play two-on-two or even one-on-one.

Most were exhausted and ready for a nap or a plate of pasta. Berry, a student of basketball who had come to Washington to test himself at one of America's best factories, was always up for it. He liked seeing how more talented teammates, those on scholarship who rarely needed to prove themselves after arriving on campus, reacted to the tricks he had simply taught himself—how the details he had obsessed over paid off. When he was in high school, he watched videos of Tim Hardaway and John Stockton and how one telegraphed move seemed to always give them a cushion. Their crossover dribble was effective, and Berry wanted to learn it. He hit rewind and then play, seeing how Hardaway dribbled the ball high and let it float in his hand as he leaned in one direction and then broke the other way; rewind and then play, watching again and again how Stockton bent almost into a crouch and protected the ball with his speed—his eyes and head sending one signal, and then when the defender committed, there he went. Berry took his lessons to the playgrounds, trying each of his heroes' moves, loving how it dared a defender to come get the ball and then, in a flash, he was gone.

They were playing pickup one afternoon at McDonough when Iverson asked about it. How the hell did Berry, who was a year younger than Iverson, keep getting so open? Why could they not stop him? Someone at Georgetown had finally found Iverson's weakness: He could not defend Berry's crossover.

"Hey," Iverson called over. "You gotta show me that."

Berry obliged, and he waited for Iverson to tighten his defensive cushion, and then it was time. A hard bounce to lull Iverson into thinking this was it, but this one was a bluff. The first one, always a bluff. "You want that person to believe that you're going to the right, but first *you* must believe it," Berry recalled explaining to his student. "You believe that that person is going to the right, if you'll lean and turn your shoulder that way." Iverson nodded, telling himself he would not fall for it this time; he would sit back in his stance, refusing to commit.

So Berry took his time, slowing things, making Iverson wait for it. When Berry saw Iverson leaning, he hit him with the big dribble, the big lean, the big move, the big—*fuck!* He was gone again.

One more, Iverson kept begging, determined to stop it first and then learn it himself. Berry took the ball toward center court, starting the drill again. Rewind and play, again and again, rewind and play.

TOGETHER THEY WERE building a machine, Thompson and Iverson, the gruff and hardened coach and the kid who would stop at nothing to achieve greatness, so many possibilities attainable with them in it together. Thompson had provided the structure he had promised Ann Iverson, but his young guard had given the coach a chance at one more Final Four before his career geared down. In return, Thompson handed over the keys to his offense, giving Iverson freedom to run the floor most times—and, on the occasions he had pushed Iverson into a coaching box, regretting caging such a bird.

"When we got home," Thompson was quoted by the Associated Press as saying in February 1996, "I'd say I wished I'd let him go. We're [messing] around disciplining him, saying, 'Take your time and follow everybody else.' I wish I'd said: 'Go get it! Go get it for us.' "

Thompson relaxed his exterior as a no-nonsense disciplinarian, explaining defensive positioning with a dance move or howling with deep-voiced laughter when Iverson would show the team his hand-drawn caricature of Thompson and his enormous belly. With Iverson as Georgetown's centerpiece, the Hoyas played at a suffocating pace that few teams in the Big East Conference could defend. At the University of Arkansas, coach Nolan Richardson had won a national championship with his patented "forty minutes of hell," a full-tilt, lung-ravaging approach that simply wore out most opponents. Now Thompson was perfecting it, stifling his own instincts and wiping his brow with that terry-cloth towel he kept on his shoulder and telling the kid to do his thing, for Christ's sake, and bring home the damn victory.

Iverson perfected the crossover, never satisfied until he could stop Berry and until Berry could *never* stop him. His determination to perfect the move made it effective, but Iverson's speed made it lethal. And he wanted to try it on everyone; who could possibly stop it? "He tried it in the game every time," Berry would recall. "Every time he would get an opportunity, he would hit it. He knew that it was that good of a move, that he just wanted to do it every time."

Iverson, learning lessons that would bring on chronic headaches for his future NBA coaches, learned to improvise—using tricks he had taught himself on Hampton's playgrounds—and win games himself. "Three passes?" Thompson described in that same Associated Press account, getting inside his best player's mind. "To heck with three passes; I can beat this man right now." If Georgetown struggled, it was because Iverson's teammates, not the opponent, were unable to keep up with his frantic pace; they would often stand near the baseline or at the top of the key and watch as Iverson made something happen; if he did pass the ball in their direction, an increasingly unlikely occurrence, it was just as likely to bounce off a pair of stony, unprepared hands.

Iverson was strong-willed and impossibly determined. No situation seemed to intimidate him, and when his sophomore season was finishing, he was named Big East defensive player of the year for the second consecutive season. The highlights of Iverson's best moves—the fast breaks against Villanova and Syracuse, the crossover victimizing Boston College's Duane Woodward and Arizona's Jason Terry, the acrobatic drives and steals and three-point shots befuddling Syracuse and Connecticut—were played repeatedly on television, and NBA scouts were starting to notice.

The success was addictive, but Thompson became increasingly sensitive to suggestions that he might lose the kid after only two years. When Georgetown's home crowd began chanting for Iverson to stay in school—"Two more years! Two more years!"—Thompson turned and faced the student section, slinging his towel into the crowd. Thompson, one of America's most powerful college basketball coaches, and therefore one of higher education's most influential men in this sports-crazed country, thought he was strong enough to chase away the possibility of Iverson leaving, if only he kept the predators away from his prized pet. "I don't need every agent running up and down this campus because you imply that he's going to leave school," Thompson told reporters in March 1996. "When that happens, we got to bolt all the doors down. I start seeing mystery people floating around out here. . . . The wolves are circling the house now. The buzzards are flying over the top, and I start getting an attitude because you got to get ready for the wolves."

Thompson had always been protective of Iverson, but now he was part of something special with the kid. He did not want to risk losing it and, more important, having Iverson do something he would regret. Thompson overreacted when, during a game at Villanova, students raised signs that read "Convict U," and another called Iverson the next Jordan, only "Jordan" was crossed out and "O.J." scrawled in its place, a reference to O. J. Simpson. Earlier in a game at Pittsburgh, the student section chanted "Jailbird! Jailbird!" when Iverson shot free throws. "I'm overly protective, very conservative, and proud of it," Thompson told reporters later. "I'm not going to change."

Georgetown's coach was fighting a losing battle, no matter how he tried to convince himself it was not true. When the Hoyas lost in the Big East tournament championship game to Connecticut, Thompson noticed Iverson crying in the locker room. The coach told himself, along with longtime confidante Mary Fenlon, that Iverson had been through so much and that the disappointment of the loss had spilled his emotions. But it was not true. Iverson was crying because an important chapter of his life was coming to a close.

IVERSON KEPT MAKING his way to Hampton, during slow periods and holidays, to visit family during birthdays and to make future plans with Tawanna, who had been thrown out of her mother's house for defying her rules and was now staying at the home of Iverson's aunt Jessie. He met his newborn daughter, Tiaura, albeit not immediately, and listened to the stories about how Iiesha, his eighteen-month-old sister, needed care from a medical specialist. Iverson enjoyed the college experience and the tutelage of Thompson, he would tell friends as they sat on familiar stoops as night turned to morning, and leaving Georgetown would be difficult.

While on his breaks to the Peninsula and throughout the years prior, Iverson heard about Michael Freeman, the father of Ann Iverson's two daughters and the man whom Iverson had referred to as his dad for most of his life. Freeman had worked for a while as a welder, and he had been employed at a shipyard when he met Ann, moving in with her in 1975. But the job paid like shit, and soon Freeman was looking for other ways to provide. He was convicted in 1991 of intent to distribute cocaine, telling fifteen-year-old Iverson to look after the family while he was gone—and that basketball was his and the family's way off the Peninsula and out of this desperate life they had come to know so well.

Freeman was paroled in 1992, and less than two years later he was back inside after turning once again to selling cocaine when legitimate jobs either were not hiring or did not pay enough. The kids had to eat, Iiesha needed medicine, and the point to the stories, Iverson came to know, was that sometimes a man has to do what he must do, not what he wants to do, if there are others depending on him. In April 1996, two months after Freeman's release, police raided a home in Hampton. They found Freeman and his brothers, Baggies and a scale, cash and cocaine. Just like that, he was gone again. Iverson wrote a letter to Freeman, promising that upon his release Freeman would be taken care of—moved with the rest of the family to whichever NBA city he would call home.

About 175 miles north, on the campus overlooking the Potomac, Thompson was still swatting away the flies, even as the swarm thickened. He described the "sacred" tradition of Georgetown players remaining in school all four years, resisting the NBA's pull. And he discussed how, if Iverson were considering deviating from the custom, it would not be Thompson who would be caught by surprise. "If Allen Iverson leaves," he told reporters in March 1996, "be assured I have told him to go, or he will go nowhere."

When Georgetown lost in the Big East tournament final, Thompson heartened but misguided by his All-American guard's tears, the Hoyas dropped in the minds of those on the NCAA tournament committee. The team entered the Big Dance as a number-two seed, cruising through the first three rounds. Then it faced Massachusetts for a chance to reach the Final Four, the fringe of history and a chance for Thompson to reach the national semifinal for the first time since Ewing delivered him an NCAA championship eleven years earlier. Iverson crossed over Marcus Camby, giving those NBA scouts one more highlight against a fellow lottery pick, but in the second half, with the game in his hands just as Thompson had reluctantly given it to him so often, Iverson lost control. He made one of his ten shot attempts, a sign that perhaps his mind was elsewhere, and he lamented later that he usually made those baskets. The Minutemen won, eliminating Georgetown and ending Thompson's hopes of reaching one last Final Four. Three years later he would step down at age fifty-seven, following his first losing season since 1971–72 and citing an attempt to save his marriage. He was never again this close to cutting down the nets.

A few days after the team returned from Atlanta, Iverson ventured to Arlington and that Mercedes-Benz dealership, driving away with that sweet S600. Thompson, still holding on to hope that Iverson would return for his junior season, heard about the car and immediately confronted Iverson about it. "Take the damn thing back!" Thompson thundered at the kid, and he eventually did. But the damage was done: A high-dollar car, driven off the lot for free, almost definitely violated NCAA rules, effectively ending Iverson's amateur career.

Thompson called a meeting, summoning Ann Iverson from Hampton into the same office she had visited a year and a half earlier. They talked once again about Iverson's future, and Thompson brought in a secret weapon: David Falk, the NBA agent who represented Michael

Jordan, Iverson's childhood hero, along with several former Georgetown stars. Thompson told Iverson and his mother that the kid should stay with him at least one more year, and Falk chimed in, saying Iverson was not yet ready for the NBA. "I told him the league is a very difficult market to play in," Falk would recall years later. "The fans are tough, TV was tough, and that he was used to a very protective environment at Georgetown."

Iverson kept firing back: Iiesha needed medical care that was beyond his family's means, Tiaura and Tawanna needed financial support, and he was unable to provide either as a college player compensated only with a scholarship. Thompson and Falk kept at him, but he deflected their reasons. "He listened for about two hours," Falk said, "and said: 'Thanks, but I have to do this.' "

Iverson and Thompson agreed to disagree. The kid hired Falk as his representative in the Georgetown way and the school prepped for a news conference on the floor at McDonough. Ann Iverson sat at her son's left, leaning over and kissing him and thanking Thompson for guiding her son into manhood. Thompson sat at Iverson's right, handing him a statement and thrashing the "antiquated" NCAA, whose rules made it impossible for Thompson or the school to provide financial assistance to Iverson's family, even while profiting from his remarkable ability. He made it clear that he disagreed with his protégé's decision, saying he was certain Iverson's skill was NBA-ready but adding that he was "scared as hell about those other twenty-two hours" of the day when he was not playing basketball.

When it was Iverson's turn to speak, his left cheek adorned with his mother's bright red lipstick, he thanked Georgetown and assured the audience that he planned to complete his degree requirements. He said it was not necessarily what he wanted to do. But as he learned back home, when others depend on you, hard choices must sometimes be made.

• • •

THEY APPROACHED HIM on the street and on the Jersey Shore boardwalk, chasing him sometimes as he walked away. "Pat! Iverson!" they screamed, trailing him into work at the Sixers' practice facility or out at dinner. "Yo, Pat!" they'd call toward him. "Iverson!"

"I thought my name was Pat Iverson," recalled Pat Croce, who in spring 1996 was a newly minted millionaire and in his earliest months as the Sixers' president. "I'm telling you, everyone yelled at me."

He had watched Iverson at Georgetown, almost immediately falling in love not only with the kid's ability but his killer instinct. His motor. His drive and intensity. There was something attractive and familiar about that, because Croce too had once known modesty, if not poverty. He was a South Philadelphia kid who made his name as a physical therapist, taking a job as the Sixers' strength and conditioning consultant to oversee special assignments like trying to help Shawn Bradley, the team's seven-foot, six-inch center, pack on muscle. He wound up staying ten years, building a chain of therapy centers in his spare time, pulling himself from the streets of South Philly by any means necessary, screaming to everyone that he feels great, baby. And you should, too, because he did it with a smile, whether he was taping ankles or delivering speeches or winning two national karate championships, leaving the daily grind in the dust when he sold the company for $40 million. In 1996 he redirected some of the money into a minority interest in the NBA team he grew up following, and after installing himself as team president, inherited a team at a crossroads. The Sixers were not just bad, they were boring, and Croce was among the first to promise a revolution. All they needed now was a little luck.

Croce tucked his father's holy medal in his pocket and ordered a Waterford crystal basketball flown in from Ireland, his mother's native land, and sat as the NBA draft lottery began. As the other teams' names were assigned the later picks, Croce's leg started jumping under the dais, faster as Milwaukee and Vancouver and, my God, they had told the men to sit stoically and avoid celebrations, an edict directly from NBA commissioner David Stern. But fuck that, Croce thought, this was showtime. And so when Toronto was assigned the second pick, Croce smiled and leaned forward, pumping his fist and slapping the hand of the executive to his left and then standing to high-five the Raptors representative at his right, then everyone behind him as the other men could not help but laugh. “I thought: I’m in!” he told Bob Costas afterward, going on to slow-play his team’s intentions.

The fans wanted Iverson, and the truth was, so did Croce. Boy, did he want him, because he was exactly what this franchise and this city needed: a kid with skills and attitude and not an ounce of fear in him, because that was the Philadelphia way. A few weeks after Iverson’s news conference at Georgetown, officially declaring for the NBA draft, Croce assigned a private detective to take a deep look into the kid’s home life. He arranged an interview with Thompson, who provided an honest but favorable review of the player he had grown so close with. Croce wanted to know what really happened in that bowling alley, and when the detective came back with vanilla, obvious information that Croce could have found himself in the *Daily Press* archives or by making phone calls to those on the Peninsula, he organized a one-on-one meeting with Iverson. Croce walked into the lobby of an Embassy Suites hotel near the Philadelphia airport and found the kid lounging on a sofa, maybe half awake and wearing sweats.

Croce introduced himself, telling Iverson that Sixers general manager Brad Greenberg was on his way, and they walked together toward a table and two chairs, where Croce grilled him about his background, about his homeboys, about how he liked it when Coach Thompson drilled that size-sixteen up his ass. Iverson looked at this spindly white man with the red goatee and wondered what the hell planet Croce was from. Then Croce asked about that night at Circle Lanes, turning up the volume on Iverson, making sure he was really awake now. The kid slid into the chair, telling Croce that, as he had told everyone, he was barely involved.

“So you didn’t fight?” Croce asked, studying the kid’s body language.

"Nope," Iverson said.

"So you're telling me that a guy calls you a nigger, and you don't hit him?"

Iverson looked into Croce's eyes. He had Iverson's attention now, right where he wanted him, and he studied the kid, his eyes turning to slits behind his John Lennon glasses, waiting to see how Iverson would react. Still, he stood his ground. "Yeah," Iverson said.

"Well, you're a *fucking pussy*!" Croce said, raising his voice.

Iverson looked at him, perplexed, wondering what he was supposed to say. Then he just smiled, and so did Croce. He had been testing him, and Iverson knew it. He explained to Croce that the fact was, he did not have to fight. His friends were there, and after all hell broke loose, they were the ones who jumped in. Iverson, who went on to detail his support system back home, might even have respected Croce for bringing it up. "I'm telling you," Croce would recall much later, "you could see him: There are certain times when Allen lights up, when you really get in and the lights are fully on inside him."

Croce left the meeting satisfied and validated—but wary of Iverson's crew from back home. Iverson would not break easily, and given where this team would be when he joined it, that was a necessary skill. Croce returned to Sixers headquarters, relaying to the organization's basketball men what he had learned—but keeping to himself the secret that he already felt drawn to Iverson, something like an older brother. He told himself that if the personnel department recommended Camby or Georgia Tech's Stephon Marbury, he would go along with it. The thing was, yes, the personnel department knew basketball, but Croce knew people, making himself nod when they reminded him of Iverson's slight frame and bad temper and so many red flags in his past. Drafting the kid from Georgetown would be a risk, but he had looked into his eyes. There was something there that Philadelphia, the Sixers, and Croce all needed.

"We suck!" Croce said later. "This guy was a scoring fucking machine. He knew how to win. The guy was—it didn't matter if he was only six foot, a hundred and sixty pounds wet. We needed someone that we could put the franchise on his shoulders, that wouldn't fold. So here's a scorer with—yeah, maybe he had this tough upbringing. Maybe he had this attitude of me against the world. But that's what we needed."

When he lay down at night, the draft approaching and the last of the preparations being done, Croce kept hearing the same name, again and again, just like he had on the boardwalk. *Pat,* he finally admitted in honest moments, realizing he'd known it all along: *Iverson.*

THE COWORKERS GATHERED a few nights a week at Scott Hewitt's house near Canton, Massachusetts, three hopefuls in their early to mid twenties meeting to talk about Allen Iverson. They did not know him beyond what they had seen on Georgetown television broadcasts, the lightning-fast guard zipping through the lane or stripping the ball from a dribbler and zooming toward the basket. But the three young Reebok employees wanted to train their minds to think as if they *did* know him.

They read newspaper articles, clipping them from the broadsheets and taping them onto Hewitt's living room wall. Next came magazine articles and photographs, the wall covered now as Hewitt's wife frowned at her home's unusual decor. Personality pieces were the best. Why did he do what he did? What led him to say the things he said? His attitude, his upbringing, his life—they wanted to absorb it and learn it as if it were their own. "Our Allen Iverson shrine," said Todd Krinsky, one of the ambitious young employees in that small house in Massachusetts.

Krinsky was climbing the corporate ladder the hard way, and like Croce, he saw himself in Iverson. Krinsky had played basketball and spent time as a deejay, and his first job at Reebok was in the mailroom. He worked in product design now, and he had fallen hard for Iverson. So had the other two, including a young marketing prodigy named Que Gaskins and Hewitt, a shoe designer and the owner of the A.I.

Wall of Fame. When they felt they knew Iverson, or knew him well enough, Hewitt began sketching: a white high-top with a leather upper and pearlized red overlays, along with a translucent outsole. They held up the sketch, studying it, but something was missing. They called him "the Answer," right? Were there not questions about how his size, personality, and background would fit in the structured, corporate NBA? Hewitt grabbed the paper and a minute later he held it up again, this time with a circle containing a question mark. They would call it "The Question."

"We basically wanted to color the toe and color the heel," Krinsky said, "so when you saw him going so fast north–south on the court, it was almost like this Porsche car going up and down."

Not long after Iverson declared for the NBA draft, Krinsky traveled to Washington, D.C., to meet with Iverson and Falk. They waited in Falk's office, the minutes passing and the young men checking their watches. After an hour, in walked Iverson wearing a two-piece, cream-colored linen suit, falling into a chair to hear the latest proposal. Iverson did not say much; these were hardly the first pitchmen he had hosted. But Krinsky was enchanted. "He certainly had this incredible aura of confidence," he said. "He had this swagger to him, even back then."

They left, nothing promised or guaranteed, and returned to Massachusetts. Reebok had Shaquille O'Neal and Dennis Rodman under contract, but to the three young employees, Iverson represented the future and, really, what the company's irreverent mission was supposed to accomplish. Executives were negotiating with Falk before the NBA draft, and Krinsky sat in on a meeting with top decision makers, many of them older and more accomplished than the three hotheads with the Iverson shrine.

"Listen, we can't go crazy here," said Paul Fireman, the company's chairman. "There will always be another Allen Iverson."

Krinsky fidgeted in his seat, feeling part of his destiny slipping. He had no business speaking up, but to hell with it; he did it anyway. "No, there won't," he said. "There *won't*. We can't think like that on this one."

He would explain much later that he wanted the executives to see what he, Gaskins, and Hewitt had seen. This was not just about signing a player who might score thirty points against the Atlanta Hawks. This was a potential fashion and marketing icon. He was strong, determined, and potentially dominant in a normal-sized body—far easier for the average basketball fan and shoe customer to relate to. Krinsky's passion, a former mailroom worker's willingness to speak up to the brass, got the executives' attention. If he felt this strongly, essentially wagering his career, maybe he was right. "We kind of felt we had a responsibility to speak up because we know what the company was trying to achieve," Krinsky said. "We were trying to be young. We were trying to be in the basketball culture, in the game. And this was the guy."

SHORTLY BEFORE STERN, the NBA's commissioner, walked toward a lectern at Continental Airlines Arena in East Rutherford, New Jersey, Sixers general manager Greenberg grabbed a microphone at the Philadelphia Spectrum. Four thousand fans, representing a tortured fan base that had endured losing seasons and busted draft picks and soured hope, had packed inside for a draft party. They deserved to know first.

Four days earlier, after ordering two Sixers jerseys with the names of their two finalists on the backs—IVERSON and MARBURY—Greenberg and Croce made their decision: It would be Allen Iverson leading them into the future, risks and warning signs be damned. The team's biggest worry was the crew Iverson hung with in Hampton, and early plans were discussed to help distance Iverson from the group. "If they care about him," Croce said at the time, "they'll stay away."

The day before the draft, Iverson and Falk sat at a table as Reebok representatives announced the company had signed Iverson to a ten-year endorsement deal, banking on Krinsky's and Gaskins's foresight paying off in a big way. Iverson could barely contain his excitement:

The same young athlete who had basketball shoes only because his mother used that month's rent money would now *have* his own basketball shoe.

At Falk's suggestion—and indulging Reebok's willingness to copy anything Nike had done with Jordan, including assigning him a body man named Howard "H" White—Gaskins would move to Philadelphia to marshal Iverson through the transition into the NBA and into a new life as a very rich man. Iverson would make $50 million during the contract's life, allowing the company to move forward with its plans to release "The Question" sneaker line and make Iverson the face of its future. Amid his excitement, Iverson made a promise to Jamil Blackmon, his friend from Hampton Roads who had coined the nickname "the Answer," a moniker that was now worth millions: For every dollar the name generated for Iverson, court records would show that he promised Blackmon, his friend would be entitled to twenty-five cents—a verbal contract that would later tear apart the longtime friends.

But for now, the new fortune allowed Iverson, who had returned the preowned S600, to indulge his love of cars. He replaced the Benz with a Lexus LX450, making plans for a new Benz in a different color. But that would wait until after the draft. Iverson boarded a jet at Washington's Reagan National Airport, sipping a 7-Up and napping as the plane lifted off and pointed its nose toward New Jersey.

Back home on the Peninsula, where Iverson's road began and took several unexpected detours, a parade was being planned for Hampton's new favorite son. Mayor James Eason, whose house was spared from burning years earlier after Butch Harper intervened, would declare July 6 "Allen Iverson Day," rekindling old tension and fanning protests about misplaced priorities. "He's one of ours," Eason told the *New York Times* at the time, "and it's the right things to do."

When Stern walked toward the lectern in East Rutherford, making the announcement—"The Philadelphia 76ers select Allen Iverson from Georgetown University," he said into the microphone—Iverson stood, baby Tiaura cradled in his right arm, and kissed his mother's cheek. He shook hands, handing his daughter to Ann, who would soon be driving the red Jaguar her son had once vowed to buy her. Iverson kissed Tawanna as he made his way toward the stage. Wearing a gray, two-piece suit and a massive Reebok pin fastened on his left lapel, he was handed a Sixers hat with the tag still dangling. Before greeting Stern, a handshake to begin a relationship that would rarely be so peaceful, he had one more stop to make.

Iverson walked toward a corner, and he slapped the hand of Rahsaan Langford, one of his best friends from Hampton, falling into Langford's arms. Arnie Steele, another close friend, wrapped his arms around both of them. One of them, as they had once dreamed, had made it. Now a promise from childhood was about to be fulfilled—along with everything that came with it.

CHAPTER 8

THE COMPANY YOU KEEP

The whispers traveled through the Crum Basketball Center, on the Dallas, Texas, campus of Southern Methodist University, passing from the basketball offices on the ground floor to the underground practice gym and film room. Larry Brown, the Mustangs' coach and a man forever linked with Iverson, had a surprise for his players not long after the 2013–14 season began: His former pupil was coming to Dallas.

Brown had pulled a few strings, including a surprising commitment he never thought he'd have to make, but the payoff outweighed the cost. And unlike Brown's past visitors—he had invited faces from his sprawling career, including Kiki Vandeweghe and former New York Knicks coach Mike Woodson—the youngsters were actually interested in hearing from Iverson. Keith Frazier, the Mustangs' shooting guard and SMU's first McDonald's All-American recruit ever, considered Iverson a role model; he wore tattoos on both arms and occasionally wore a headband to salute the star he had grown up watching. When Brown announced that Iverson would be visiting, Frazier cried. "The crossover, like, the bagginess of him, like the tattoos, like everything," Frazier said one afternoon, sitting in a corner of the Mustangs' practice gym. "Like, *everything:* I mean, I idolized Allen Iverson."

He walked in looking fresh as always, cargo pants and a denim vest over a green shirt, tied together with a camouflage New York Yankees cap, the bill pulled slightly to the left. His goatee was manicured, and diamonds were clipped into both earlobes. "He looked good," said George Lynch, Iverson's former Sixers teammate who was now Brown's strength and conditioning coach at SMU. "I mean, he didn't look like a drunk."

He stood in front of them and spoke, the kids hanging on every syllable. It was an innocent moment, one of those sweet and thoughtful times that so many never saw. He praised Brown and his former teammates, telling the young players to listen to their coaches as he usually had not; do as he said, Iverson told them, and not as he so often did. Iverson stood there and listened to a few questions, if you can call them that: Frazier raised his hand and, unable to say much else, managed only one word: *"Practice?!"*

Iverson smiled at the reference to his iconic news conference in 2002, and that reminded him of one last message before he left: Never, ever, ever speak with the media when you're angry. It will haunt you, he told them, and when he finished, Iverson posed for pictures with players and Lynch's son. "A blessing," Frazier would recall, "I'll never forget."

When Iverson left, all anyone could do was smile. It was perfect. Well, except for one thing—that single thread that hung free, threatening to unravel the innocence of the day. Iverson had maintained a fondness for Brown and, deep down, a sweetness in his soul. But on this day, a school employee would later say while lamenting Iverson's financial situation, the appearance was not exactly an act of kindness. Iverson's appearance had cost SMU $5,000.

BY EARLY 2003, Iverson's posse from back home—the foundation of young men who had supported him through every hurdle, never questioning him as long as he stayed true to his roots, and whom Iverson had financially sustained for years—was beginning to crumble.

Jamil Blackmon sued Iverson in 2003, alleging that seven years earlier, Iverson had promised him 25 percent of whatever earnings Iverson would rake in as a result of being called "the Answer," the nickname Blackmon had given him one night while he folded laundry. Blackmon had counseled Iverson on his marketing strategy, later moving to Philadelphia at Iverson's urging, according to court documents, and even met at one point with Iverson's attorneys. But Blackmon could never pin down Iverson on consummating a written contract, and so there he went in Pennsylvania's eastern district court, looking for his slice of an Iverson pie now worth tens of millions. Although the suit was eventually dismissed, the personal damage was done: Iverson and Blackmon were finished, more than a decade of history gone.

Five years later, Iverson's career entering its twilight, Arnie Steele—one of three best men in Iverson's wedding and one of the three men celebrating with their friend at the 1996 NBA draft—was arrested for trying to extort money from Iverson. In 2008, Steele claimed he had damaging information about Iverson, and he would keep his secrets only if he was paid. The charges against Steele were eventually dropped, but one more childhood confidant, a face on the other side of the fence at the Newport News City Farm, and one of the many friends whom Iverson had dropped tens of thousands on—a taste of a life they had once dreamed of on the Peninsula—had betrayed him. First Blackmon and now Steele, the Cru was dying a painful death.

Iverson withdrew, increasingly uncertain of whom he could trust. Other than family, the answers were scarce. And that's where it dawned on him: *family*. Gary Moore was not Iverson's father, but since Iverson was eight years old Moore had filled as much of that void as anyone. When Iverson was a youngster, Moore approached Dennis Kozlowski, the football coach at Bethel High, and bragged about a kid with otherworldly talent. Moore claimed to have discovered Iverson, and when the time came, he wanted young Allen to play for Kozlowski. In return, Moore asked, what could Kozlowski do for him? He asked to be part of the team in some capacity, along for whatever ride Iverson was leading them all on, and sure enough, Kozlowski offered Moore a seat in the press box, naming him the Bruins' official statistician.

Not that the benefit was undeserved. It was at Moore's home that Iverson crashed on nights when his family's home was a revolving door of strange faces, loud noises, and illicit substances. Moore had straightened Iverson's bow tie before his junior prom at Bethel, the kid wanting so badly to make a good impression on Tawanna. Moore, another of the best men in Iverson's wedding, had counseled his protégé through the legal maze of the bowling alley ordeal, connecting him with the defense attorney Herbert Kelly, and counseled him also when relationships soured and dreams dissolved. Moore would later confront him when things at home with Tawanna occasionally became untenable, coming to know the most personal and intimate details of one of America's most famous athletes. "He told me one time," said Butch Harper, one of Iverson's earliest coaches, "that Gary Moore buys his drawers."

It was usually Moore who called Brown or another Sixers official some mornings, explaining that Iverson would be unable to practice. Iverson rewarded his old mentor's loyalty with a place on his payroll, first putting Moore in charge of his charity back home, the Crossover Foundation, and later elevating Moore to become his personal manager. He occasionally traveled with the Sixers, sometimes even on the team's chartered flight, and when the parties ran late it was common to see Moore—twenty-one years older than Iverson—by his side, living the good life right alongside the rest of the Hampton crew. "Gary Moore let him get away with so much shit," Kozlowski would say later, "it wasn't even funny."

Even after Iverson could no longer afford to pay Moore as a full-time manager, Moore looked for other ways to remain close. In August 2010 he became certified as an NBA agent, later expanding his entertainment and management company, centered mostly on Iverson and a small cluster of second-tier basketball players, many of whom played professionally in Europe. Moore began advertising himself for corporate speaking engagements, posting photographs of himself with

Iverson and Larry Brown, among others, as part of his own "press kit." He drove Iverson home from the bar when Iverson got falling-down drunk, directed pussy in his direction when his man needed a pick-me-up, saw to it that Iverson arrived at appointments on time—or within a few hours of on time—and explained away Iverson's faults as part of the legend. If someone suggested Iverson's NBA days were finished, Moore disagreed; if an outsider questioned Iverson's habits, Moore blamed the rumor mill and gossipmongers. If a person suggested Iverson needed help reining in his drinking or his spending habits, Moore assured them that Iverson had it under control.

Moore saw him as a son, sure, and the way fathers see sons is that they can do no wrong. Especially when they can get you paid. "He definitely had a love for Allen," said Que Gaskins, who as Iverson's corporate handler for Reebok spent years at his side. "But I also think Gary is looking at Allen as his way out."

As the years passed, most everyone in Iverson's life—teammates, coaches, Tawanna, the kids, many childhood friends, and those he had financially supported—disappeared. Everyone, of course, except Moore.

HE EXITED THE elevator a little before noon, walking into the lobby of the Ritz-Carlton in downtown Philadelphia in late February 2014. At the time two months from his sixtieth birthday, Moore had requested that any meeting take place no earlier than eleven, and when he wandered into the lobby, he looked groggy, as if his alarm clock had just gone off. He wore a sweatshirt and a day's worth of stubble, flecks of gray in his beard.

Moore was a man who came to hone his radar for opportunities. And why not? This is what managers do. But as the years passed and Iverson's fortune dissolved, others who had cashed in on his soft spot for loyalty still were occasionally seen with their hand out. "You develop a dependency on a person," Harper said, "and that person has a lot of money, and you want to keep that dependency going, that drug."

On this cold and windy morning, Moore was in Philadelphia to begin preparations for Iverson's jersey retirement ceremony at halftime of the following Saturday's Sixers game. There were plans to finalize, partying to do, opportunities to seize. Maybe this was one of those. A book was being written on Iverson, examining the good, bad, and ugly of his life and career. A few weeks earlier, Moore had seemed interested in possibly making Iverson available for such a project. He had offered a preliminary meeting near Hampton Roads before changing the venue to Philadelphia. Indeed, Moore had allowed, Iverson deserved a chance to explain himself and the turbulent past few years in his own words, and he seemed to be entering a period of reflection. A documentary had been produced and would be shown two months later at New York's Tribeca Film Festival; Moore would be listed as an executive producer and walk the red carpet and sit in on a panel discussion alongside Iverson. This time the gatekeeper listened for a few minutes, nodding and occasionally checking the time on his phone. After a few minutes, he had a question.

"So," he said, sitting at a long table, "who profits from this?"

The only thing being offered was a chance to answer questions and explain complicated subjects the way Iverson saw them. There was both wonder and nastiness in Iverson's life, no doubting that now, and maybe there were reasons in Iverson's mind for it all. Maybe he saw it differently than it appeared to someone who had not lived as a transcendent athlete.

"Uh-huh," Moore said, his attention beginning to sag.

He sat for a few minutes, contemplating each word and committing to nothing, and when it was made clear that no money was being offered, he checked the time on his phone once again and said he needed to go. Meetings lay ahead, and this was an important week, you know, and anyway, he would ask Iverson what he thought. Then he stood, shook hands, and retreated toward the elevator. Two weeks later, Moore sent an email: Iverson would simply write his own book, with a writer of his choosing, in language that would support the narrative Iverson and his people would craft themselves (a year later, no such project had been green-lit).

Gaskins, who had become close enough with Iverson that Gaskins and his wife accompanied Iverson and Tawanna on their honeymoon, laughed when he heard the story. Then he groaned when told about the visit to SMU, Iverson's impassioned address to Brown's players—and that it had cost the school $5,000. "I promise you Allen did not know that Larry had to pay him," Gaskins said. "I promise you Allen didn't ask for five grand. I *promise* you."

But this phenomenon was nothing new. Gaskins said that when Reebok grew tired of setting up photo shoots or personal appearances only to find Iverson running hours late, the company decided it was smarter—and possibly cheaper, considering the cost of wasted studio time—to simply distribute some side money to make certain Iverson arrived on time. "Five or ten thousand," Gaskins said, "just to get Allen to do his job."

When Iverson announced his retirement from the NBA in October 2013, he did so in front of a backdrop, though that much is hardly unusual. Team officials and celebrities often conduct high-profile news conferences with company logos advertised behind them. But this time, the logo belonged not to Comcast SportsNet or Xfinity. It instead was plastered with the logo of Moore Management & Entertainment.

Gaskins said he stepped away from Reebok in part because of the company's willingness not just to overlook Iverson's bad habits but in some ways to validate them. Gaskins said NBA teams grew wary late in Iverson's career of Moore's insistence that he be consulted for all matters regarding contracts and sponsorships, leading some executives to keep their distance. "He hasn't been smart in the sense that there have been people that wanted to help Allen," Gaskins said, "and there's probably been opportunities where people wanted to do deals with Allen. But Gary will get in the way as opposed to just being the manager and the facilitator of the deal. People will say: 'Well, I'm not doing this deal with Gary.' "

Iverson seemed to know the score. He joked sometimes that, these days, Moore was probably richer than Iverson. "At times, Gary's needs, even if he's not putting them before Allen's," Gaskins said, "he's putting them on the same level as Allen's."

But the other key voices in Iverson's life had mostly stepped aside, some of his closest confidants having betrayed him. So through Moore's loyalty and because of the attrition, Moore by 2013 had become the most important person in Iverson's life. Stephen A. Smith, the longtime Philadelphia columnist who would become a household name appearing on ESPN debate shows, challenged Moore in 2010 to offer tough love for Iverson, telling a Newport News *Daily Press* reporter that he understood how difficult that would be, considering the skin Moore had in the Iverson game. "Sometimes when you are protecting someone, you play the role of enabler, because you've been an apologist and protector all his life," Smith was quoted as saying by the newspaper.

Moore offered mild alternatives for Iverson, the strongest of which came when Moore offered ways—through Tawanna as an intermediary—to get Iverson into Alcoholics Anonymous in early 2012, but he rarely pressed any issue if Iverson pushed back. In return, Iverson empowered Moore. No decisions were made without Moore's blessing, no deals signed without the terms being just right, no interviews or speeches given unless the circumstances aligned just so. "The rise of his power," Gaskins said of Moore, "had a lot to do with Allen's demise."

At Iverson's retirement news conference, there was Moore sitting at the table with Iverson, along with three of Iverson's children. The week before the Sixers lifted his number-three jersey into the rafters, Moore staying out late and sleeping in, the team's public relations director, Michael Preston, allowed Moore, of all people, to have final say over which reporters would or would not be allowed to cover the night's game against the Washington Wizards. When that Saturday night arrived, an evening that wrung out Iverson's emotions like a rag and confirmed that the best part of his life was finished, there was Moore in the receiving line on the arena floor. Standing between Julius Erving, Pat Croce, and the NBA's newly installed commissioner, Adam Silver, Moore could not possibly have been farther from scribbling statistics in the Bethel High press box.

CHAPTER 9

STRAIGHT OUTTA HAMPTON

He brought the ball from the wing toward the top of the key, pausing as the crowd rose to its feet. This, whether they knew it or not, was a changing of the guard, from old to new, as a twenty-one-year-old Iverson faced Michael Jordan, his thirty-four-year-old role model and the face then of the NBA.

"Michael!" Chicago Bulls coach Phil Jackson yelled toward Jordan in March 1997. "Get up on him!"

As Jordan tightened his defensive cushion on Iverson, the kid dribbled through his legs and paused. Jordan, one of basketball's great defenders, waited with his hands on his thighs. A year or so earlier Iverson had told his friends that when he reached his game's largest stage, its greatest star in front of him, he would try the crossover dribble he had learned at Georgetown from teammate Dean Berry and perfected during the Hoyas' Big East schedule. If it could beat Jordan, it could beat anyone.

The time, fifty-seven games into Iverson's young career, had come. Iverson dribbled to his left and Jordan hopped to his right, a dialed-down version of the crossover, just as Berry had taught him. "Textbook," Berry would say later, years after watching his student in his biggest test. Then, after another quick pause, he brought the ball up and leaned his body hard to the left. Jordan committed this time, and in an instant, this rookie had moved the ball and his body to the right, stopping near the free-throw line for a jump shot, and in the process putting a clown suit on the game's greatest player.

IN HAMPTON, RESIDENTS saw the play and then watched the highlights on repeat. Some, not knowing what else to do, ran outside and honked their car horns. Their boy had arrived. Others recognized familiar faces in grocery stores or on sidewalks, slapping hands and beginning conversations about the hometown kid who had survived everything to cross over Michael Jordan.

He would not change, they told each other in the aisles and waiting rooms and gymnasiums. Not Bubba Chuck, no matter how famous he became. The game would change first.

In the late 1990s, America was undergoing an interesting cultural shift. Its heroes were no longer men who wore ties and obeyed the rules. Movies such as *Fight Club* and *American Beauty* blazed a new frontier with characters who had grown tired of being marginalized and went on to kick the establishment in the teeth. Tony Soprano became the first of many dramatic television antiheroes, and the pro wrestler "Stone Cold" Steve Austin represented a new feeling in America: that convention could be and should be challenged, middle fingers raised and beer guzzled as traditional authority figures were sidestepped as sellouts and pussies. Music had capitalized on this movement like nothing else; grunge and hip-hop had moved earlier in the decade from regional cults to nationwide explosions. In neighborhoods like Los Angeles's South Central or the Bronx, places where heroes had forever been scarce, Dre and Biggie now illuminated the paths toward something better, accessible by anyone who kept their shit real.

And then there was the young man with the speed and the crossover, the Sixers rookie who acted like they did back home. Only he was no longer riding the street corner, waiting for a lift to practice or someone to offer shelter; he was on the private jet, returning from South America and his first international tour for Reebok. Que Gaskins, himself a rising star in the company, had agreed—somewhat reluctantly, considering he had been valedictorian at Florida A&M and had earned a master's degree from Northwestern University's prestigious Kellogg School of Management—to be, as he would later put it, Iverson's "corporate babysitter." For the foreseeable future, if Iverson went somewhere, Gaskins would be his shadow. Now they were heading home after a three-week corporate tour, building a new partnership and a growing friendship.

Iverson shared his story, and Gaskins told his: how he had grown up in Southeast Washington, D.C., pulling himself out of the ghetto with his mind, in the same way Iverson had risen above the Peninsula's temptations using his quick legs. No matter how you learn to feed yourself, they told each other, hunger is hunger, and the threat of its return is never gone.

"Damn, my hair's long," Iverson said during a quiet moment on the plane. "Look how long it's getting."

Iverson and Gaskins had taken to getting their hair cut each week, keeping everything neat.

"Might as well let it keep going," Iverson continued, "because I'm gonna get cornrows."

Gaskins laughed and did not immediately say anything. But in his mind, the marketing man was screaming about Iverson getting a hairstyle most common among prison inmates: *Man, you better not get no cornrows.* Could not say that, though, and so Gaskins blamed it on the league, and then they would chuckle about how uptight David Stern is.

"The NBA will not let you have no cornrows," Gaskins said, and it took hearing his own words to realize his mistake.

"What? Won't *let* me?"

Uh-oh, Gaskins thought.

"Reebok," Iverson fired back, "won't let *you*!"

"Man, Reebok don't even care about stuff like that."

Then it became a bet. Who could grow their hair fast enough, braid it tight enough, become the first one with "hangtime," or what urban kids called it when their braids were long enough to reach the middle of their necks. In February 1997, Iverson arrived in Cleveland to play in the Rookie Challenge during All-Star weekend, unveiling for the first time his modest cornrows. Somewhere in Gund Arena, Gaskins sat and watched, his own hair tightly braided and his mind wondering what the hell he had just gotten himself into.

Two years later, as players funneled back to their teams after the NBA lockout, Iverson arrived at the Sixers training camp with several fresh tattoos, company for the lonely bulldog on his left shoulder. Above it was a cross with words he believed represented his upbringing—words he wanted to carry with him and wear as a badge of honor: *Only the Strong Survive*. "A weak person will break. They'll give up," he would say later in a video interview with *Slam* magazine. "Whatever I go through in life, whatever it is, I'll fight through it. I don't think God would put you through nothing you can't handle."

Iverson found his way often to Body Graphics in South Philadelphia and recognized his boys from Hampton with "Cru Thik" immortalized in blue ink on his left forearm. His right arm was soon covered in words and symbols: "Hold My Own" in calligraphy on his shoulder, a skull wearing a battle helmet on his biceps, and the grim reaper lurking on Iverson's right forearm. The names of his first two children, Tiaura and Deuce, now appeared on his chest, along with a pair of hands locked in prayer. It wasn't just decoration for Iverson; his skin was now a canvas that told a story of experiences, triumphs, and philosophies. "He was pretty distinct about what he wanted," said Danny Balena, who would eventually become one of Iverson's favorite tattoo artists. "It wasn't like: 'I don't know what to do here.' It was like: 'I want this here, and I want this here.' "

Even while Balena was putting ink on Iverson's hands, smoking out a dollar sign and the graffiti-style "Money Bagz" on the left and negative-shading two stacks of cash on the right, he wondered how this would fly in the NBA. This was a universe that Jordan had occupied for nearly two decades, moving from player to pitchman—and finding himself rewarded for it with salaries in the neighborhood of $30 million annually, along with huge endorsement dollars. Jordan had been the face of Stern's NBA, saying and doing the right things and keeping everyone from worrying too much. Jordan was a gentle, approachable, suburb-friendly superstar; he liked golf and cigars, the same as any corporate fat cat and weekend warrior.

But Iverson wore oversized white T-shirts and held up his sagging pants, just like they did on the streets of every city in America. Several thick chains bounced as he walked, and he mumbled and cursed during interviews and news conferences. Every few months the clean-cut rookie with the neat hair and blank skin died a little; in his place was a kid whose very adult life would be a mural to acknowledge his childhood, the despair he had once known, the rise he had promised himself and achieved. "We saw the transformation clearly," said Reebok executive Todd Krinsky, who along with Gaskins had recruited Iverson to join the shoe company shortly after Iverson left Georgetown. "Every day, we'd be hearing: Oh, he's getting another tattoo."

The NBA did not like the message that Iverson's look was supposedly sending, even if Iverson was becoming a folk hero in black America. When Iverson appeared in January 2000 on the cover of *Hoop* magazine, the league's official publication, Iverson's tattoos had been airbrushed out of the photograph. His earring and a gold chain also were absent, though he had worn them during the shoot. Amid an uproar, the league eventually apologized and later ran a more authentic photograph in one of its issues, but Iverson was outraged. How he looked was a matter of personal expression and one of the ways he kept in touch with the men and women who honked their horns when he had crossed over Jordan—the same people who had helped him get onto this stage in the first place, those he represented and the new generation he wanted to inspire. "They could have used somebody else if they didn't want to accept me as a whole," Iverson said at the time. "This is who I am. It kind of hurts, because I've got my mother's name on my body, my grandmother's name, my kids, my fiancée. That means something to me. Airbrushing them, that's like a slap in my face."

Reebok, whose approach was irreverence compared with the wide-ranging appeal of Nike and Adidas, was more judicious about the concerns that some older executives were raising during meetings. The company organized focus groups to learn whether, as the NBA feared, Iverson's off-the-streets look was scaring away potential customers. Reebok had a decision to make, between two decided risks: Support Iverson, potentially firing on the gates of the NBA in defense of his broad appeal, or ask him to tighten his image, possibly declaring war on Iverson himself. When the results came back, Krinsky was relieved that he would not have to opt for the latter option. Younger customers, particular those in places like Detroit and North Philadelphia and Los Angeles, identified with Iverson—far more than with cleaner-cut celebrities. "He is me. Allen Iverson is me," Krinsky said the research showed, time after time. "They could relate to him. Obviously he could relate to them because he was a small dude playing the game with giants.

"But the way he handled himself, the way he talked, the way he dressed and hung out with his friends, the music he listened to? He *is* me. Like, I can identify with him, and I can aspire to be more because he was a guy from the hood that did it."

The company gave Iverson license to be himself, whatever that might eventually become, and if the NBA did not like it, then, well, fuck the NBA. Jadakiss, a rapper who appeared in a Reebok commercial for Iverson's Answer 5 sneaker, was among those who became fascinated with the young star and, more than that, the way he became a symbol of his time and place in the world. "Excuse my French," the rapper said. "But when you're young, black, and you don't give a fuck, you become kind of a hero like that."

AT THE T.G.I. Friday's on City Line Avenue in Philadelphia, colorful lights dance off the necks of liquor bottles and staff members hustle to accommodate those seated around the U-shaped bar. Big-screen televisions show sports highlights from the hours and days before; eyes train on the action as plates are slid onto the tabletops and plastic cups are kept full.

What more could one of America's most famous men want?

In the late 1990s, this was Iverson's favorite hangout. Early in Iverson's career, his agent, David Falk, visited Philadelphia to attend a Sixers home game against the Bulls. Falk also represented Jordan, and so he invited his two most famous clients to dinner on consecutive nights. The first night, Jordan, Falk, and the president of the floral company FTD went to the Striped Bass, an upscale seafood restaurant on Rittenhouse Square. The men dined and relieved the restaurant of several bottles of expensive wine, and when the check arrived, the bill for the three of them came to about $3,500. The next night, Falk asked Iverson where he wanted to go—anywhere in the city, kid—and, naturally, Iverson asked Falk to take him to Friday's. And would he mind if Iverson brought a few friends, just so they would not feel left out? Of course not, Falk said, and this time when the bill arrived, the agent paid the tab for Iverson, his mother, the FTD president, and nine others—all for less than $300.

There were no velvet ropes or bottle service there, but at least it was convenient: three blocks from the Sixers' practice facility and a staff always willing to make him feel welcome. And besides, the way Iverson grew up, Friday's seemed highbrow. "That was going out for them," said Gaskins, who shared hundreds of meals with Iverson over the years.

When Sixers home games ended, waiters and bartenders began preparing for Iverson's arrival. He could arrive at any minute, flanked by an entourage twenty or thirty strong. And so the bar was stocked with Iverson's favorite imported beers, and Table 70, a long booth in the corner and Iverson's favorite spot, was kept vacant and marked as reserved. Staff members were reminded not to ask for autographs, not even on the paper dinner napkins, and fans and groupies would be kept at a distance.

"We used to think: You know, hey, this guy doesn't have to be here. He could go anywhere in the world. He could be on a jet to New York, have dinner, and fly back home. Whatever he wants to do," said Tim Hampton, who was Iverson's regular waiter at Friday's. "But it just shows that he wanted to stay connected. I believe he had the feel of the people of Philadelphia. And Philadelphia is a working town. You know, blue-collar workers, regular people. And so he was able to connect just because of that."

When Iverson's Bentley stopped in front of the main entrance, usually in one of the handicapped spots, Hampton or someone else retrieved the Monopoly board the staff kept for Iverson behind the bar. Then a bartender reached into the cooler, pulling out frosted bottles of beers Iverson saw as exotic. "It wasn't like he was drinking Hennessy or Rémy Martin or vodka or stuff like that," Gaskins said. "In the beginning, or at least what I saw all the time, it was mostly like Heineken and fucking Corona." Sometimes he drank and played for hours, the bottles and phony five-hundred-dollar bills collecting—Iverson still insisting that he act as the banker—as the Friday's employees allowed the group to finish its game long after the bar closed and the doors were locked. Other times Iverson stopped in for a quick plate of fried shrimp or chicken fingers before heading to the titty club with a teammate or a rapper. His crew watched the highlights on the televisions near the bar, waiting for Iverson to appear, and when he crossed over a defender or sliced through the lane for a drive to the basket, everyone erupted—and Iverson sat and smiled. Three or four nights a week Iverson and his friends occupied Table 70 and the surrounding area, and special occasions were no different: When Ann Iverson celebrated her birthday one year, her son took her to his favorite place on City Avenue, and Tim Hampton led the staff in song.

I don't know but I've been told
Someone here is getting old!
I don't know but it's been said
Someone's face is turning red!

Iverson had arrived in Philadelphia a simple man, of simple tastes, and in private he remained that way. He was thoughtful and caring, even if occasionally he hid that side of himself. He was not perfect and did not claim to be, but he was more good than bad, more hard worker than among the blessed, and in the city he now called home, there was some commonality in that.

"This city don't take no bullshit," said Aaron McKie, a Sixers teammate who was born, raised, and educated in Philadelphia. "You can't fool these people. And that's him. . . . For all of the small people, whether it's business, whether it's sports, whatever—if you're an underdog at your job and people don't give you an opportunity, he gave all of those people hope."

He would stay at Friday's until the staff playfully kicked him out, promising to see him tomorrow, and then he went to whichever bar would have him or, shit, who was up for a run to Atlantic City? Then he would arrive late for shootaround the next day or spend the first quarter of afternoon games suffering the alcohol shakes, his teammates rolling their eyes and waiting for Larry Brown's head to explode, the players wondering how the hell Iverson did it. He did not sleep on the team plane, and God help anyone who did. There were spades to be played and money to be made, so wake up, Aaron, wake up, wake up, wake up!

"A.I., give me a half hour, man," McKie would tell him, his head resting on the airplane's wall.

"Ah, man, fuck that!" Iverson would reply, and if McKie kept his eyes closed, Iverson sat there and threw popcorn at him until McKie had enough.

"Heck with it," McKie said finally, reaching for the cards. "Come on, man, let's go."

Iverson's voice carried through the plane, telling jokes or talking about George Lynch's muscles or how Tyrone Hill looked *just like* Skeletor, and when the plane landed in Oakland or Seattle or Phoenix at three or four in the morning, Brown dazed and his glasses sitting crooked on his face, Iverson kept going. "It's just quiet as can be, and he's just yelling: 'Yeah, I won all the money! I won all the money, da-da-da-da!' " McKie recalled. "Coach Brown used to just be looking at him, like, this guy, do he *ever* shut up?"

Iverson never lifted weights, barely stretched, and ate like hell, and before games he would sit in the players' family lounge until a half hour before tip-off, wearing a tank top and making plans for after the game. Then he would run downstairs and slide on his number-three jersey, and five minutes before the public address announcer introduced him—"a six-foot guard from *Georgetoooooooown*"—he choked down four hot dogs, all the fuel a high-performance body needs. "You go in Allen's room, and he might have like steak, some french fries, a Sprite—three Sprites—and a bowl of ice cream," Gaskins said. "And then he'd drop fifty on you. What the fuck?"

When the games started, he would dazzle and shine, and more than that he would take zero shit, even from Jordan. Iverson shoved Dennis Rodman during one game against the Bulls, and Scottie Pippen and Rodman later ripped Iverson in the media for his behavior. "I don't like too many of these young players," Rodman was quoted as saying, and considering Rodman's own reputation as a shit-stirrer, the remarks were both ironic and biting. "But I like him the least. You've got to respect the game and the players you're playing against. He doesn't respect people. He thinks he's God. He thinks the court is his street, his playground, and he can do anything he wants and say anything he wants."

Iverson was immature and unseasoned, the veterans said, and they were not alone in those opinions. He feuded with Charles Barkley and NBA official Tim Donaghy and teammate Jerry Stackhouse, at one point coming to blows with Stackhouse and compelling the Sixers to trade Stackhouse, choosing one first-round draft pick over the other. "The guy is showing disrespect. You come into the league, and you have to do something, or your team has to do something before you talk," Bulls guard Ron Harper said. Later, Jordan approached the kid and tried to offer some advice; instead, the *New York Post* reported at the time, Iverson told his boyhood hero to "get the hell out of my way," and Jordan rolled his eyes and did as Iverson asked.

Iverson dived across the floor or hurdled the scorer's table to chase loose balls, craned his neck upward to get in the face of any opponent who challenged him or tried to get in his head, and talked back to anyone who dared stand in his way. Street ball, *got dammit,* the game he learned and one he was bringing with him from the playgrounds of Hampton into the arenas of the NBA. Then he would light up the scoreboard and, as he put it so often, play each game as if it were his last, draining a clutch shot or slamming home a dunk and then jogging toward the sideline and cupping a hand around his ear, nodding his head as the cheers thundered through the arena. They might hate his ass everywhere else, but in Philadelphia he was becoming one of their own.

"Here's this guy getting beat up and knocked down underneath the rims by these behemoths, and he gets right back up and looks them in the eyes and keeps on going with a smirk and a smile," said Pat Croce, the former Sixers president and a Philadelphia native. "And we just fuckin' loved that."

WAS IVERSON JUST being himself, the tattoos and restlessness and anger just side effects of his upbringing, or was Reebok's marketing department pulling the strings on a brilliantly timed character during the Rebel Movement?

"He was not that way. That's not the way he was," said Bill Tose, one of Iverson's youth coaches back in Hampton. "Sure, he hung out and did those kind of things. But that's not how he carried himself in high school, and that's not how he carried himself at Georgetown.

"They wanted to create this hip-hop guy, because that was the hot thing going at the time. So now they give him this money, and then they created this image, a hip-hop image, so Allen's got to live up to that."

Gaskins, for his part, said Tose's suggestion that Iverson's image was a corporate creation was fair but not exactly accurate. "One of the things I kept telling Reebok, especially from a marketing perspective," Gaskins said, "is that we don't have to do *anything* to try to market him to be cool and authentic."

Nevertheless, past mentors encouraged Iverson to distance himself from the most unsavory parts of his past, but whichever powerful force was guiding him—loyalty or his endorsement deal—he refused. In September 1996, a little more than a month before his rookie season started, Iverson and two friends visited Hampton University and played a pickup basketball game. Afterward, Iverson asked the friends, Alex Rhoden and Michael Powell, who had a felony conviction on his record, to wait in his idling Mercedes-Benz while he made a quick stop inside a dormitory. As they waited, another car drove up, spraying bullets into the body of Iverson's luxury sedan, and though no one was hurt, the incident was enough to draw attention. Three days later, two rooms at the Ramada Inn in Newport News, both registered to Iverson, were trashed, and it was revealed that Iverson was so concerned about his safety that he kept a .45-caliber Glock pistol, along with a fully loaded clip of bullets, in his car.

A year later, Iverson was a passenger in his Mercedes when it was pulled over for speeding in Virginia. The police officer smelled marijuana and discovered two joints, including one under the front passenger seat, not far from Iverson's Glock. "He did do crazy shit," Croce said, now making light of an incident that at the time made the Sixers front office wonder if it had made a mistake in drafting Iverson.

If Reebok truly had not created Iverson's persona, as Tose and others back home suspected, then it at least had allowed it to grow without much resistance. And why not? The focus groups had spoken, and Iverson's Question and Answer franchise was a sensation; along with retro releases it eventually would become the second-best-selling franchise ever, behind only Nike's Air Jordan. Reebok understood that tampering with the formula could have consequences, and besides, the company's chairman, Paul Fireman, was infatuated with Iverson and his attitude.

Once, Fireman asked Krinsky to set up a meeting with Iverson. Krinsky reminded the Sixers guard several times that Fireman, one of the most powerful men in sports, would be visiting his home in suburban Philadelphia. But Iverson forgot about the meeting anyway, arriving two hours late. Krinsky squirmed, cursing himself for promising to deliver Iverson, his habitual tardiness almost as famous as that crossover, to his boss.

Finally Iverson pulled up, and Krinsky breathed out a sigh. *Thank God,* he thought, but Iverson's reaction to seeing his visitors deflated his hope for a successful meeting. "Oh, today?" Iverson asked Krinsky.

"Yes, Allen, today," Krinsky said.

Iverson shook hands with Fireman, who in essence was paying Iverson as much as the Sixers, and Fireman beamed as he unveiled a suede-bound book with an outline of Iverson's future with the company. Fireman began his presentation, and Iverson's mind wandered. By the time Fireman flipped to the second page, just beginning his proposal, a sleepy Iverson had seen enough. "Listen, big Paul," he said to Krinsky's horror. "It's time for A.I. to lay down."

Iverson said nothing more as he walked upstairs, passing through the French doors that led to his bedroom, then closing them without further announcement. Krinsky was already considering the fitness of his resume when he looked at his boss. "Is that it?" Fireman asked, and Krinsky bit his lip and nodded.

Then Fireman smiled. "That was one of the greatest exits," the chairman said, "I've ever seen!"

Iverson's legend was growing, and so were the profits associated with him: On the strength of Iverson's brand, Reebok's stock had increased, and the company sold $1 million in Iverson jerseys. But those closest to him worried about how he was adjusting to being among the nouveau riche. In his mind, he was on a one-way ride to the top, and along the way he was honoring the pact he and his friends had made years earlier. Those who had been with him through the bad times were now experiencing the glory with him. At T.G.I. Friday's or an expensive club downtown, Iverson always picked up the tab. When Iverson wanted a new tattoo, arranging for Balena or another artist to conduct a private session in a hotel room, several others wanted ink, too, and Balena said that at the end of each marathon sitting, Iverson would step forward and hand him a wad of cash—sometimes double the amount Balena had quoted him.

Iverson looked the other way when an old acquaintance in Washington, D.C., charged a $7,000 watch to Iverson's account, and a few months after buying a $40,000 Lexus, Iverson bought a new Range Rover and gave the Lexus to an aunt. If he bought a new piece of jewelry, the piece it replaced went to the first friend who requested it. Iverson paid for travel so that his crew could watch him play on the road, then party with him after games. They charged thousands in room service and phone calls, all of it eventually deducted from Iverson's paycheck without even a hint of protest. "They were his family, just like you're loyal to your family," Croce said. "It just so happens his family extends outside his four walls because, really, the hood is his four walls."

He took care of friends and old neighbors, past coaches and mentors, family members and even new friends who would have no trouble paying their own way. Jadakiss, himself a millionaire, once spent six hours drinking poolside with Iverson at a Miami hotel, and when the $19,000 tab arrived, Iverson reached for it. "Never had to go in my pockets around Bubba Chuck," the rapper said. "Never."

Closer friends lived with Iverson, who allowed them to drive his cars and eat his food. They came to expect Iverson to pay for everything, no matter how much a meal or a suit or a bottle cost. "They end up buying champagne for three hundred dollars a bottle," former Sixers player Roshown McLeod said, describing a typical night out with Iverson and his entourage. "And they're with you, so owners and bartenders and waitresses assume that it's on your tab, and so a lot of times it's things you don't even spend that cause the problem. And then the bill comes, and you feel as though, 'I've got it, so I might as well go ahead and do it, because these are my friends and we're here together, and I've got it and they don't.' "

Before the All-Star Game in 1997, when he debuted his cornrows, Iverson arranged for two longtime friends, Eric Jackson and Rahsaan Langford, each of them aspiring rappers, to perform for Reebok executives. His success was their success, their pact now coming to life, and it was time for the music world to learn the names "E" and "Rah The Illicit."

However it had been done, an image and a brand had been conceived and brought to life. Now it was growing, spreading almost out of control, and with everyone around him having such a good time, Iverson had no idea why anyone could possibly have a problem with it. "He's a very loyal guy," said Boo Williams, Iverson's former AAU coach back in Virginia. "Maybe too much."

ANN IVERSON WAS growing concerned that the image was consuming her son, that the aggressive and violent Mr. Hyde was overtaking the calm and loving Dr. Jekyll. She drove to Philadelphia early in Iverson's career and discovered a group of her son's friends living in his condominium, Iverson himself nowhere to be found.

The flickering candlelight of her son's innocence seemed darkened by a spreading set of bad examples and a lack of discipline. He was drinking more now, staying out later, and Ann's phone rang occasionally with panicked calls from Tawanna, her son's longtime girlfriend. Long after his days at Georgetown, when he smiled at hecklers in arena stands, Iverson in 2001 screamed profanity at one fan, calling him a "faggot." Over a relatively short period of time, Iverson seemed less entertained by things like the lighthearted birthday song at Friday's; instead he withdrew into a recording studio to put down lyrics over the sound of gunfire, a rap single called "40 Bars" to be the first offering of an album called "Non-Fiction." His rap name, Jewelz, was a nod at *Pulp Fiction,* a movie he and

Tawanna had watched dozens of times, and Samuel L. Jackson's character, a contract killer who also believed in righteousness—and grappled with where he stood on the spectrum of good and evil.

You got the wrong idea nigga I'm CT fool
Get murdered in a second in the first degree
Come to me wit faggot tendencies
You'll be sleepin where the maggots be

It was a raw, unfiltered look into how Iverson saw the world, for better or worse, and some worried that, yes, Iverson *had* changed. Now he was a caricature of who he had once been, other rappers even noticing how hard-core his viewpoint was, and even those who loved him wondered if it was possible he could come back.

Niggas screamin he was a good boy
Ever since he was born
But fuck it he gone
Life must go on
Niggas don't live that long

The NBA blasted the single, Stern calling the lyrics "coarse, offensive and anti-social." The commissioner reportedly had to be talked out of suspending and fining Iverson, though he did threaten such punishments. The Sixers star apologized for the lyrics and eventually killed the album, ending his rap career before it truly began.

Ann Iverson kicked her son's friends out of his condominium and asked her brother, Gregory, a former marine, to move in, shadowing Iverson and making certain he stayed out of trouble and performed his responsibilities in a timely manner. Not that Ann was above enjoying her own lavish new lifestyle. She drove that red Jaguar and traveled and collected jewelry and clothing and poured hundreds of thousands of her son's dollars into converting an old Chinese buffet in Hampton into her own restaurant and sports bar—giving up on the project after four months and $360,000 in renovations, numerous health code violations, and Ann's public suspicions that her staff was stealing from her. "I've learned," she told the Newport News *Daily Press* shortly after the restaurant closed, "that you just can't trust people."

In 1998, as threats intensified that NBA team owners would, in reaction to an impasse in collective-bargaining negotiations with players, lock out the players and jeopardize the 1998–99 season, Falk, Iverson's agent, advised his clients to begin hoarding money. Iverson would not listen, and after the lockout went into effect and players no longer received paychecks, Ann—who had been granted power of attorney when her son was eighteen and sitting in jail—called Falk on a Friday, threatening to fire him if an amount of money was not released to her. She had been unable to board a flight to Philadelphia because of her son's unpaid bills to a travel agent. "I begged her to leave the monies alone because the lockout was coming," Falk said, "and he needed that to live." Ann kept making threats, and Falk kept balking, two headstrong personalities, each of whom cared deeply for Iverson and had their own stake in his financial future. Falk stood strong, and so did Ann. She fired her son's agent, as promised, and it was not the last time responsibilities would be stripped and relationships soured because someone made an attempt at curbing Iverson's self-destructive tendencies. "It was a very simple expression of why blood is thicker than water," Falk said. "His mom wanted certain things we weren't in position to provide. And she pulled the plug."

Others tried to adapt to a rapidly changing landscape. Reacting to season ticket holders' complaints about how Iverson's friends were behaving at Sixers games, Croce moved the friends' seats at the First Union Center. Reebok—now trying to control what it had given life to—fidgeted over its future with Iverson, even as Gaskins tried like hell to rationalize Iverson's thinking. "He liked taking on that responsibility of taking care of his family," he said. "I think that's the thing that motivated him to go out on that floor every night and kick some ass.

'I've got to do this for my family. I've got all these mouths to feed. I've got to go take care of this shit for my family. I've got to go take care of my business.' Like, I really think he kind of carried that attitude with him every time he came out to play."

Gaskins, trying to balance his loyalty to Iverson and responsibility to Reebok, witnessed Iverson's exorbitant spending, such as buying first-class airline tickets for a New Jersey hairdresser named Dionne Matthews, arranging limousines for her, and covering all expenses so she could tighten his cornrows. Iverson wasn't just attracting attention for his game; fans were on the lookout for the next creative braid design or a new tattoo—all of the expenses adding up but Iverson barely noticing. "I used to tell him all the time: 'I know you're going to make mistakes, man,'" Gaskins recalled. "'But it's not a mistake unless you do it twice. So let's just try to be smart.'"

Iverson dropped tens of thousands a week, keeping his friends and family afloat and fulfilling his own material desires. Reebok executives were conflicted: The buzz was unmistakable and lucrative, but the company was growing increasingly concerned about its star's financial future. "There's a lot of rumors about how much he's spending, and we really, really like him and want to continue with him," Krinsky said. "But it's not really responsible for us to just keep paying him if he's going to keep spending it."

As it finalized a contract extension in the form of a lifetime deal in 2001, installing company-friendly triggers that could alter or void the agreement if necessary, Fireman suggested a deferred trust be added. Iverson would be paid millions, but rather than make every dollar accessible, $32 million could not be touched until he turned fifty-five. After Iverson's career ended, he would receive an $800,000 annual interest payment, protecting him—or so the executives hoped—long-term.

Along with the run-in with the league about the rap album, the growing concerns of Iverson's family actually compelled him to pause and consider regaining control of his life and, at least for now, keeping

Mr. Hyde at bay. At one point Larry Brown made his move to save Iverson's soul, catering to his soft side by reminding him of the habits of his hero. Iverson had grown up wanting to be like Jordan, right? And did he realize that Jordan refused to appear in front of a television camera in anything but an expensive suit? "If they see you with your hat crooked and your jewelry and your pants down below your ass," Brown told him, "that's the impression they're going to have of you. And I know you're not like that."

So Iverson indulged his coach, going to Boyd's, Philadelphia's landmark department store, and buying a Versace suit. He wore it to the arena for a Sixers playoff game, and Brown hoped that he had finally made sense to his best player. What Brown did not know was that Iverson knew his boys from Hampton would see him wearing it, and this simply could not happen.

Before the game, Brown walked into the Sixers' locker room and looked toward the corner, where the suit was crumpled on the floor like garbage. Brown looked around but saw no one. Iverson, or at least the version of him that some of them wanted him to be, was already gone.

CHAPTER 10

ON DEFENSE

How long has he been doing this?" Tawanna was asked during a divorce hearing in 2013.

"Years," she said simply, looking back to one argument before they were married. Iverson had lost his temper and opted to throw Tawanna out of the house, even getting three-year-old Deuce to help haul his mother's belongings through the front door—and, following his dad's instructions, calling Tawanna a whore.

The couple's problems began in 1997, Tawanna would recall, shortly after they moved in together in Philadelphia. Iverson was a young superstar, emboldened by fame and power and told only what he wanted to hear by those who depended on him, and although Tawanna also needed Iverson for financial support, she was the only adult who actually lived with him full-time. In those early days, she would testify, Iverson came to think he was invincible, living the NBA life and drinking increasing amounts of alcohol. He had always been moody, eager for confrontation—an attribute that, in an ironic twist, would both make and break him—but alcohol brought out the worst. "I didn't think it was an issue until a couple of years in the league," Tawanna would tell the court, "and it just progressed. . . . He's gotten worse. It was bad, and it got worse."

Early in Iverson's career with the Sixers, the young couple lived in a townhouse outside Philadelphia. He had decided one night to unwind with friends after a game, leaving Tawanna at home with Iverson's mother, along with Ann Iverson's boyfriend and another man who had been her high school basketball coach. They talked and passed time in the living room, and then Iverson came in drunk, walking toward Tawanna as if he wanted to greet his then girlfriend with a hug. The group smiled, assuming they were about to witness a tender moment with a pair of high school sweethearts, but then Iverson rested his Timberland on the top of Tawanna's bare foot, grinding her skin with the hard sole like he was putting out a cigarette. She shoved him away, further infuriating the tipsy Iverson, who responded by grabbing Tawanna's hair and dragging her upstairs as Ann Iverson screamed for her son to stop.

Another time he punched Tawanna, hitting her in a place on her lower back that left her gasping for breath, and later, after she asked Iverson just what the hell that was, he chuckled. "Aw, that's a kidney shot," Tawanna would testify that Iverson said.

"I couldn't even catch my breath," she would recall. "I didn't even know what a kidney shot was, but he laughed at it because he thought it was funny."

THE CONFRONTATIONS WORSENED, following Iverson's pattern of self-destruction as he approached and passed age thirty, developing full-on anger and alcohol issues that many—especially those who relied on him—were reluctant to bring up. Larry Brown, the Sixers' coach during much of Iverson's career in Philadelphia, tried to stay out of players' personal affairs. His teammates saw Iverson not as a threat to himself or his family but as a superhuman wonder who could abuse his body until the wee hours and then come back the next night and score forty points. The great ones could do this, so many of them told themselves, like Michael Jordan staying out all night in a casino, drinking scotch and puffing on cigars as the next hand was dealt, because they had somehow been touched by the finger of God. "There's a motor inside of them that no one else has," Iverson's former Sixers teammate George Lynch said of these legends.

Pat Croce, the team's president during Iverson's first five NBA seasons, occasionally had no choice but to bring up the turmoil creeping more often into Iverson's life, usually doing so after a skipped practice or an especially heated exchange with Brown. The talk would typically begin with Iverson trying to ignore Croce or firing back at him, prompting the streetwise Croce to get in his best player's face.

"Shut the fuck up! I'm talking!" Croce remembered screaming at Iverson on more than one occasion. "That's the only thing he understood, because when he's off, he's off. You've got to play street with him. Otherwise he's going to run all over you. Remember, this is one of the most competitive athletes there is. Even when he's wrong, there's no way. You've just got to come back at him."

Tawanna learned this, and sometimes standing up to Iverson stunned him into ending an argument, and other times it incited him. She slammed on the brakes once while driving on an interstate that runs through Atlanta, and another time she picked up an empty champagne bottle—Iverson had drained the contents himself—and hurled it at him, the thick glass missing Iverson and bouncing off the wall with a thud. She admitted during court proceedings that she punched Iverson, once drawing blood, and threw insults toward him, his mother, or Gary Moore.

At the same time Tawanna had no choice but to rely on Iverson, riding the highs and lows of his changing personality. She also was often at the mercy of those who knew her husband best, and so sometimes she had no choice but to call Ann or Moore to beg for assistance. "He's not getting up doing what he has to do," Tawanna said, replaying a typical conversation with Moore, "or he's drinking too much, whatever, those type of issues, where I felt like Gary had that voice and he was the one that could convince him to do the right thing."

Moore, with his own stake in the unsteady Iverson empire, usually tried to avoid taking sides unless the problems boiled over. Ann spoke with her son occasionally, and Iverson promised to be a better man, and Ann opted to believe him. Then, a short time later, Ann's phone would ring again. He had thrown Tawanna's cell phone so hard once that it passed through a wall, leaving two holes in the drywall—one in the foyer, where the argument raged, and the other in the powder room, where it landed. Another time, as police made their way to their home in Atlanta, he pulled the phone out of Tawanna's hand and pretended to throw it into the woods. He referred to Tawanna as "TD Turner," recalling her father's playful nickname; Iverson used "TD" as a way to throw it in his wife's face that she was nothing more than a way to score. He called her a "prostitute" and a "dirty dog," and his favorite was calling her "water girl," once a term of endearment—a callback to her role as manager on her high school's girls' basketball team. The position had once allowed her to attend road games and be with Iverson outside the context of the school or home routine, and at the time, he enjoyed her company. Now it was nothing but an insult, Iverson using it to demean Tawanna as a groupie who became interested in him only because he was a talented basketball player who might someday make it big. Whatever the reasons, the moniker hit a nerve. "I would say that Mr. Iverson pushes my buttons," Tawanna told the court, "and he knows what buttons to push."

She testified that, when things were at their worst, Iverson threatened to have Tawanna killed, along with any family member who had gotten sideways with him: Tawanna's mother, her brother, her one-year-old nephew. After one of their many separations, Iverson complained about paying for Tawanna's apartment. She replied that he was lucky that was all he had to pay for. "Bitch," she testified that Iverson had once said, "you lucky you ain't dead."

He then reminded Tawanna that, through the people he knew, he could pay for someone to say that she was having an affair, or, if it came down to it, spend $5,000 and, as she recounted it for the court, "get me if he wanted to, or anybody."

Holidays, supposed to be a peaceful time, were no match for Iverson's temper and the thunderstorm that was the relationship between him and Tawanna. When Iverson spent Christmas one year in Turkey, playing for a professional team in Istanbul, Tawanna planned for the family to spend the holiday with him on foreign soil. Their five children were packed and ready, but the night before the family's flight, Tawanna and Iverson had a championship shouting match, and Tawanna stayed home, allowing the kids to go to Turkey and herself finding holiday peace only in solitude.

The day before Easter one year, Iverson came home drunk, chirping at Tawanna for one thing or another, and Tawanna just sat there in silence, trying like hell to ignore him. It was her go-to strategy, Tawanna always the quiet one, and if getting in Iverson's face was just as likely to intensify the run-in as defuse it, so was saying nothing—Iverson would grow increasingly angry that she would not respond. This time, she testified, Tawanna put on her shoes to leave the house and Iverson chased her, screaming as he did it. "Yeah, run," Tawanna told the court he said. "Leave." When he caught up to her, Iverson punched her in the back.

Tawanna ran downstairs, hiding under the dining table as Iverson stalked through the house, looking for her. When he found his wife, Iverson stood next to the table, and all she saw was her husband's hand holding a cell phone, Iverson daring her to call the police.

SHE BEGGED HIM to get help and involved more and more outsiders, telling them more and more troubling details—his mother and his teammates, Moore and team officials—but without a close-in view of reality, all most people chose to focus on was the image of Tawanna and the kids smiling near the basketball court's baseline, Ann Iverson wearing her Iverson jersey and handing out her own trading card, the family all together in the arena's corridors for a postgame gathering. Iverson, whether he intended it or not, had become a master at manipulating his image, and because of this, nobody asked too many questions. Plans for an intervention did not come until much later, when Iverson's life was falling apart in plain view, everyone around him scrambling to fortify the walls before his empire collapsed. "Toward the end, the last five years," Que Gaskins said in summer 2014, "I've had people call me and be like: 'Yo, I just seen your man in the club drunk as hell.'

"I haven't been in an environment where I've been around him socially within like the past five years, but I do know that he has a drinking problem. Big-time drinking problem. But I don't know if he—and I don't know if Gary or anyone has said anything to him about it."

Aaron McKie, the Sixers teammate who was closest with Iverson, either never saw the confrontations or turned a blind eye toward them. He instead remembered only the times when Iverson sat alone after road games in the rear of the team bus, assuming no one could hear him as he whispered loving words to Tawanna into his phone. " 'Hey, baby, can't wait to get back,' " McKie remembered hearing regularly. " 'I love you. I love you.' "

There was no doubt that Iverson loved Tawanna and the children; to those closest to him, though, the ones who were not afraid to stand up to Iverson, there also was no doubting the height of his ferocity. It became what they both loved and hated about him, the thing that built and would eventually topple him, and Iverson also became a master of the apology. "His history," Tawanna said during a divorce deposition, "is that he'll say what he needs to say to reel me back in, and not follow through."

He was both one of the most thoughtful, caring people they knew—and also one of the most unpredictable. The problem was that it often took Iverson losing his temper for him to realize his mistakes, and then he would turn into the man they all hoped he would be.

"I would know that in a quiet moment, he'd be the gentle A.I. that I knew," Croce said, "when he was upset after the fact. He could do something crazy, whether it was pot and a gun in the car, whether it was misogynistic rap songs or whatever it was. But afterward when he was remorsed, you could see the real Bubba come out."

Sadly for those who spent the most time with him, that image was usually short-lived. He would spend a few hours or days at home, showing his tender side to Tawanna or the kids, and then he would go out drinking and turn into the monster that only the family knew. These transformations happened more often, gradually driving Tawanna away.

"What, if anything at all, would you do differently in your marriage," she was asked during the deposition, "if you had a do-over?"

She answered almost immediately: "I would have left sooner."

CHAPTER 11

THE RIGHT WAY

They could hear it through the brick wall and the window, past the curtain and onto the court.

Sixers players were told to keep practicing, but this was just too good to miss. A few minutes earlier, team president Pat Croce walked onto the floor, looking first at Iverson and then at Larry Brown.

"Excuse me, guys," Brown told his team on this morning in December 1999, its two most important pieces leaving the floor, distance clearly between them, through a doorway and into a conference room connected to the practice floor. Two days earlier, Brown had benched Iverson against the Pistons, and Iverson let his coach have it like he had so often. But this was different. Every night there was some reason to take a seat that Iverson could not understand, and he was neither hurt nor tired; this time it took all the restraint he had to not fight his fifty-eight-year-old coach. Instead, Iverson called Croce that night, demanding that Brown be fired; Brown called his boss, too, saying that if Iverson were not traded, ending this personal hell, he would quit. One of them had to go, and each man was asking Croce to make his choice. Croce suggested to both of them that they talk one more time before the organization did anything rash; one more attempt at peace before the war tipped one way or the other.

After they walked through the doorway that morning, Sixers players paid no attention to the assistant coaches, pleading with them to continue their drills, and before long, Brown's assistants were eavesdropping, too.

"Fuck you!" they heard Iverson screaming as Croce and general manager Billy King tried to mediate. It was over. Philadelphia's most talented team in years was collapsing, the realization heartbreaking to the men on the other side of the wall—but, as it usually went with Iverson and Brown, kind of funny, too.

"No," Brown said, his voice raised like players had never heard it. "Fuck *you*!"

BROWN SAT AT a table in May 1997 and talked about his challenges. He was an older coach with a clear vision, and, yes, there was a way to save this franchise. Look at its cornerstones: Jerry Stackhouse and Allen Iverson, talented as anyone in the NBA; they just needed direction and leadership.

Croce had been desperate after his team lost sixty games in 1996–97, finishing last in the Atlantic Division despite Iverson being named rookie of the year. He had averaged more than twenty-three points per game, showing that trademark speed that first grabbed attention at Georgetown, but he had also led the league with 337 turnovers, one of the many reasons for Philadelphia's losing record. Johnny Davis, the Sixers' fifth coach in six years, was already packed and gone. Croce's top choice to replace Davis was Rick Pitino, the University of Kentucky coach who had led the Wildcats to the national championship two months earlier. Croce wondered if Pitino, who had coached the New York Knicks two seasons in the late 1980s, might be ready to test himself again at the sport's highest level—especially with Iverson as his centerpiece.

But as the coaching search progressed, Brown's experience and resume seemed perfect for the Sixers and their young stars. He had won his own national championship nine years earlier at Kansas, and in twenty-five years he had endured two losing seasons. *Two.* Croce liked his odds. Plus, as he had done while falling in love with Iverson before the 1996 NBA draft, Croce searched for common ground with his new coach, along with an inspiring tale of hard work and a refusal to give in—a necessity, he believed, in the high-stakes world of professional sports.

Brown had played at North Carolina decades earlier, learning at the feet of the legendary coach Dean Smith as a player and assistant coach, adopting a coaching style that did not just value defense, hustle, and unselfish play—it treasured it. Of leaning equally on members of the *family*, because to Brown, that was what a basketball team was. Hell, it was more a family than the one he had come to know as a child; at least once the seasons began, this family would not desert you, leaving you to fend for yourself and those who relied on you for guidance.

He was the grandson of Russian immigrants who treasured respect and the act of giving; this was not just the way to succeed but the way to survive, and when Brown reached Chapel Hill, Smith making so much sense to Brown and calling his method the *Right Way*, Brown had no choice but to make it not just a philosophy but a way of life. They set picks and distributed the ball and relied on each other, one man's abilities and desire no more important than anyone else's, because without the sum of the team, the machine could not run. It was as simple as that: one machine, made possible because of many parts working in concert.

Croce liked the way this sounded, and when Brown shared his background and beliefs, the Sixers president was sold. "He had box office appeal and an incredible amount of expertise," Croce wrote in his memoir, *I Feel Great and You Will Too*. "It was like the Playmate of the Year also had a Ph.D. in biochemistry." Brown was reluctant, but Croce was determined. He abandoned months-long plans to pursue Pitino, recruiting Brown with such enthusiasm that he promised that, when they were finished, a statue of Larry Brown would replace the one of William Penn, the man the damn *state* was named for, on top of

Philadelphia's city hall. When Croce accidentally called Brown shortly after the coach's wife had gone into labor, giving birth to their first child, Croce quickly sneaked the gender out of Brown—a girl—and called a local florist, offering his credit card number to order sixty-two pounds of flowers—insisting that he wanted the hospital room to look like a damned mafia funeral parlor.

Then, when things calmed down, Croce kept working Brown. He would have total control over basketball operations—draft picks, free agent signings, trades, you name it, Coach! Then he delivered his kill shot, and his biggest lie: that Iverson was an angel; Larry, you guys will get along *beautifully*! "I told him what I believed he wanted to hear," Croce would write later, and it worked; Brown agreed to join the Sixers, who with help from the local sports network Comcast offered Brown a five-year, $25 million deal to restore Philadelphia to its glory days.

Now, the details finalized and the ink dry, here the men sat at the CoreStates Center, talking about the future and the combination of Iverson and Stackhouse, the Sixers' two young stars. "I'm not worried about handling them," Brown confidently told reporters that day.

A few days later, Brown arranged a meeting with his twenty-one-year-old point guard. Many years earlier he had noticed the kid's talent during a summer league tournament in Lawrence, Kansas, and had met Iverson during his rookie season at a joint shootaround between the Sixers and Brown's old team, the Indiana Pacers. Although Iverson had been late to the shootaround, Brown smiled anyway and told him he admired his heart. Iverson, for his part, had been unimpressed with Brown, and disappointed when the Sixers hired him after learning that the Pacers had won only fifty-two games the previous season, losing in the first round of the playoffs.

But now Brown was his coach, and that changed the game. Brown drove himself to the Marriott in nearby Conshohocken, and Iverson arrived in a limousine, covered in jewelry and surrounded by friends. They spoke in the lobby, talking about the future, and Iverson mustered enough energy to assure his new coach that he could not wait to give Brown everything he had.

They shook hands, both eager for what lay ahead, and Brown thought that this would be easy. What had David Falk, a friend of Brown's for decades and at the time Iverson's agent, been talking about? Before the meeting, Falk encouraged Brown to research Iverson's time at Georgetown, what John Thompson had done with Iverson that had been so effective. Thompson had not coddled Iverson, Falk told Brown, and if Brown hoped to manage Iverson, he would be well served to follow Thompson's lead.

Brown shook it off, though, assuming a player of Iverson's drive would welcome coaching after agonizing through five dozen losses. Heartened by his brief meeting in the hotel lobby, and eager to get started, Brown scheduled an exhibition at Temple University's McGonigle Hall between the Sixers' rookies and an all-star team assembled by Philadelphia legend Sonny Hill, who tried to curb inner-city violence and gang activity through basketball. It was a way for Brown to get a look at the nucleus of his own squad long before training camp, and so he jumped at the chance. Iverson would play with Hill's all-stars.

Brown walked into the small arena, each of the field house's 3,900 seats packed and ready for a show. The Sixers' rookies were there, and so were the other all-stars, but Iverson was nowhere to be found. Brown took his seat in the bleachers alongside King, whom Brown had handpicked to be the coach's personnel man and a kind of consigliere with the Sixers. The game was about to begin, and Iverson wasn't there. Brown's rookies dunked and drove the ball irresponsibly, taking far too many shots for Brown's liking, and whether this was learned or innate, defense was clearly not a priority. Brown told himself there was more work ahead than he had imagined.

The coach was watching when he heard a roar, his eyes finding the doorway with Iverson strolling in. The game started at 7:30. Iverson entered at 7:27, a cool three minutes to spare. The young player walked to the bench, pulled off his T-shirt, and slid on a jersey; then, with no warm-ups and no thought of looking toward his coach for instructions, Iverson jogged onto the court and subbed himself into the lineup. The first time he touched the ball, he barely looked at anyone else, cutting through defenders and the crowd's screams on his way to the basket. He did it again and again, the principles that defined Brown's life and outlook not even entering the kid's mind—but finishing with forty-seven points and the adulation of everyone in the building. Well, almost everyone.

Brown looked at King, shaking his head, knowing they were about to begin the challenge of their lives. "I ain't got no shot here," Brown said.

NOT SURPRISINGLY, BROWN'S first training camp had a distinct North Carolina flavor. The Sixers held training camp in Chapel Hill, and four players on Brown's preseason roster had played for the Tar Heels. Brown even scheduled an exhibition with the Bulls at the Dean E. Smith Center, the sprawling arena named for his mentor.

Iverson was not impressed. Early in camp, Brown instructed his players to execute a Smith favorite: the twelve-minute run, a drill in which each man was given a dozen minutes and asked to run as many laps as possible around an oval track. Some players welcomed the chance to show how much they had worked during the offseason. Iverson thought it was stupid. Why were they running when they could be *playing*?

Two of the Sixers' backup point guards, Rex Walters and Doug Overton, planned to win the event, maybe make a good early impression on Brown. They were hard workers but fringe NBA players, the kinds of men who would go on to become coaches, and little things like strong first impressions and offseason work can go a long way in winning one more roster spot, one more meaty NBA paycheck. They lined up on the track, Iverson shaking his head at the idiocy of it, and Brown blew the whistle. Walters, who took pride in winning the twelve-minute drill as a player at the University of Kansas, playing in Lawrence a few years after Brown left for San Antonio and his first NBA job, started out in front before noticing Iverson out of the corner of his eye. There he was, keeping pace with the others—running backward. He kept going in reverse for three laps, Brown seething at the kid showing up his teammates and his new coach and, most important, the treasured Right Way, and when he finally turned and faced the finish line, Iverson won the race by two hundred yards.

Brown bit his lip, though, maintaining his patience, trying to show Iverson the way. *Here* is what happens when you pass the ball, Allen, and when you set a pick; the whole *team* gets better. Brown demonstrated the movements and explained the details himself. Iverson rolled his eyes. "Y'all shouldn't have drafted me," Walters would recall Iverson telling Brown. "You should have got Muggsy Bogues," referring to the diminutive point guard who was regularly among the NBA's most selfless players and one of its sharpest passers. If Brown brought up defense, Iverson reminded his coach that he was tenth in the NBA in steals as a rookie. Brown countered that, sure, he had noticed that, but he had also noticed that Iverson had led the league in turnovers. Already, two strong forces were developing tension, and the season had not even begun.

Fine, though, Iverson said one time. He would pass the ball, just as Mike Bailey, his former coach at Bethel High, had wanted him to do. Brown was relieved. Finally he had broken through. During shootaround before that exhibition against the Bulls, cameras centering on Iverson and Brown and comparing them with basketball royalty in Bulls coach Phil Jackson, who had once pulled the best out of Michael Jordan, Iverson made good on his promise. And it was just as much a public fuck-you as it had been to Bailey so many years earlier.

Each time he caught the ball during shootaround, a teammate or team manager dishing the ball his way, Iverson passed it. Then again. And again. Every time.

"I'm Muggsy Bogues!" he called out as he sent the ball toward a teammate, stealing a look at Brown.

Then someone would toss Iverson the ball again.

"I'm Muggsy Bogues!" he said again, his voice raised an octave and the ball bouncing off a teammate's back or knee or the poor player's head.

Brown had made his point. Now Iverson was making his. Teammates were laughing, avoiding Iverson's missiles, and the Bulls stopped to watch with confusion and pity, some of the same Chicago players who had criticized Iverson a year earlier thinking the little shithead had not changed a bit.

"I'm Muggsy Bogues!" Iverson kept going as Brown watched the farce play out on hallowed North Carolina ground. Iverson was mocking Brown's philosophy on its home court. "You should have seen the steam coming out of Larry Brown's ears," said Walters, who is now a college basketball coach. "I was literally not shooting at that point, either. I was watching [Iverson]."

A COLD WAR had begun, and most days it seemed to intensify. Other times, usually in flashes, there was hope. Brown refused to budge, and Iverson would not conform—though as a matter of desperation, Brown's resolve was beginning to erode. During games, Brown rested Iverson for the last few minutes of the first and third quarters, the idea being that his best guard would be fresh in the final minutes of the second and fourth quarters—when the game was on the line. Only Wilt Chamberlain had famously played all sixty minutes of a game, because if the seven-foot, two-inch legend came out, folding himself into a chair, his muscles would stiffen.

The problem was, Iverson claimed that he did not get tired. As in, never. So each night, the seconds ticking out of the first and third quarters, Brown pulled Iverson from the lineup and sent him to the bench, and just as customary, Iverson would walk past his coach and tell Brown to go fuck himself. "He had so much belief in his ability that he would think he was going to win the game by himself," Brown said, joking years later about the confrontations and saying that someday he would write a memoir with a title being something about having been motherfucked twelve hundred times—twice a night by Iverson for nearly six hundred games. "My biggest challenge was trying to figure out: Wait, how can I help him? How can I make him see how we need him to play?"

Brown kept chipping away at Iverson, but he also reminded Croce that his patience was running thin. He did not need this shit, not at this point in his career, and besides, had Croce not called Iverson an *angel*? The Sixers lost fifty-one games in Brown's first year, and Brown, always fearing that he was in the wrong job, began wondering if Philadelphia was really the best place for him. He told King that he wasn't sure how long he could keep this up, not at his age and with so little else to prove. And besides, he refused to discipline Iverson, believing professional athletes were above such hand holding, no matter what Falk had emphasized about John Thompson's approach. Iverson had never missed a practice at Georgetown, fearing whatever punishment Thompson might cook up. In one season with the Sixers, he missed seventy of them, because he knew the only thing Brown would do was ask Croce to speak to Iverson. "If you want to know, can the guy conform to rules and stuff, the answer's yes," Falk said. "But you have to have a certain level of respect in order to do that. John commanded it, and others didn't."

Iverson asked Croce to get Brown to lighten up; Brown asked Croce and King to help break down the wall between obstinate coach and stubborn player. They told him to keep working with Iverson; keep trying to find common ground between an aging, Jewish white man who believed basketball was an equation that had one right answer and a kid from Hampton with cornrows who saw each day as a chance to improvise and do what felt right. Iverson just wanted to play at that breakneck speed of his, and he did not understand why Brown could not understand that if he removed the reins, they would win. "He didn't want to stop to hear Coach Brown teach him where to go," longtime Sixers forward George Lynch said. "He just wanted to play."

Croce and King kept talking Brown off the ledge, and Brown kept trying to solve Iverson, twisting the sides and top of the Rubik's Cube, hoping to somehow align the right colors. He came to realize that he would never make all the squares Carolina blue, eventually distancing himself—painful as it was—from his original plan. Brown and King traded Stackhouse and Eric Montross, both former Tar Heels, and took their chances with Iverson, who was becoming a star. A moody, generous, complicated, inspiring star—depending on the day.

As much as Iverson frustrated Brown, he was heartened by the kid's acts of generosity and his genuine desire to make an impact on those he cared about. Brown heard about Iverson handing his friends $250,000 to start a record label, a chance to push them toward a better life of their own, and when the team gave each player nine hundred dollars for meals and expenses during road trips, Iverson slipped the cash quietly to the equipment manager. In private, Iverson was gentle and thoughtful, and this much gave Brown hope. But in public, Croce tried to impress upon Brown, Iverson was protecting an image, and the old white coach was no match for this. Not only that, but Brown had his own image, as the team's leader, to consider. "He never wanted us to start looking at him like, 'Man, you ain't got no control over the situation,' " Aaron McKie said.

Iverson staggered into practices some mornings with alcohol still on his breath, his braids having come undone, and, if he could find them, sunglasses hiding his bloodshot eyes. Sometimes a friend from back home was with him; other times it was Ann, his mother, still bleary-eyed from another late night alongside her son and his crew. "We worried about practice every day," Walters said. "How was he going to walk in? Who was he walking in with?"

If he showed up, Iverson went through the motions during warm-ups; he refused to stretch, and he would not perform push-ups. He lay on the floor like a fish, barely lifting his shoulders off the floor while his hips and legs stayed down, jawing with Brown or joking with teammates until practice began, and away Iverson went, as always the best player on the floor. After a while, nobody bothered asking where Iverson had been, what he had been doing, why he had not slept. "He had the bags under his eyes, so you knew," McKie said. "His eyes were a little puffy, so it looked like he was in a fight or something. Like, there was a fight in Atlantic City the night before, you knew that he was going to be down there. And he was going to come in the next day with a coin toss as to how he would be."

Other times, Brown or a team trainer would receive a call shortly before practice, Gary Moore usually on the other line. Deuce had fallen and needed stitches, one of the reasons went, or Tiaura had a fever. Somebody was always sick. Someone in Iverson's house always was the subject of some terrible misfortune. One of the reasons used was that Tawanna had had a miscarriage, which Brown later learned was bullshit. The months passed, Brown hearing the same excuses again and again, eventually keeping a list of the more tired explanations on a notepad in his office. "I heard *that* one before," Brown would recall.

Eventually, Brown started hoping that Iverson *would* stay home. Rather than bicker with Iverson, he could get so much more accomplished. Maybe he would work with the other players, teaching them a thing or two about the Right Way. Then Iverson would glide in, late as ever, and Brown took a passive-aggressive approach, complimenting the players who were *always* on time, who *always* listened, who *always* did things as they were told. The coach knew this was shaky ground, and Iverson did not care. But if Iverson had so little respect for his coach, it occasionally felt good to Brown to return the contempt—especially knowing how much Iverson hated to be chastised in public, in his mind an ultimate show of disrespect.

"In front of the group," Brown said, "you couldn't say anything to him. He just couldn't handle it. He would become real defensive. He could not in front of his peers think that you were disrespecting him or calling him out."

In December 1999, the tension, always at a healthy simmer, boiled over. Again trying to get his star player's attention, trying to break through, Brown benched Iverson and four others in a loss at Detroit. It was, as Iverson viewed it, a public humiliation. Afterward, Iverson addressed the media: "For some reason, my style doesn't fit this team anymore," he said, sounding exasperated. "If that's the way it is, something needs to happen. Something's got to give. If I'm hurting this team, I need to get out of here."

Hours later, Iverson called Croce, issuing an ultimatum. Brown did the same.

CROCE POINTED TO chairs on opposite sides of the conference room table, Iverson in one and Brown in the other. *Sit across from each other, talk it out, and do not leave until you make peace.*

Brown spent the first few minutes snarling at Croce for demeaning him like this in front of a player, a kid he was supposed to have ultimate authority over, or had Croce forgotten his promises? Iverson sat there, slumping in his chair with his arms crossed and staring at his coach, like a cobra ready to strike. Iverson pointed at Brown, telling him he talked about family only when it was convenient, but the thing was, family members do not try to humiliate other family.

Brown fired back at him: "Are you finished?"

Iverson's Sixers teammates and Brown's assistant coaches were a few yards away, listening as the men inside the room lost their tempers—"Fuck you!" and "No, fuck *you*!"—leading them to wonder, amid their giggles, if after this meeting there would be much of a team left.

When there was silence, Brown melting into his chair, Croce got to the point: "Larry," he said while gesturing toward Iverson, "I'm *not* trading him. And Allen, I am *not* firing that coach."

They sat there, saying nothing.

"Allen," Croce would recall saying, "you can't motherfuck this coach when he gets you off the court. That's disrespectful. That's your father. And every time you do that to him, he's insulted. He wants to come back at you."

Brown smiled.

"And, Coach, Allen thinks you're like the white prison guard that told him sit the fuck down."

The white-haired coach's jaw dropped. He could not believe Iverson thought that. What's more, he could not believe he had *made* his best player think such a thing. Brown's philosophy was about widespread respect, not alienation; he wanted to push Iverson toward greatness, not make him think Brown was the enemy.

He apologized if Iverson truly thought this and admitted that he had never put himself in Iverson's shoes. He told his own story: When Brown was six, his father, a furniture salesman named Milton, died suddenly from an aneurysm, leaving only young Larry to care for the family. Like Iverson, Brown had grown up without a father and had developed habits that, although different, proved successful. They did not always make sense to others, but they worked for him. He was proud of his way. It felt right. He knew that if everyone bought in, it would work here. All it took was commitment and trust, and just think, Allen, how good they could both be if they took a leap of faith in each other.

By now Brown's voice had softened and Iverson was leaning forward, his hands now on the table instead of wrapped around his ribs. When Brown was finished, Iverson spoke, admitting that his body language sometimes masked his true feelings: that he respected Brown and wanted to learn from him. Just because he raised his eyebrows or slumped his shoulders did not mean he was tuning Brown out. But he promised to work on how he accepted his coach's teachings and promised to tighten his bad habits. Together, Iverson told Brown, they could reach greatness.

See? Croce cut in. "Look at both of you guys," he said. "You're just like each other." They had spent the previous two years looking only at their differences, missing the most important thing of all: They both wanted to win so badly, certain their method was the only right way, that they had missed how much they shared the same goals—and, oddly enough, even some of the same childhood challenges. Ten or so minutes after the meeting began, Iverson stood and walked to the other side of the table, wrapping his arms around Brown. He told his coach that all he ever wanted was to have a relationship with his coach like Jordan had with Jackson, like Magic Johnson had with Pat Riley, like Iverson had with Thompson.

Then the door opened, the other players scattered like their parents had just come home, and Brown began yelling instructions for the day's practice. Iverson walked toward McKie, who asked what the hell had just gone on in there. Iverson shook his head.

"We cool now," he said.

IT WOULD BE a stretch to say that after the meeting there was peace in the land. But the worst of the war had passed. Iverson still arrived late for most practices, sometimes hungover or still drunk from the night before, but he at least gave his entrance some thought before walking through the doors. "He mouthwashed the shit out of himself. His hair was all . . ." Brown said, his fingers illustrating above his head that Iverson's usually immaculate rows were messy. "And his pants were down, and he looked shitty. But in his own way he was respectful of me."

Brown, who would for years carry a grudge against Croce for disrespecting him and calling such a meeting, no matter its result, looked deeper into his reservoir of creativity. He hoped to eventually find the formula that worked for Iverson. He tinkered with the lineup the way Thompson once had, coming to install Eric Snow as point guard and relieving Iverson of the pressure to run the team *and* score points. Brown invented a new and intricate kind of ball screen to take advantage of Iverson's speed: Most screens, including the dusty old plays Brown had learned years earlier and relied on throughout his career, centered on the ball carrier running on a vertical plane, high to low and back high. But because Iverson could cover so much ground in such little time, Brown drew up a horizontal screen, asking a teammate to set a pick and then letting Iverson run until he was open. The "Iverson cut," as it came to be called, satisfied both player and coach. Brown was being creative and smart, and Iverson could create his own shot and usually ended up with the ball in his hand. "I didn't grow up in a program like that," Brown said. "I'd never been taught that way, but the competitiveness is the thing that I've always loved more than anything.

"And so I tried to get him to understand that, if you just trust me enough to let us move the ball, then I don't care how many shots you take."

Brown also experimented with Iverson's psychology, taking advantage of his star's competitive drive. Rather than exploding when Iverson staggered in or loafed through warm-ups, Brown approached him and spoke in soft tones. "Hey, Allen, how are you feeling today?" he asked, barely louder than a whisper. "You feel like practicing?" Brown would offer the day off, even urging Iverson to take it easy, then hitting on the incentive-based motivation that high school and summer league coaches had learned years earlier would get Iverson's motor humming. "Can you give me a half hour?" Brown would ask, knowing that once Iverson started, a teammate would challenge him or he would discover something to prove, but regardless of what kicked him into high gear, he would not stop.

Sure enough, Iverson accepted the small challenge—yeah, he could give Brown a half hour—initially keeping his focus on blowing out of the facility after thirty minutes. Then the balls were distributed, and away Iverson went, Brown hiding a victorious smile. "He was giving Allen that opportunity," McKie said. "You know how it is with some people who don't like authority figures, who don't like direction? They want to do what you're asking them to do, but if you *ask* them, then they don't want to do it. Leave it up to them, *then* they'll do it."

The Right Way was gone, left to die in the past with short-shorts and red, white, and blue basketballs. The clashes would continue, and eventually they would realize some of their worst fears and many of their most ambitious goals. Sometimes the old habits would reemerge, Brown asking Iverson to find another open shooter, to stop forcing so many damn shots, to stop turning the ball over. Then Iverson, usually calmly, would remind Brown that, yes, he had completed 60 percent of his shots, but he had taken only twenty shots—not enough, in Iverson's opinion.

"We can't win this way, Coach," he would tell Brown during timeouts, and deep down, the coach knew Iverson was right. "You're not going to get the best out of me."

Brown thought about it a moment, his instincts telling him to overrule Iverson. But then a different instinct—the one he actually shared with Iverson, a drive to win more than everything else—kicked in. "I said: 'Screw it,'" Brown said. "Let him go. That wasn't the Right Way. But it was the right way for us."

CHAPTER 12

ROCK BOTTOM

In spring 2013, Larry Brown called often, during quiet periods at the Southern Methodist University coaching offices, on his drives back to an apartment he rented during his first season coaching the Mustangs, when he sat at home and wondered how his old pupil was doing.

Brown heard the stories and read the reports, snapshots like the dazzling highlights that had once defined him: Iverson was going through a bitter divorce with Tawanna, was drinking increasing amounts of alcohol, had somehow plowed through millions of dollars. Brown had clashed with Iverson years earlier, but as the years separated them, the coach came to feel nostalgic about their times together. Years after their paths diverged, he came to think of Iverson as a son—a surly, moody cuss of a son—and Brown occasionally wondered if he had done enough to support him; if his purpose in life was greater than winning a national championship at the University of Kansas and winning an NBA title with the Detroit Pistons in 2004. "You know," he said one evening in a conference room at SMU, a marathon practice and teaching session now behind him, "looking back on it again, I was put here to coach him. I just know. I think God put me here to coach Allen Iverson."

But mostly Brown felt the nagging pang of sorrow. Always the wanderer and wonderer, his mind always looked forward or backward. Now on his third marriage and twelfth head coaching job since 1974, he had a well-earned reputation as a worrier, with curiosity among his most potent emotions—second only to regret. There was always the next coaching position or the one he never should have left, the player whom he gave up on too early or had not pulled the plug on fast enough, and now this one, the big one lingering on his mind at age seventy-two: that transcendent talent he had known long ago, an unlikely kindred spirit, both of them still searching for whatever it was that drove them.

So Brown dialed the numbers sometimes, wanting to tell Iverson about the kids he had met recently at an airport. They had barely recognized Brown, knowing him only as Allen Iverson's coach. He wanted to tell him about the youngsters he saw in high school gymnasiums on recruiting trips or on Dallas blacktops, some of them with a sleeve on an arm and others wearing cornrows or tattoos. "I didn't realize this as much as I do now: He maybe had a bigger impact on our sport than anybody," Brown said, and maybe if he told Iverson that again, it would help somehow. He wanted to share the stories of laughter and reflection, how Eric Snow and George Lynch, two of Iverson's teammates in Philadelphia, had moved into a new phase of their lives and careers—both were now on Brown's staff at SMU. They still ribbed their boss about the confrontations and the disappointments, the weird things Brown got bent out of shape over, and the important things he had somehow taken in stride. More than anything, Iverson's new predicament setting the table so often for these melancholy talks, they spoke of how when either of them was in a pinch, Iverson would be the first to offer help.

But Brown's calls usually just went to voice mail, and he ended the call and tossed his phone on a table or in his passenger seat. On the rare occasion Iverson did pick up or call back, Brown invited him to Dallas; come on down, Allen, and be around the game again and some people who love you. Iverson, when he thought about it, liked the idea of getting the band back together, of shooting hoops with Snow and Lynch as Brown stood by, a taste of the old days, and maybe imparting wisdom on the next generation of players. He was proud now of his story, albeit one laced heavily with his own regrets. *Do as he now said,* Iverson thought of telling their young ears, *not as he had done.*

Brown was building something in Dallas, the same as he had done in Philadelphia and Lawrence and Detroit, and Iverson's mood would lift when Brown talked to him about it. He told Brown and Snow about his comeback hopes, how he was determined to return to the NBA, and they chose to believe and support him. His mood buoyed by the prospect of hope and that familiarity he had lost, Iverson agreed several times to step out of his rut, come to Dallas, and maybe rediscover his passion.

Brown was relieved, and then he would call Iverson's number again in a few days or weeks to discuss specifics. The phone rang and rang, the voice mail again ending the call and weeks or months sometimes passing before Brown heard anything. More invitations were tendered and accepted, and then Iverson went underground—no explanation, no reasons, no response—leaving Brown to wonder and worry, a feeling he has come to know well. "Yeah, I worry about him," Brown said. "A lot."

PAT CROCE CALLED a year or so earlier, speaking with Stephen A. Smith, the former *Philadelphia Inquirer* sportswriter who had become close with Iverson, coming only as close to Iverson as Gary Moore—turned away like so many others by the gatekeeper. Croce, like Brown, had heard the rumors. They weren't true, were they? Iverson was *broke*? He and Tawanna were divorcing? That could not be.

"I hear Bubba's in some tough straits here," Croce said he told Moore. "I just want to see if I can help."

"No, no," Moore replied. "He's doing fine."

"How about alcohol?"

"No, no."

"How about finances?"

"No," Moore said finally, seemingly turning a blind eye toward reality when it came to Iverson, and besides, Moore might or might not have maintained a decade-old grudge against Croce for issuing a last-minute edict that Moore couldn't board the Sixers' plane. "Everything's good, Pat."

Croce asked Moore to pass along his concern and his phone number, the same one Iverson used to call when Brown had pissed him off and Iverson wanted out of Philadelphia. Moore agreed, but Croce's phone never rang. Croce had left the Sixers after the 2001 NBA Finals and distanced himself from professional basketball. He lived in the same Philadelphia suburb as Iverson, though, and sometimes he would be out for a run in Villanova when a Bentley slowed next to him, a familiar high-pitched voice emerging from its driver's window: "Pat! Pat!" Iverson would call out, and they would catch up for a few minutes as the motor hummed and Croce's heart rate normalized and Iverson's kids screamed and laughed in the backseat. Then Iverson was gone, and eventually, he just stayed gone—traded to Denver, then Detroit, then Memphis and out of Croce's immediate universe.

But like Brown, Croce wondered how his old protégé was handling his career's twilight, all the trades and the shuffles toward the bottom of the lineup. Deep down, he knew, though Croce was an optimist and held out hope for the best. Maybe the reports were just rumors, as Moore had indicated; maybe his situation had been exaggerated as a way to bring a giant down to a relatable size. But he kept hearing those grumblings from people in Philadelphia, read the same reports everyone else had seen—about boozing and dissolving his fortune—and even though Croce once feared his tough-love interactions with Iverson were warning signs, this was just too hard to believe. "Listen, we don't change. People don't change," Croce said. "We may bend, but we don't change."

Croce was among those who believed Iverson had no chance of returning to the NBA, at least not without a massive physical and emotional overhaul. Could Iverson, whom teammates *never* saw in the weight room or on the treadmill unless he was forced, pull a Rocky Balboa, as Croce described it, and rebuild himself by chasing chickens or jogging through North Philly? Could Iverson humble himself in such a way, admitting to himself and outsiders that, yes, he needed to train, to change, to be saved? "There's no freaking way he can play in the NBA if he doesn't train," Croce said. "And he didn't train back then; how the hell is he going to train now? That's my biggest pet peeve with him: I was a physical conditioning coach. And it would bother me to no end that he wouldn't train and he could come and run a mile in less than five minutes.

"He doesn't do what Kobe and the other guys do, working in the off-season and condition for the sport. If he didn't do it then, when he's getting paid fifteen or twenty million, who's to think he's doing it now?"

Croce was not alone in his concern as spring 2013 inched toward summer, Iverson's divorce going final and his NBA comeback effort dead on arrival and laced with denial. Lorry Michel, the longtime athletic trainer at Georgetown with whom Iverson became close and who felt comfortable speaking with Iverson about anything, reached out when she heard the rumors about the finances and the divorce. Sometimes weeks would pass before she received a text back, usually with Iverson saying he would be okay. Then she would text back, changing the subject, and good grief, could he believe Georgetown would no longer be playing Syracuse again after the 2012–13 season, conference realignment reshuffling such an important part of their lives? He would flood her phone with messages, the subject briefly commanding his attention and enthusiasm, and then he would disappear again for months.

Aaron McKie, one of Iverson's closest friends on the Sixers, texted him occasionally, and if things sounded bad enough, McKie would call. "Sometimes, man, with that invincibility that others may see," McKie said in March 2013, "people on the inside know better. I was somebody that he always felt free and used to talk with, and I think we all need that."

McKie would ask how he was getting along, and if Iverson said he was fine, McKie would accept his friend's word and move on. Iverson chuckled at seeing McKie on the Sixers' sideline, in his sixth season as an assistant coach. Iverson had always thought the cerebral, thoughtful McKie would follow his playing career with a segue into coaching, and McKie used the opportunity to ask Iverson how he saw himself in the future. McKie thought his old friend could write a book or join the public-speaking circuit, sharing a story sometimes too difficult to believe, and after a moment or two of listening to McKie's ideas, Iverson would interject, preferring to steer the conversation toward old times—the past a more comfortable place than the present or future. McKie would oblige, recounting stories from their days together in Philadelphia, when Iverson was one of America's most famous men, when money and household drama seemed to pose no threat. "He'll deal with it his own way," McKie said, "and I just let him know I'm a friend and I'm here for you."

Others were not so willing to change the subject or allow Iverson to keep living in the past, dwelling on memories and images that no longer defined him. There was a new, starker reality they wanted to address—and believed Iverson should address, too. In spring 2013, Croce again went about trying to track down Iverson. "I'd say come up here and sit in front of me," the former Sixers president said. "I want to eyeball you. No different than what I wanted to do before we drafted him. I want to look into your eyes, and I want to see right into your soul. I'd be looking for commitment, intent—and a clear gaze, for sure."

SO MANY OF those who knew and cared about Iverson were now filled with regret, worried about how he was handling the adjustment to life after basketball, marriage, and full-time fatherhood. But why, then, did they wait until his life was approaching "rock bottom," as former Sixers teammate Roshown McLeod would call it in spring 2013, to reach out, blowing up Iverson's phone and offering alternatives?

They all had professional skin in the game back then, everyone along for the ride, and protesting too loudly got you fired or downsized or distanced from. David Falk, the NBA agent who represented Iverson when he left Georgetown after two years, was fired in part for trying to impress upon Iverson that he needed to save his money. Tom Shuttleworth and Larry Woodward, Iverson's longtime attorneys, were stripped of their responsibilities as financial advisers in 2003, Iverson appointing Tawanna as the family's money manager. Those who continued riding the Iverson train were smart, even if their reasons were rooted in self-preservation or perhaps even greed, to overlook problem behavior, even as years later each news story and rumor pushed the knife deeper into their consciences.

"I can imagine some of the pickup games as a youth, him trying to get on the court with the bigger guys, them saying no, and him having to wait," Lynch said. "And there was a fire that burned inside him, but for him to be as successful as he was, he had to be determined and have that little chip on his shoulder and that inner voice telling him: 'Do it your way, Allen.' And that's probably his downfall."

Others tried to be proactive, worried that Iverson had not yet actually hit bottom. What if this instead was just a grotesque look at his slide, the ground waiting to smack Iverson later? When Tiaura, his eldest daughter, was in tenth grade, she moved in with her father. She was, as Tawanna would later testify, concerned about her dad because "everyone else was leaving," and because Iverson was spending an increasing amount of time alone—a jarring and disturbing change for a man who was once constantly surrounded by people.

In June 2013, a video emerged that sent shivers down the spines of those familiar with Iverson's recent run of misfortune. It was part of a reality Web series starring the boxer Adrien Broner. Nearly six months after the final ruling in Iverson's divorce, doors continuing to close on any possibility of a return to the NBA, there was Iverson in the center of the dimly lit frame, sitting in the seat of a parked car. He was laughing as the camera focused on him, the slight man swallowed by a hoodie, and a moment later, Iverson's smile faded. "Me and you," he told Broner, who mumbled something back to Iverson.

"Because I'm ready," Iverson said, his words badly slurring, "to play Russian roulette."

"With a fully loaded pistol?" Broner said in a scene turning uncomfortably dark.

"*Damn* sure ready to play Russian roulette," Iverson said.

Broner made light of it, pointing out that this would not be Russian roulette, in which one bullet is inserted into the chamber and the remaining five slots are left empty and the chamber spun, just before the muzzle is pointed at the player's own temple and the trigger squeezed. No, with a loaded gun, it was suicide. "This is a *fully* loaded pistol," the boxer said.

"You think I don't know?" Iverson replied.

"It don't matter how many times you spin it, the first shot," Broner said, "you dead!"

Iverson looked at him, an eerie smile stretching his face. "You think I don't know?" he said again.

Those closest to him don't like images like that, whether or not he was joking or it was an out-of-context moment between friends. They tell themselves Iverson had been at rock bottom before; hell, he spent his childhood and teenage years there. They tell themselves he is, at his core, still a man filled with hope, not a person who would give up. Others were not so sure Iverson was the same man who had grown up on the streets of Hampton Roads. "It's one thing," McLeod said, "to grow up in the inner city and see it every day. But when you made a transformation into a good life and now all that [is] being taken from you, you worry about a person in that sense—because do they still remember how to fight?"

Just in case, throughout 2013 Brown kept calling, trying to reach his former star, kept leaving hopeful messages and trying to get him to Dallas so that he could, in Brown's mind, rediscover the joy and passion he had once known—and maybe Brown was trying to ease his own conscience in the process. "I don't know," Brown said. "I just don't like to see it end this way."

CHAPTER 13

THE CAPTAIN

He pushed away from his opponent, jogging toward the wing and stopping in front of the Los Angeles Lakers' bench. Iverson stood for an instant, the crowd screaming—"Defense . . . defense!"—and caught a pass from Vernon Maxwell, the Sixers' point guard.

Lakers guard Tyronn Lue was shadowing him, Lue's assignment throughout the 2001 NBA Finals, and Iverson held the ball upward, deciding which way to go. Five years earlier, Iverson had crossed over Michael Jordan, his boyhood hero, as Chicago Bulls coach Phil Jackson watched. Now the Lakers' coach, having formed the league's most dominant team, Jackson had a front-row seat for another show of offensive mastery. The Sixers had blown a fifteen-point, third-quarter lead in Game One, Shaquille O'Neal and Kobe Bryant leading the inevitable comeback, and Iverson had gone cold in the fourth quarter. Now in overtime, the seconds ticking away at Staples Center in downtown Los Angeles, the Sixers had scored seven consecutive points. The Lakers needed a defensive stop to prevent an unthinkable upset on their home floor.

Lue pressed against Iverson, who raised the ball above his head. Iverson leaned to his right, dribbling toward the baseline, and Lue trailed him. Then Iverson threw himself in reverse, dribbling through his legs and pivoting for a jump shot. Lue tried to correct himself, throwing his body toward Iverson; he lost his balance, tumbling to the hardwood, sliding on his ass, and looking helplessly up at Iverson as the ball went through the net. It happened in a flash.

Then, the cameras still locked on perhaps the world's most exciting basketball player, Iverson looked down at Lue, scowling and stepping over him, the Sixers guard's right foot stomping the floor.

THE CALL CAME during the summer of 2000, Pat Croce reluctantly delivering the bad news he had been unable to squash. The Sixers' president was on the Jersey Shore, where he had once pondered the pros and cons of drafting Iverson, and his phone had been ringing for days. Now that the unavoidable trade was all but finished, it was time to let his favorite player know that he had been a pain in the ass one too many times.

When Iverson answered, Croce wasted no time: "Bubba, I'm just calling you to let you know that you're on the trade block right now," he said.

Throughout his time as the Sixers' top executive, Croce had played peacemaker and counselor, so often stroking the egos of two of America's best basketball men, trying to push his team forward through a seemingly impossible coexistence between Iverson and Brown. Croce had, perhaps stupidly, begun to think the war was over; things would be different now. Then he ran into Brown in Miami during a Sixers road trip, Croce on his way to his vacation home in Key West for a few quiet days.

"Your boy missed practice today," Brown said after Croce dropped his bags at the team hotel. The coach told his boss about Iverson going clubbing the night before, hitting it so hard that he was now nursing a bad hangover, hours after he called and said he could not drag himself out of bed for practice. Hell, at least he had been honest.

Croce stood there a moment, then he fumed. "Fuck! Fuck!" he said, his voice rising and his mind saying goodbye to those easy days on the islands. His next call was to Iverson, whom he had backed so many times, still groggy from the night before.

"What the fuck are you doing?" Croce barked, knowing that he had spent much of his political capital with Brown during their group confrontation in the conference room at the Sixers' practice facility. "I'm watching the front door and you're fuckin' running out the back door. You can't do that, Allen. You can't leave me out here stranded. You missed practice. Now you're not going to play."

Iverson shook out the cobwebs, asking Croce to repeat what he had just said. Yes, Croce told him, he was suspended. So deal with it. Croce's next call was to Ann Iverson, who always appreciated hearing bad news about her son before reading it in the papers. Mike Bailey had offered Ann such courtesies years earlier, and Croce did the same. Ann liked feeling like part of the Sixers' nerve center, and it was a slick political maneuver by Croce; he knew if Iverson complained to his mother, she would back Croce because he had the good sense to call her and get her on board. After all, Ann believed Pat cares about you, Allen, so try not to take it personally.

But now, the 2000–2001 season on the horizon, Croce feared this call would be one of their last. Brown had talked to Croce about burning the candle at both ends, getting sick of the head games between himself and Iverson, tired of the meetings every few weeks when Eric Snow, a team captain, or Aaron McKie would enter Brown's office, the coach asking two of his damn *players* to work shit out with another player. And Brown was sick to damn death of the talks with Croce, who kept trying to *explain* Iverson to Brown and Brown to Iverson. It just had to stop, Brown told his boss, or he needed to walk away—as he had nearly done a year earlier when Dean Smith had personally called about becoming coach at North Carolina, Brown's alma mater. That fell apart, though, and Brown agreed to return to the Sixers with fresh eyes. But now? Brown was ready to make a change.

Croce had, during the previous weeks, begged Brown and general manager Billy King to give him one more season with Iverson as the team's centerpiece. One more, and if it went to hell, as Brown and King had predicted, then Croce would sign off on whatever they wanted. Those were his wishes, he told them, but as always, he would defer to his basketball men for on-court matters. But he called Iverson anyway, a man-to-man heads-up just as Croce had telegraphed the one-game suspension after Iverson got drunk in Miami. "I've got to let you know this: Larry Brown wants to trade your ass out of Philly," Croce told him, outlining a possible deal to the Los Angeles Clippers, at the time one of the worst-run franchises in the league.

Wait, Iverson interjected. He *liked* it in Philadelphia. He might not show it often, he told Croce, but this felt like home now. The people of southeast Pennsylvania worked hard and were proud of it, and because this is the way they saw Iverson and he saw himself, they *got* him. They did not want Iverson to change his attitude or cinch on a necktie; that would not have been real. So, what, Pat? What did he have to do to stop this? He did not wait for Croce to answer. Iverson kept talking. He was turning twenty-five soon, had Croce not considered that? Did he not understand what that meant to Iverson? People from where he grew up did not often live twenty-five years, or at least they did not plan on it, and so they live like they are dying, even if it becomes a self-fulfilling prophecy. But it was happening, Pat, June 7, and he would be a man then, and, yes, it was time to grow up. He knew that now. He admitted it. Did Croce know that he and Tawanna had talked about getting married? Next summer, he told his boss; the gears were already turning. Iverson could not promise to be perfect, but man, he would try.

"He was begging. Truly begging," Croce recalled. "'Pat, Pat, listen, I'm tellin' ya: I want to be cocaptain with Eric Snow. I'm working out this summer, I promise. I'll do everything necessary. I'll be on time!'"

Croce just listened, not just hearing the words but feeling them, like the first time he had heard Springsteen: It changes you and everything you had once thought normal or possible. Iverson kept going, hammering one point harder than the others. "Tell him," he told

Croce, referring to Brown, "I want to be a captain. I want to take leadership."

Croce made no promises, but he was heartened by the passion in Iverson's voice. It was always Croce's soft spot. He called Brown, who was sitting with King at the time, and told him about the conversation he and Iverson just had. "If he does half of what he says," Croce said, "we'll be in heaven."

But it was too late. An offer had come in that was too good to pass up. A four- or five-team blockbuster, between ten and twenty-two players, depending on whether Miami was in or out: Iverson and center Matt Geiger to Detroit, and among all the other moving pieces, Lakers forward Glen Rice, Charlotte guard Eddie Jones, and Detroit forward Jerome Williams—Iverson's old friend and roommate at Georgetown—would come to Philadelphia. It was all but done, King told Croce; just a few small wrinkles left to be smoothed, and they would say goodbye to Iverson after four seasons—along with the headaches that had come with him.

THE ANSWER WAS no, and Geiger was not budging. *Goddamn David Falk.* The agent who had brought Iverson to Philadelphia, negotiating his first contract with the Sixers, a deal with Reebok that validated and amplified Iverson's hip-hop, don't-give-a-shit-about-shit attitude, and in January 1999 finalized a simple and obvious six-year, $70 million extension, was—months after Iverson and his mother had fired him—*keeping* the son of a bitch in Philadelphia.

Falk represented Geiger, a talented but injury-prone player whom Brown was almost as sick of as Iverson, and when the four-team trade was agreed upon, Falk pointed out that a clause in Geiger's contract called for a 15 percent raise if he was traded—that is, unless he waived it. Brown and King made their calls, worked their phones, did their things, and sorry, guys, he's not willing to just give away $3.3 million a year. And at that price, the Pistons would be unable to fit its payroll inside the NBA salary cap. Two months before the new season was set to begin, a period of new beginnings, the deal fell apart.

Christ, Brown thought. He was stuck with Iverson. More than a dozen years later, Brown would still hold a mild grudge against Geiger, though more would come into play than just his refusal to waive his trade escalator. A trade would indeed go down, many of the key players finding new homes, but the Sixers were not involved. Brown, his restless mind now looking toward new on-court possibilities, started thinking—and he started by accepting Iverson's request to be captain, hoping this new equity in the team would mean renewed accountability. And, Iverson indicated to teammates, he would accept it along with everything the assignment entailed. "He was like: 'I'ma show these motherfuckers,'" McKie recalled. "Like, you know, it's on. You know what I mean? He was laser-focused and he was just ready to go. I mean, from the beginning of the season, he was just ready to go."

When Iverson arrived at training camp at Penn State University, he brought with him a new attitude. Iverson was not just on time for practices; he was early. He reintroduced himself to John Croce, Pat's brother and the Sixers' trainer, and agreed to perform dry-land training, lift weights, and do whatever else team officials suggested to help his game. "He's already gone up about twenty-five pounds this season," John Croce would tell the *Washington Post* that November. "He's great at this squat-and-jerk lift I have him doing. To be honest, I never would have been able to get him to even *try* that last year."

When Brown designed plays, Iverson carried them out, passing to Snow or Raja Bell or McKie—because almost always, the ball wound up in his hands when the time came to shoot. Once, he showed up for a game with his cornrows ragged and barely fastened; he had known that making his hair perfect would make him late for shootaround, and so he opted for punctuality for once, rather than a polished appearance. This was something the old Iverson would have never so much as thought about.

When the first single dropped from his forthcoming rap album, which had now been renamed *Misunderstood*, the lyrics of "40 Bars" seen as homophobic, sexist, and violent, Iverson met with NBA commissioner David Stern and leaders of the National Association for the Advancement of Colored People, apologizing and agreeing to eliminate the most vile of the words, eventually killing the album entirely.

The Sixers won their first ten games of the new season, blistering opponents from all angles. Iverson was the team's only star, and later, his teammates and coaches within other organizations would agree that this was perhaps Brown's finest achievement as a basketball coach. He built a team on which, although its other players wanted touches, they did not care who scored. McKie and Kevin Ollie and George Lynch and Eric Snow and Theo Ratliff—they defended and played the role of backup band to Iverson's lead and understood the dynamic and wants of Brown and Iverson better than even Brown and Iverson ever had. "We just built a team," King said, and once the Sixers' front office realized what it had that season, the building would continue.

Brown moved Iverson permanently to shooting guard, and with peace now within the organization, Iverson directed his anger toward opponents. Slights, or those he conjured and fanned in his own mind, had always fueled Iverson, the heartbeat of a Napoleon complex that had pushed him from the streets of Hampton to the top of the NBA. During a game in Philadelphia in March 2001, the Sixers squared off against the New Jersey Nets—and, more specifically, Iverson was matched against Stephon Marbury, whom the Sixers had considered a finalist for the number-one overall draft pick five years earlier. A rivalry had formed between them, and on this night it occasionally flared. At one point Marbury drilled Iverson in the lip with an elbow and Iverson retreated to the bench, dabbing the blood from his lip with a towel.

"Hey," six-foot-eight forward George Lynch called over, "you want us to get him?"

Iverson tossed the towel away. "Nah," he said. "I got this."

The old Iverson might have rumbled with Marbury, getting in his rival's face and leading officials to separate them and maybe drawing himself a suspension. Instead Iverson was smarter and more cunning about it. His motivation now fueled by revenge, he scored fourteen points in the fourth quarter, finishing with thirty-eight amid chants from the home crowd of "MVP! MVP!" The Sixers won, 102–94, and the Nets were shamed; the loss guaranteed their third consecutive losing season. Even so, Marbury might have gotten off easy. "If Allen didn't say, 'Look, I got this under control,' the whole team was out to hurt Marbury that game," Lynch said. "He probably scored the next thirty points on Marbury. And it wasn't like, 'I'ma give you thirty quiet points.' It was thirty with a crossover, thirty with a step-back. You know, he gave him everything. It was personal."

Seven months after Brown pushed to trade his most talented player, Iverson was leading the league in scoring and received the second-most All-Star votes for the Eastern Conference, behind only Vince Carter. When the game rolled around, the surroundings, Washington, D.C., were familiar, and so was the East's coach, Larry Brown. Iverson scored twenty-five points, the most of any All-Star, and was named most valuable player. With Iverson's All-Star teammates surrounding him, the NBA commissioner touched the elbow of the new symbol of his league, cornrowed and tattooed as he was.

"We know," Stern said, "that great play can be wrapped, if you'll pardon the expression, in very small packages."

Iverson chuckled at Stern's corny remark, lifting the MVP trophy high, and when Ahmad Rashad asked him on camera about the moment, he began scanning the crowd for a face that, a few months earlier, had been unfriendly. In fact, it had wanted him the hell out of Philadelphia; wanted him out of his life. Now there was something interesting brewing—and they were in it together.

"It's definitely special," Iverson said, wanting to share it, pausing as he searched. "Where my coach? Where my coach?"

IVERSON CALLED HER his wife during a Tuesday afternoon news conference, smiling about it when a reporter picked up on Tawanna's new title. She had for years been only his fiancée; now she had badgered him about something important, sending Iverson to the doctor to get a wart removed. "My wife," Iverson said on that day in late November, "thought it was a piece of glass."

Reporters congratulated him, though he would reveal few details other than that the wedding would be the following summer, after the season. Tawanna, who had insisted upon the secrecy, had become a fixture at Sixers games, along with young Tiaura and Deuce. There they were in the lower level, watching Daddy do his thing while Ann went nuts, wearing Iverson jerseys that became increasingly garish. Reebok had customized the jerseys years earlier because she had become a character in her own right. First it had been enough to have "MOM" embroidered under Iverson's number three. Then she wanted sequins, then she wanted his shoes—"The Answer" took the place of "The Question" and was a monster success—before they ever hit the market, the executives back in Canton, Massachusetts, knowing the cameras would focus on what she was wearing almost as much as what her son had on. "Her outfits to the game became very calculated," said Todd Krinsky, who was on his way to becoming a vice president at Reebok, contemplating such things as whether to station a handler in Philadelphia for Ann just as Que Gaskins managed Iverson.

Ann spent the games mingling with fans, holding signs—MY SON IS THE ANSWER, one read in cartoonish red and blue—and passing out trading cards the Sixers had printed with her face on them. Tawanna, always poised and measured, stood there cheering quietly. She enjoyed the lifestyle her fiancé's success had brought, comfort now and presumably forever for the family, but the circus was not her thing. She took classes at St. Joseph's University and dabbled in art, bringing the kids to the arena sometimes and waiting afterward to reunite with Iverson. "She was a simple girl," McKie recalled. "She wasn't no woman that was high-maintenance or anything. And that was the beauty of it. She was real, real simple."

But she was also living the good life now, cashing in on Iverson's fame and fortune. They collected cars and jewelry, and their home on Monk Road in Gladwyne, a posh Philadelphia suburb, sprawled out onto 8,100 square feet, within which there was a billiard room, home theater, and heated marble floors. Tawanna maintained a personal assistant, and when she would undergo surgeries later for a breast reduction, tummy tuck, and liposuction, it was the assistant and not Iverson who cared for Tawanna, bringing her Gatorade while she recovered. Tawanna completed a few household chores, but her main responsibility was being there for the man she had loved since high school.

Particularly during the 2000–2001 season, Iverson's supposed transformational year, Tawanna was seen as the woman who had tamed the bad boy. Look at them, the cameras sometimes focusing on her, Iverson's high school sweetheart, the mother of their two children, and soon to be his wife. Maybe Iverson was not as bad as people made out. Teammates and team employees saw Tiaura beam as her dad walked into the family lounge, scooping up his daughter and tickling her. Then he would kiss Tawanna, draping an arm around her, and away they would go. McKie heard Iverson whispering into a cell phone sometimes on road trips, telling Tawanna that he missed her. Their relationship was not perfect, but how many are? "That was his sweetheart. He loved her. She loved him," McKie said. "I don't think he was the greatest—in my opinion, and I'm quite sure he would say the same thing—husband at times. But I know for a fact, and he knows for a fact, that that woman has been in his corner and loved and cared about him.

"It takes a strong woman to sit in there and hang in there. And you can ask any of these women that's married to the superstars. Their lives is different."

Tawanna had not pressed the issue of marriage, perfectly content to continue living as they always had. But Iverson wanted to make things official, and she agreed. Just as they had planned to have their first two children, now they were preparing for their dream wedding. And, not surprisingly, Tawanna wanted it to be a small, intimate affair. No television cameras, no throngs of fans waiting outside. The invitations, printed on parchment, asked that no uninvited guests attend and for cameras and camcorders to be left at home.

Inside the framed announcement, which kept the specific location a secret, was a message: "Love," it read, "has brought us here today."

OUT WEST, JACKSON was building a dynasty. Bryant was one of the stars of the 1996 draft class, realizing the potential that the Sixers were in no position at the time to wait for, and O'Neal was the NBA's most dominant big man. The Lakers had depth, size, talent, coaching, versatility, and, as the regular season entered its twilight, one hell of a hot streak in front of them.

On April 1, 2001, Bryant went scoreless in his return from an ankle injury, and the New York Knicks smothered O'Neal, keeping him in check for a one-point win and the Lakers' fifth loss in eight games. They were listless; the chances of repeating their NBA championship from the previous year were dimming, with only eight remaining regular season games and the playoffs beginning in less than three weeks. "Right now," Jackson said then, "we're not executing with the kind of precision that we have to."

That was the last time the Lakers lost for more than two months. Bryant got healthy, Jackson refocused his team, and when the playoffs started, it seemed no one could slow this veritable dream team, let alone beat it. Entering the playoffs as the Western Conference's number-two seed, they swept Portland and then Sacramento, and took the drama out of the conference final against top-seeded San Antonio by sweeping the Spurs. "Throughout the body of the regular season, the Lakers probably were a little bored," said Kevin Harlan, who alongside former Georgetown coach John Thompson called games in three Lakers playoffs series in 2001 for TBS and TNT. "I really don't think Phil put the throttle down hard enough or shifted into the gear that they needed until that final month.

"The way they finished the regular season, they just plowed their way right into the playoffs where there was just very little hesitation with what they were doing with the teams they were playing."

The Lakers were making a statement: They would not lose a playoff game. They were too strong, too determined, too well built to slip up, even for a night. After cruising into the NBA Finals, the Lakers had a nine-day layoff, time to rest and a chance for Jackson to study his final opponent. He saw a team that had gradually improved during the regular season, mostly because Brown never stopped tinkering. The Sixers had, at Thompson's urging, acquired Dikembe Mutombo at the All-Star break, trading the injured Theo Ratliff, along with Toni Kukoc and two others. Brown went on to be named the NBA's top coach, McKie its best "Sixth Man," and Mutombo its top defender. Iverson, his promise kept to the Sixers and his responsibilities as a team captain somehow exceeded, was the only player to appear on every ballot for the NBA's most valuable player award. In May 2001 he became the shortest and lightest player to ever be named MVP—Bob Cousy, who won the award after the 1956–57 season, had been an inch taller and ten pounds heavier—but more important, he dominated the voting. Iverson received ninety-three first-place votes; San Antonio's Tim Duncan finished second with eighteen first-place votes.

But now, the regular season finished and the awards distributed, the Sixers were being held together with duct tape, and Jackson and anyone else could see that. McKie had recurring shoulder tendinitis, Snow was suffering from two fractures in one ankle, Lynch had a broken foot, and Geiger always had some ailment that kept him from playing. Years later, and perhaps with his grudge over the failed Iverson trade still lingering, Brown thought Geiger was not as much hurt as he was lazy. "I thought that was bullshit," the coach said of Geiger's constant complaining about a leg injury. Iverson had a bruised tailbone, missing a playoff game in Milwaukee and watching alongside Gary Moore as his teammates somehow won without him. Earlier in the season, Iverson's right elbow had developed bursitis, and the team's trainer cut a piece of bandaging into a sleeve. It was supposed to reduce inflammation, but it also apparently helped Iverson's shooting touch: He scored fifty-one points that night, and not wanting to tinker with a good thing, added the sleeve to his uniform—an accidental fashion statement that became as famous as Iverson's others. "I'm watching on TV or I'm watching a high school game or something like that," Brown would say much later, "and all little guys have (jersey number) three, they all have a sleeve."

Jackson watched as the Sixers, who needed seven games to defeat Toronto in a semifinal, also went seven games against Milwaukee to win the Eastern Conference title—a chance to bring Philadelphia its first professional sports championship since 1983. Jackson saw Iverson in agony, trying to shake off the symptoms of the hurt tailbone, and the strategist in Jackson saw an opportunity. If Iverson was injured, Jackson wanted to amplify the pressure on him. During Finals prep, he assigned Lue, a little-used, twenty-four-year-old guard with quickness and determination, to *be* Allen Iverson. Though Lue wore cornrows, he was seen as a sort of anti-Iverson: He did not drink, and he wore no tattoos; he was from the quiet midwestern town of Mexico, Missouri, and when he went to the University of Nebraska, he was usually in bed by ten thirty at night, rarely leaving his fifth-floor dormitory in Harper Hall.

But this was Tinseltown, and Jackson wanted Lue to act. His role during practices was to portray Iverson, and that meant, as Lakers teammate Ron Harper put, taking "all the shots," even if they were off balance or low percentage, and later charge through the lane without regard for elbows or big bodies. It would give the Lakers a taste of what it would be like to defend Iverson—and give Lue a taste of what Iverson put himself through during games. "A lot of bumps and bruises," Lue told reporters.

Along with the Lakers' other advantages, they were confident. Lue's practices made his teammates think that getting in Iverson's way would be no problem. Shoot, Harper chirped shortly before the Finals began, Lue might even be *faster* than Iverson.

• • •

IVERSON READ THE quotes as he always did, taking the *Philadelphia Inquirer* with him into the practice facility's bathroom stall and coming out fuming. Tyronn fucking *Lue* was faster than him? "He was like: 'It's on,' " McKie recalled.

Brown's plan was simple: Have Geiger bring O'Neal out of the low post, making enough jump shots to give Mutombo a cushion inside, and let Iverson engineer the rest. As much as it pained Brown to let Iverson improvise, going against each of his own coaching philosophies, this was what had gotten them here. It was not working, though, at least early in Game One against the Lakers. The Sixers—and Iverson—were off target and sloppy, allowing the Lakers to look every bit as dominant as advertised. Bryant and Derek Fisher gave Iverson little breathing room, but then he hit a quick-release jumper, an off-balance fadeaway, and away he went. It was classic Iverson: He missed six of his first eight shots, but he kept chipping away at the Lakers and himself, finishing the first quarter with four baskets in five attempts.

Lue checked in during the third quarter, taking turns guarding Snow and Iverson, preventing Iverson from getting open and leading to a seven-minute scoring drought. Lue, nipping and grabbing, pushing Iverson away from the ball and staying in his way, was like a persistent gnat in Iverson's face. He gave the MVP fits; at one point Iverson shoved him away, clearly frustrated that Jackson's plan was working. "You can't shoot the ball if you don't get it in your hands," Doug Collins, the broadcaster and former coach, said during the game broadcast.

The Lakers, meanwhile, had erased the Sixers' double-digit lead, and when the game moved to overtime, the Lakers quickly built a five-point advantage. It was happening: Los Angeles was going to win again, their twentieth victory in a row. Its players were too big, too strong, too good. And Lue had caused problems for Iverson, who had four points during a twenty-two-minute stretch. Then the Sixers guard ran up the floor with about a minute left in the extra period, pulling up on the wing, nailing a three-pointer for a Sixers lead and pumping his fist toward the court's other end. "This Sixer team will not go away, will it?" Collins said.

Croce, sitting courtside, was enjoying the moment. "Every time I stand up and cheer," he said, "the whole stands are yellin' at me: 'Sit down, Croce. Fuck off!' "

On the next play, Maxwell brought the ball up court, and Iverson faked to his right and then ran to the left, Lue trailing him. He caught Maxwell's pass, holding it up as Lue swiped at it, a wall between Iverson and the basket. He dipped it low, his eyes looking up at this pain in his ass, and made a move that more than a decade later would still link these two men. As of summer 2014, nearly a thousand articles would mention Iverson and Lue together, and retrospectives of Iverson's career would invariably show or describe the next few seconds as the very definition of badass.

Iverson broke to his right, and Lue followed. Like a lightning strike, Iverson stopped, took a step back, and jumped to shoot. Lue, in a panic, lunged toward him, losing his balance and tumbling as the ball slipped through the nylon. Lue slid to a stop and then looked up, Iverson glancing down in disgust at the man who had, for parts of three periods, hounded him—responding with a sneaker-on-hardwood show of dominance. "And steps *over* Tyronn Lue!" TV announcer Marv Albert shouted into his microphone.

Across the nation, fans howled and cheered at what they had just seen. It was, in effect, a three-second "fuck you," played again and again, further propelling Iverson into icon status, the play mimicked on playgrounds and debated in sports bars as perhaps Iverson's signature moment—skill and high stakes and attitude combining, forever and amen. Croce, whose politicking had led the Sixers to this point, stood up when Iverson drilled his shot and, because it made as much sense as anything, screamed toward the actress Sharon Stone, sitting in the same row. "In your face!" Croce shouted as he pointed at her. "In! Your! Face!"

A minute later, the clock expired and the horn blew at Staples Center. The Sixers won, 107–103, on the forty-eight points and Iverson's refusal to quit. "I'm glad no one bet their life on it," he would say afterward, "because they definitely would be dead now."

THE NEXT FOUR games were, they would remember, mostly a blur. The Lakers won each of them, winning their second of three consecutive NBA championships, and depending on who is retelling the story, either the stronger team was reawakened by the Sixers, or with a few more dashes of magic or hard work, Philadelphia would have won. "I know it's heresy saying this," Brown said, "but if George was healthy, if Geiger would have played, if Eric was healthy, if Aaron was healthy, we'd have beaten that team. There's no doubt in my mind. They had no answer for Allen."

But that was not how it went, and there were consequences—some of them as soon as the final buzzer sounded in Game Five, the Lakers winning 108–96 and the coaches turning to congratulate each other. "I had to shake fucking Phil Jackson's hand," Brown said, looking disgusted and then raising a flaccid right hand. "He gave me the fish."

In the immediate aftermath, no one in the Sixers' locker room realized what the team had just accomplished. Players sat on their stools, telling each other that they would be right back next year; that Iverson would return a year older and wiser and better, and after a few months of healing, his supporting cast would be stronger. Yes, they told themselves, the Sixers would be right back in the Finals the following year.

In the months following the Finals, an unsteady empire would begin to crumble. Brown would contemplate retirement before changing his mind. Croce, feeling lied to by Sixers co-owner Ed Snider, would resign, cutting out the energetic heartbeat of the Sixers' front office. He was the man who always had Iverson's ear, the man who somehow played peacemaker better than anyone else. Mutombo lost a step, and Lynch would be traded to Charlotte early the next season. The band would be broken up, and the all-important support beams for the fragile Brown-Iverson dynamic gradually went their separate ways. Without them the Sixers would rock and sway in the slightest of breezes, coming as close as ever to toppling in the stronger winds that would soon arrive.

For now, though, the men smiled through their tears and tossed their jerseys and soiled towels into the locker stalls at First Union Center, saying see you when I see you. A few, including McKie, would at least see Iverson in a little more than a month; he was among those on the wedding guest list. Until then, though, Iverson left the locker room and reunited with Tawanna, Tiaura, and Deuce, walking toward the pressroom, where he would conduct his final news conference of a remarkable season. What he had learned and the regrets he had anyway, whether he was satisfied being the MVP with no championship, how he would approach the next few months and the follow-up season.

When he walked in, there stood Kobe Bryant, waiting for O'Neal to finish his remarks. Iverson was ready to get this over with. When O'Neal ended his conference, Bryant started toward the table, and so did Iverson. Then the Sixers star stopped, turning to Tawanna. "Let's get the fuck out of here," he said, disappearing back into the arena corridor.

TAWANNA WAS AT lunch with her bridesmaids in August 2001 when her phone rang. Iverson's sister Brandy was calling, telling her that Iverson's lawyers needed to speak with her.

This is it, Tawanna thought. The subject no man is ever comfortable bringing up with his future wife: the prenuptial agreement. Iverson had, less than two months earlier, completed his second season of a six-year, $70 million contract, and there was talk of an unprecedented lifetime contract with Reebok. He was one of the richest men in sports, with an unquenchable thirst for late nights and big parties, so of course Iverson's attorneys would want protection for him. Not that it would make the conversation between bride and groom any easier, and besides, Moore had already called a few wedding guests, telling them earlier that the wedding had been postponed, and then—oh, wait, false alarm, it was back on. Such was the drama of Iverson and Tawanna, even then.

But as the wedding approached, Tawanna was already stressing out, the final touches being put on a ceremony nearly ten years in the making. They registered at Bloomingdale's and would be married in Voorhees, New Jersey, not far from Philadelphia, and hotel shuttles would transport guests to the mystery location. Iverson had actually helped plan the ceremony and reception, selecting the music and many of the key players, in particular best men Michael Freeman, Moore, and Andre Steele, one of the Cru Thik friends from back home. Groomsmen would wear black, seven-button jackets and white, six-button vests—a nod at the 76ers. Deuce would walk his father down the aisle, the Jackson 5's gentle ballad "I'll Be There" filling the air, and then he would meet his twenty-five-year-old bride-to-be, exchange vows, and light a unity candle for Tawanna's late father and Iverson's grandmother, Miss Ethel.

With the hours now counting down and her phone ringing, Tawanna told Brandy that she would deal with it later, whatever it was. The calls from Brandy kept coming, but Tawanna ignored them. As evening approached, her phone rang again. This time it was Iverson. "What time are you gonna be home?" he asked. "I've got something for you to sign."

There it was. She was calm, maybe even resigned. The time shortly before the wedding had mostly been one of peace, a rarity with them, and of course this meant it had been too good to be true. Still, Tawanna would read the agreement, determine if it was fair, and if so, she would sign it. Fair was fair; he was the one with the basketball career.

That night, Iverson came over, holding the papers so Tawanna could see them. She said nothing. He kept them between his fingers, and as Tawanna waited for him to offer the document, she felt the tears on her cheeks. At that moment, neither of them saying a word, Iverson brought out a lighter. A prenuptial agreement had indeed been drafted, but he would not allow Tawanna to read it. Iverson touched the papers to the flame, and together they watched them burn.

CHAPTER 14

COLLATERAL DAMAGE

Iverson's talent and heart bought him otherworldly, transcendent fame, which attracted fans and admirers around the globe. Websites devoted to Iverson were born during the boom of the Internet, kids found themselves on playgrounds emulating the crossover and the braids and the swagger, a generation of young Americans stepping into Reeboks and balling their fists to say fuck you to the way things used to be.

Iverson was, even if unwittingly, influencing the next generation, and a young player named Bradley Beal mimicked Iverson on the St. Louis blacktops years before the Washington Wizards drafted him and Beal wore jersey number three in honor of his hero. Young ballers wore cornrows and compression sleeves not because they were taking a social stance but because Iverson had done it, looking so damn cool in the process. "You know, my whole thing was just being me," Iverson would say during his retirement news conference in October 2013. "And now, you know, when you look around, you see all the guys in the NBA now, all of them got tattoos. All them guys wearing cornrows. You used to think that the suspect was the guy with the cornrows. Now you see the police officers with the cornrows."

With the fame came power and entitlement. His penchant for tardiness became a bigger problem for his teams and for Reebok, whose representatives eventually stopped scheduling events before noon. Que Gaskins, Iverson's former body man for the shoe company, said he eventually started lying to Iverson about when he was supposed to be somewhere; if an event truly started at three in the afternoon, Gaskins told Iverson it began at noon. Iverson came to expect a certain lifestyle, of disconnected velvet ropes and bulging groups of friends and onlookers, of favors and women and money. He indulged his car collection, at one time owning nearly a dozen luxury cars, including the marble-white Bentley he liked to park in spaces reserved for the handicapped. Who was going to stop him or tell him to move it?

During shouting matches with Tawanna, police officers were occasionally called to break up the disputes. Usually they gave him a quick warning and, in part because he was Iverson and it was cool that *they* had been here and allowed to decide *his* short-term future, they went on their way. Lawyers and judges and authority figures came to admire Iverson as much as anyone, even when they were supposed to be impartial, and in return he came to believe he could manipulate anyone to say or do whatever he wanted. "Do you know who I am?" he reportedly asked an Atlanta police officer in 2011, and on top of him being Allen Iverson, he was also a man who had not renewed the license plates on his Lamborghini Murcielago two years after they had expired. Iverson unleashed a tirade on the officer, who eventually let Iverson walk away, though not before the car was towed.

He told Tawanna occasionally that he could pay friends or associates to do all manner of favor for him: After Tawanna threatened to leave him, she would testify, Iverson told her that a friend would happily accept a million dollars to testify that she was having an affair with him. This amount on top of his $5,000 estimation, according to Tawanna's testimony, to have her killed. Tawanna, though, would later be seen as perhaps Iverson's fiercest enabler—a person who felt both empowered and trapped because her husband relied on her. Iverson simply had no idea how to do most common tasks, and Tawanna never forced him to learn.

"This ain't EASY these r things you've ALWAYS done!" Iverson texted to Tawanna during a difficult time. "Yeah I should have been do n this stuff but when we were fine with each other its wasn't a problem. I made the money & u took care of us & our business. I don't know what else 2 say this is something both of us know."

"Don't keep talking about it. Do something about it," Tawanna responded.

"I'm trying I'm just asking 4 help that's all."

One thing Iverson did know how to do was get others to do things for him. He rarely drove his own cars, and there was a network of sycophants and coattail riders who were happy to do all manner of task: keep his schedule, buy his clothes, book his travel. Even when his playing career faded and his fortune dissolved, Iverson retained his sense of entitlement—and several of the contacts who would do anything for him. Fame is a powerful thing in modern America: Without personal history or prior relationships, many people want little more than to please a well-known personality or sports figure—favors offered and normal standards abandoned. It is warm and comfortable even in close proximity to fame, that glow too snug to jeopardize with honesty and tough love, explaining the entourage phenomenon that Iverson came to know so well.

During a meeting in late 2012 with Dawn Smith, a court-appointed investigator who during divorce proceedings would make a recommendation on child custody, Iverson accused Tawanna of drinking just as much as he did, and of using cocaine. "Tell me about it," Smith recalled saying to Iverson during her investigation. "Who should I talk to?"

"I'm not going to tell you any of that," he replied, apparently believing that Smith worked for him. "I can get paid witnesses to say anything I want."

OVER THE YEARS, LeRoy Reese had developed and honed a routine. He always asked for clients to conduct evaluations at his office in Decatur,

Georgia, paying attention to whether they were early or late. He looked into their eyes and listened to the sharpness of their words, and then he began calling most anyone the subject interacted with. His spouse and parents, his colleagues and superiors, his friends and enemies—trying his best to understand even the most complex individual. "Your goal," he said in the summer of 2014, "is to be able to answer a question as well as you can reasonably answer it."

A bookish man with glasses, a shaved head, and graying goatee as he approached fifty, Reese was a clinical psychologist who made extra money by lending his services to divorce attorneys. During many cases, an impartial and respected voice is a powerful weapon against bias and made-up minds. Sometimes Reese recognized the famous names, the rules for them no different than for the factory worker or mailman, and in Reese's mind their fame and money would not affect the routine. It was too precious, the bedrock to his credibility, and other than his honesty and thorough nature, he was proudest of one fact: that he could not be bought.

He had studied at Wooster College, a prestigious liberal arts school, and Ohio State University, later working for the Centers for Disease Control and now settling into a life as a research professor at the Morehouse School of Medicine. If he agreed to an investigation, understanding that he would present his findings under oath in court, he took weeks to properly unpack someone whose future lay partially in his hands. If an attorney offered a referral with fewer than two weeks to investigate, Reese typically declined; it simply was too little time for such a big job.

In late 2012, his phone rang, and Reese heard Melanie Fenwick Thompson's voice on the other end. A divorce attorney in Atlanta, she sometimes retained Reese as an evaluator and witness, and his commitment to thoroughness had given heft to his opinions in the local courts. Fenwick Thompson was representing Iverson, and she asked Reese to evaluate her client and deliver an opinion on whether Iverson abused alcohol, had shown an inability to parent his five children, and had issues with anger and violence.

Fenwick Thompson needed a quick turnaround on this one, a response to investigators who had been appointed by the court and who typically sided with the estranged wife and the kids' mother. There would not be time for Reese's preferred two or more weeks of investigative time. And it would be Iverson retaining Reese for his own evaluation—the kind of situation, Reese would describe in general terms nearly two years later, "that almost never happens."

Reese thought about it, turning the case over in his mind like a rock tumbler. He would be given a contact list of "collaterals," or people who knew Iverson in one capacity or another, and a chance to interview Iverson at his office in Decatur. Reese, an NBA fan who had followed Iverson's career, decided to take a magnifying glass and hover it over one of sports' most compelling personalities. He responded to Fenwick Thompson, telling her to send him on over.

IVERSON ARRIVED ON time for his appointment, a rarity for him, and showed Reese the side of himself that so many others longed to experience more often. Iverson was charming, thoughtful, clearheaded, patient, and remorseful. "When the season wasn't in, I should have been taking care of home," Iverson told Reese. "I was hanging with my homeboys." For two and a half hours Reese conducted a clinical interview with the little man who had revolutionized basketball and changed how an athlete—and opportunity—are viewed on the streets.

In this snapshot of two and a half hours, it seemed like Iverson was not the monster his estranged wife was making him out to be. He told Reese that he had "a couple of beers" two or three or four times a week, sometimes adding a glass of champagne if the occasion or his mood called for it. Although he would make a few calls to Iverson's collaterals, never actually speaking with any of them, the doctor offered support for Iverson after their meeting. He did not ask questions about high-profile incidents involving guns, violence, or verbal abuse toward Tawanna, and some of the stories making the rounds about Iverson's finances.

When Reese appeared in court in early 2013, he recited his impressive credentials and quickly made his thoughts known during direct examination by Fenwick Thompson. "There were no examples," Reese told the court, "of Mr. Iverson engaging in high-risk behavior."

Reese said there were no signs of alcohol abuse or dependency, no hints of a violent temper or destructive behavioral patterns, no history of issues in his workplace. It appeared that Reese somehow did not consider legendary tales of Iverson's partying and his tendency to show up late to important functions, if he showed up at all. By the time Reese arrived at the Superior Court of Fulton County, a half hour's drive from his office in Decatur, he had not completed his usual level of diligence. He had not spoken with Iverson's friends and family members, had not even reached out to personal manager Gary Moore (who was growing increasingly worried about a man he genuinely cared for), and performed no comparison of notes with Dr. Michael Fishman, the court-appointed evaluator who in late December had seen a drunken Iverson during his required alcohol test. He had not even spoken with Iverson's two eldest children to gauge the effects of Iverson's behavior on his family.

Reese had spoken with one source: Iverson himself.

Answering Fenwick Thompson's questions, Reese admitted to the court that alcohol was a "regular part of Mr. Iverson's life" and that Iverson needed to develop healthier coping and problem-solving skills. But Reese also testified that, as it fit into his five-pronged assessment, Iverson had no deep-rooted behavioral imperfections to speak of; in no way did his lifestyle interfere with his responsibilities. He could, as Iverson had insisted to Reese weeks earlier, simply give up alcohol and the late nights at any time. Reese testified that Fishman's recommendation that Iverson enroll in Alcoholics Anonymous meetings—a suggestion even Moore had backed—would be unnecessary and potentially harmful, considering AA was for alcohol dependents; Reese testified that he believed that Iverson needed no such therapy or support group. According to Reese, Iverson's parenting needed work, but he was just as capable as anyone of raising his children.

"It seemed to me that Mr. Iverson was fairly forward, candid about not doing everything he could have as a husband and a father and also communicated a willingness to do different and be different," Reese testified. "I think ultimately that's an empirical question, but I certainly think he should be given the opportunity."

Fenwick Thompson's questioning was a smooth ride, but turbulence waited ahead. John Mayoue, Tawanna's lead counsel and a clever and opportunistic attorney, could hardly wait for cross-examination. When his chance came, Reese's life inside the Iverson glow became far less comfortable—revealing yet another poor soul who apparently had gotten himself shipwrecked by the Iverson swell.

"Did he tell you," Mayoue asked Reese, "that he doesn't know where his children go to school?"

"No, sir," Reese replied.

"Did he tell you that he doesn't know the names of any of their teachers?"

"No, sir," the doctor responded, his confidence and credibility seemingly dissolving as the seconds passed and the rapid-fire questions continued.

"Did he tell you that he does not know the single name of any one of his five children's friends?"

"No, sir."

It went on, Mayoue now asking Reese—a well-known and prideful alcohol evaluator—about how little he truly knew about Iverson's alcohol use, how little research had actually gone into his full-throated endorsement of Iverson, all of it built on one conversation that spanned 150 minutes.

"Did he tell you how much he drinks?"

"He did, sir."

"Do you know that he drinks every night?"

"That's not the frequency that he described, sir."

"Then you don't know, do you?"

"No."

"Do you know that he comes home so drunk at night that he urinates on the floor?"

"No, sir."

"Do you know that he comes home so drunk at night that he passes out naked, no clothing on in front of the children?"

"No, sir."

"You didn't do a formal evaluation of any type, did you?"

It was finished. Compressed now by the weight of Mayoue's questions, the opinion of a respected doctor was collapsing in full view. Reese, who should have known or learned that there were problems fueled by destructive habits and desperate enablers, admitted that he had no idea that Iverson had twice blown off the court-ordered alcohol tests with Fishman and had missed appointments with Smith, the guardian ad litem; that Reese had not even attempted to reach Moore, whom Iverson now called his best friend; that he had not bothered to factor in the many news and Internet reports about Iverson's alcohol-fueled run-ins with the Sixers and even with the law; and that he performed no urine or saliva test to determine whether Iverson had alcohol in his system even during their meeting in Decatur.

"And you don't really know, as you sit here today," Mayoue asked, "what types of problems his alcohol has caused within his family, do you?"

Reese was defeated, standing now in the dank and cold area that the warmth of Iverson's fame could never reach. "In a concrete way," he replied, "no, sir."

Mayoue then went for the kill, breaking Reese's credibility with one hollow-point question.

"Are you an NBA fan, by chance?"

"I am."

"You knew Mr. Iverson long before he got to your door, didn't you?"

"I did," Reese said.

A few agonizing minutes later, it was mercifully over. Iverson's fame had been given life two decades earlier, its effects spreading like the kind of pathogen that Reese had once examined at the Centers for Disease Control. Now, like so many others who could not fight it off, even in its weakened state, Reese climbed down from the witness stand and left the courthouse.

CHAPTER 15

FAMILY BUSINESS

It started with a joke about Gregory Fox's lazy eye, and why someone would bring him to the sports bar to watch the Mike Tyson fight in October 2002. "What you bringing that one-eyed man in here?" Rahsaan Langford had cracked, and after the laughs quieted, the insult seemed forgotten. The fight was beginning anyway, and so they drank.

Two months earlier, Langford had taken his young family to New Jersey, where he stood alongside eight others as Iverson's groomsmen. The friends from the Peninsula had, years earlier, promised each other that if one of them made it big, then they all would. Now here they were at a mansion in Jersey, laughing about the ceremony's late start because Ann Iverson had arrived very late, to no one's surprise, and then smiling as they posed for pictures and eating cake flecked with gold leaf. Iverson and Tawanna then went on their honeymoon, inviting two other couples—Ra and his wife, Sherri Ivey, and Que and Cindy Gaskins—to join them.

The group returned home, life returned to normal, the Iversons settled into married life, and Langford went home to Virginia. On this night in Newport News, the group watched, drinking and laughing in the sports bar, as Tyson pounded a big Dane named Brian Nielsen.

Midnight passed, and soon the bar was closing. They headed for the exit, five men in two cars.

One of the men riding with Langford, Tyrone Highsmith, felt sick, and so the driver pointed the car toward another friend's house in nearby Briarfield. The other car followed. When they stopped, Highsmith got out and threw up, and another friend went to piss.

The cars idled, and soon the men heard shouting. Amid a fog of alcohol and fatigue, a cloud of tension and disrespect still hung in the early autumn air. Fox had not forgotten the joke from earlier. Now he and Langford were arguing, the darkness and quiet shaken awake by profanity and threats. "What are you going to do now?" another friend, Darren Springer, would testify later that he heard Fox say.

Next they heard gunshots, eight loud pops, and turned to see the twenty-five-year-old Fox holding a pistol. Then they saw Langford collapse, dead before his knees hit.

IVERSON LOOKED AT his teammates through eyes welled with tears, the hum of the Sixers' team bus acting as the story's sound track. He had been more reserved than usual, and finally on the ride to a road game, friend and teammate Aaron McKie asked what was wrong.

Iverson, normally quiet about personal matters, told his friend and others about how Langford had died and the meaningless things that caused it, going on to shake his head about how, no matter the big contracts and fame, a man from the streets can never run so far away that the tentacles of those streets cannot reach him.

"Life was great for him before that happened," said Todd Krinsky, one of Iverson's point men at Reebok. "Because in his life, he had both worlds. He had his friends from home, and he had his NBA lifestyle. He was able to show his friends that life.

"And when the Ra thing happened, it brought him back to that old life. I think he felt like he was never going to get away from it."

Langford had, whether the times were difficult or triumphant, provided comic relief to his circle of friends, and alongside Iverson they had laughed as children and adults, cracking on something as simple as a man's wardrobe or another friend's lazy eye. He had been devoted to his three sons, vowing as a youngster himself that he would always be there for his children. Now he was gone.

Iverson tried to channel the pain into basketball, wearing a black band with Langford's initials on his left elbow, touching it 585 times during the 2001–02 season, once before each of his free throw attempts. It helped, friends said, and thank God it was basketball season, because there were friends to lean on if Iverson needed them, along with opponents and iron rims to take his sadness out on.

When the games were finished, though, Iverson's mind wandered. He pondered his own mortality and, although he and Tawanna vowed to financially support Langford's three boys, Iverson wondered whether he had done enough for his friends from Hampton, the young men who had sworn loyalty to each other. If someone was born into a life like theirs, was he forever cursed, no matter the blessings, to see his still-young friends lie in caskets? Iverson withdrew into his own mind, wondering about trust and worrying about death.

"You watch me on the court, and you can tell me if that guy is good or bad," he told *Playboy* shortly after Langford's death. "I think you can tell who I am. I think you can tell I'm trying to get better as a person. Believe that. Because I want to go to heaven. When I die, I want to go see Ra, man. I know he's in heaven, and before I die I want to know that's where I'm going."

But for the time being, Iverson drank more and partied harder, staying out later than normal. He distanced himself farther from the media and again clashed with Larry Brown, who criticized Iverson, less than a year after being named most valuable player, for his work ethic, fanning new rumors that he would be traded.

He spent more at clubs and jewelry stores and hotels and steak houses. Anything to keep his mind off Langford, any nibble that might feed that restless mind. For a while, the story went, the Hilton near the Sixers' practice facility sold more Cristal, the champagne made famous in rap songs, than any other establishment in the country. Iverson had founded a music label, handing over a quarter million to start ABK Music Group, naming himself chairman and a few friends from Hampton as executives. Langford was supposed to be one of its rappers, but he was gone, and so Iverson kept throwing money at things to chase the ghosts away. When Iverson's longtime attorneys, Tom Shuttleworth and Larry Woodward, tried to step in to curb his spending, Iverson lashed out, stripping them of their responsibilities as his financial advisers.

He refused to set foot in Virginia, afraid of the memories it would stir and the tears and rage it would elicit. It was where he and Ra had become friends, made promises, and then made good on them, and where Langford took eight bullets. Gregory Fox, the man who shot him, claimed he had shot Langford in self-defense, but Fox was convicted anyway. Virginia was where Fox sat in prison, and, no, Iverson just could not do it.

"When I go home," he told the *Philadelphia Inquirer* in May 2002, "every place that I see, every thing that I look at, Ra saw every place that we'd been together. All I think about is him.

"I'm just having a hard time just getting myself up to have to go there. I know it's going to happen sooner or later. I'm going to have to go to Virginia. But for now, I just want to stay away from there because I think about it too much every day as it is, and when I get there, it will be worse."

On his left arm, prized real estate beneath his original "Answer" bulldog, he had Langford's first name tattooed, and on the right side of his neck he asked for ink that honored "Ra Boogie." But it didn't feel like an appropriate enough way to remember him, and so he thought of a more meaningful way, if the time ever came, than even the tattoos.

Iverson found refuge on basketball floors, but his play was more unruly than usual. His shooting percentage dipped below 40 percent, at the time the lowest of his career, and a year after coming within three wins of an NBA championship, the Sixers were underachievers. They went 43-39, finishing fourth in the Atlantic Division, and their season ended in the playoffs' first round. Now the time came to worry about how Iverson would handle the avalanche of emotions heading toward him, when basketball—the beam that so often held his life together—was taken away. "My biggest fear, my biggest concern," said Gary Moore, Iverson's personal manager, "was when he was off the basketball court."

Four days after the Sixers' season ended, Iverson and Brown argued in the practice facility parking lot before making peace. Iverson then held what would become an iconic news conference about his feelings toward practice, the humor in the often-repeated sound bite hiding a man losing an unsteady grip on his emotions.

"I'm upset because of one reason: We are in here," he said in a rarely aired portion of that same news conference, which moved from defiant to proud to brooding—so many emotions in a single media gathering. "I lost my best friend, I lost [games] this year; I feel that everything is going downhill for me, as far as my life."

WITHOUT THE STRUCTURE and distraction of basketball, Iverson sank deeper. He spoke rarely with friends and teammates, and he invented reasons to start fights with his new wife. Tawanna was, he sometimes convinced himself, cheating on him or stealing from him; it was a matter of time before she slipped up and he could prove it.

He would drink his way through his paranoia, and usually when he woke up and the hangover loosened its bite, he apologized for whatever he had said or done the night before, and despite her eroding patience, Tawanna always forgave him.

On the evening of July 1, Tawanna and Iverson argued about something that, as the years passed, neither of them would remember. As usual, Iverson preferred confrontation, and Tawanna tried to distance herself from her husband's aggression, this time checking into the Marriott near Philadelphia International Airport for a night away from the storm swirling at home.

"I'm the type of person that I walk away," Tawanna would say in divorce testimony much later. "Mr. Iverson will find me wherever I am in our massive homes and say what he has to say and continue to drill it in my head until it's—either he makes me leave or I will leave on my own."

When she returned to their sprawling estate in Gladwyne late the next day, Iverson was drunk and still angry. Still, Tawanna tried to sleep. After midnight, Iverson forced her out of the house, a chill in the early summer air and Tawanna wearing only a nightshirt.

She pounded on the door, but it never opened. And so she walked, barefoot, into the darkness. Twenty minutes passed before she found a small church, and she rested on a corner staircase near the entrance. Tawanna sat there for hours, and eventually the sunrise began illuminating the tree line. Not wanting to be seen in such a revealing outfit, Tawanna made the long walk back to the house, finding an unlocked basement window. She opened it and crawled through, tiptoeing upstairs to change clothes before finding her car keys and driving away.

Later, she stopped at a gas station to pick up Shaun Bowman, one of Iverson's cousins she had grown close with, and returned to the house to retrieve the children. Iverson had by then awakened, and, as Tawanna would later put it, "he wasn't having it."

Iverson followed Tawanna and the children outside, and as they climbed into Tawanna's sport utility vehicle, Iverson found a large rock from the adjoining lot, where a new house was being built. He heaved it at the windshield, shattering the glass as Tawanna gunned the engine and sped out of the driveway.

Iverson was not finished, though. Determined to find his wife, he went first to the Marriott near the airport, questioning a hotel employee about where Tawanna had been and where she was now. Then he went to another Marriott in nearby Conshohocken, again badgering employees for information as to his wife's whereabouts.

He stalked out of the lobby, shaking off a security guard's threats that the police would be called, and drove to west Philadelphia, by now flanked by his thirty-nine-year-old uncle, Gregory Iverson, the former marine whom Ann Iverson had asked to move to Philadelphia to keep an eye on her son and keep him out of trouble. Stopping finally at the Cobbs Creek Court apartments, the men charged to the third floor, where Iverson's cousin Shaun lived—but wasn't home. Iverson knocked first, and when Shaun's roommate cracked the door open, he shoved his way through.

"Where my fucking wife at?" Iverson asked the roommate, Charles Jones, who would later replay the scene, including Iverson's supposed intention of killing Tawanna, to a 911 dispatcher. Another man, Hakim Carey, was in the apartment and witnessed the exchange.

Iverson lifted his shirt to reveal a black semiautomatic pistol in his waistband and instructed Jones to call Tawanna. When she answered, Iverson grabbed the phone. "Don't make me have to make an example out of these two," police later said Iverson told his wife.

When he hung up, anger and desperation lingering still, Iverson again gestured toward the gun, police said. "I'm either going to die or I'm going to jail," he said. "And I guarantee you I'm not going to die."

IVERSON HID OUT for nearly a week, never leaving his mansion, under orders from Philadelphia's police commissioner. "If he is seen out on the street, or at a party, or driving his car," Sylvester M. Johnson told a starving pack of reporters, "then he will be arrested."

Iverson had hired a high-profile defense attorney, Richard Sprague, who instructed his twenty-seven-year-old client to stay indoors and to keep quiet about the nine charges, including three felonies from the night he hunted Tawanna throughout Philadelphia.

Reporters camped outside his home in Gladwyne, and when there was no immediate narrative to report on, another, perhaps more revealing one emerged: As long as he scored forty points or crossed over an eager defender, those who admired Iverson were willing to overlook behavior that later revealed itself as a collection of warning signs. Iverson was, for so many, an icon and a meal ticket; one wrong step might jeopardize that. Fans did not see his temper as a problem; this was passion and a man who made it big despite the most heart-wrenching of upbringings. Brown and Iverson's Sixers teammates overlooked the drinking and spending because, if he waited out the alcohol shakes and led the Sixers to a victory, then who cared how he spent his nights?

His gambling and spending and drinking were his business, and years later no one would admit trying to step in or even recognizing his behavior as signals of future trouble, because that might have cost them a front-row seat at the show. "Maybe I didn't do enough when I was his coach," Brown would admit more than a decade later.

They even rolled their eyes at the incident with Tawanna, believing that *something* must have been misunderstood, or chalking it up to marriage being complicated, or it was just Allen being Allen. "Quite honestly with that whole thing," McKie said later, "to us it's funny because we don't look at Allen as the baddest bear in the woods. You know what I mean? That stuff is funny to us, like how people think he's so dangerous."

Iverson was so dazzling when the lights came on that almost nobody—including those closest to him—spent much time thinking about the parts of his life he kept hidden. Only Tawanna had confronted Iverson about it, and in July 2002 she was in hiding, too, as fans circled Philadelphia's police headquarters, like everyone else paying little mind to the killing in Newport News that sent their hero into a downward spiral of grief and drinking, of anger and unanswered questions, of violence and bad intentions.

Instead, they supported Iverson, proclaiming that their favorite player, spokesman, and teammate had done nothing wrong—because, in the American sports culture, it is a comforting thought that our most talented citizens are also pure and well-meaning. "Free A.I.!" shouted a woman in a Sixers jersey. Others wore T-shirts that read THE ANSWER IS NOT GUILTY, and many brought their support to Gladwyne, waiting with the reporters outside the gates of Iverson's home. So, apparently, did the local police, who had already offered Iverson special treatment after he turned himself in, allowing him to wait in private instead of among the general population. Now they were helping him arrive quietly to court, benefits not afforded to ordinary citizens.

On the morning of July 30, with Iverson scheduled to appear at a hearing nearly a month after the argument that led Iverson and Tawanna to this, the main gate opened in front of Iverson's estate. Two Cadillac Escalades passed, and news photographers hustled to shine their lights and point their lenses on the man in the backseat with a blue towel draped over his head. Finally, after weeks, the media had their nugget, and with the five o'clock morning newscasts approaching, there seemed to be golden footage on their reels.

As they celebrated, heading to their news trucks to transmit the video, another convoy exited a private road near Iverson's home. The Escalades and whoever had been in the backseat had been a well-executed decoy. Now, in front of a Lower Merion police cruiser was a green Mazda minivan, and inside the nondescript vehicle sat Iverson, who traveled in peace to police headquarters and entered the building through a secure garage.

Some believed the Sixers had pulled strings at city hall to protect their most precious investment. "It's just part of what the 76ers had always done with Allen Iverson: They're going to do everything they can do to keep him on the basketball court," the Philadelphia radio and television commentator Howard Eskin said later.

When the hearing began, court staffers asked Iverson for autographs and handshakes, and workers from the district attorney's office sneaked into the courtroom for a glimpse. A local radio personality and several well-known lawyers were allowed to sit in the jury box for the day's entertainment. The hearing lasted six hours, and defense exhibits were labeled "A.I. 1" and "A.I. 2," part of an unusual atmosphere that led prosecutor Charles Ehrlich to wonder aloud: "Why are the rules different today?"

Charles Jones, whom Iverson had allegedly threatened and who would later call 911, testified that Iverson paid rent on the shared apartment and had every right to come and go. "That was just made up," Tawanna, herself under oath, would say in late 2012, "so he can justify his placement in that apartment that night. We've never paid the rent of his cousin's apartment." The testimony of Carey, the other witness in the apartment that night, fell apart while Sprague questioned him. Iverson and his uncle, Gregory Iverson, were cleared of all but one of the charges; they were convicted only of making terroristic threats, a misdemeanor.

Afterward, fans and city officials celebrated. Sixers executives and coaches exhaled. Reebok executives rejoiced, not only because they had publicly backed their most famous client and he had now been cleared, but because nothing sells shoes in urban neighborhoods like enhanced street cred. The *Wall Street Journal* reported that Iverson's shoes were actually selling better after the arrest. Even Municipal Court Judge James M. DeLeon, whose decision freed Iverson, seemed relieved; he told reporters that, upon his assignment of the case, he was disappointed because, as he put it, "I couldn't wear the Iverson jersey."

SHE CAME HOME not long after Iverson did, because this was the way their relationship had always worked. He engaged her in a battle, she put distance between them and thought briefly of a different kind of life, and then he pulled her back with his apologies and tenderness. Even during the darkest times years later, Tawanna could not resist the flickers of warmth that Iverson showed in times of regret. She told herself that this was the time he was being sincere; that he would truly change and the good Allen would permanently overcome the bad one.

"Love yall & I love u. I miss your pretty face & I'm sorry! Ppl make mistakes!" Iverson sent Tawanna in a typical text message years later. "This is me Tawanna! I fucked up."

Then, after another spat a short time later, another kind of message would chime in. "Groupie ass bitch!" he once wrote to her. "I will make sure u will never be trusted by a nigga again! U r a sneaky ass cheating thief & the world will know."

But in 2002, as the couple celebrated their one-year wedding anniversary with so many unpleasant memories now piled atop the joyful ones, Iverson vowed that, yes, things would be different. Tawanna returned with the hope that such a near miss would be a wake-up call for her husband. The next judge might not be such an Iverson fan, she reminded him; the next district attorney might not be overpowered by distractions in the courtroom; and the next police officer might not be so eager to walk away with only a story about how he once let a drunk and belligerent Allen Iverson walk.

Tawanna spoke with Iverson about his drinking, and he at least heard his wife out when she recommended they attend marriage counseling. Then he changed his mind. "We don't do that," Iverson eventually decided, and Tawanna assumed his pride was a race or loyalty thing, and though she would regret it later, she dropped it.

Iverson was otherwise agreeable to Tawanna's demands, and in a show of renewed faith after the gun incident, he wanted to empower her. Iverson refused to take seriously a meeting with a financial adviser they had flown in from Michigan; he arrived for the meeting an hour late and held a brief and dismissive conversation. "Let her handle it," Iverson told the money manager. "Talk to her."

When the man left, astonished that Iverson wanted no role in his own finances, not even occasional reminders of how much money he actually had, Iverson explained to Tawanna that outsiders could not be trusted. And besides, he told her, he believed in her more than anyone. He appointed Tawanna to find their homes and pay the bills, handling the expenses for Iverson's mother's two homes and the household responsibilities for his sisters, two uncles, an aunt, and all of their children. "I cut the checks," was how Tawanna explained the setup. "Allen made the money." One of her first checks was settling her husband's $300,000 legal bills for the gun incident.

But this was not enough. Langford was dead, and Iverson wanted a way for his memory to live on. He wanted another baby, preferably a son, and in the autumn of 2002, only a few months after her husband chased her around Philadelphia with a gun, Tawanna became pregnant. Iverson's behavior was not perfect as they prepared for the birth of their third child—he had promised to attend an amniocentesis test after Tawanna was diagnosed with a condition that would require a caesarean section, but he blew it off—but at least he was sober and in attendance when his wife went into labor in August 2003.

After the most turbulent two years of their adult lives and with Iverson's eighth NBA season about to begin, Tawanna delivered a baby boy on August 8. Iverson, showing unusual interest in a topic that did not involve basketball, already had a name in mind: Isaiah Rahsaan Iverson. In Iverson's mind, tattoo ink was a fitting tribute to a fallen friend. But nothing was stronger than blood.

CHAPTER 16

PRACTICE, MAN

They stood there awestruck and frozen, the words flowing from Iverson's mouth and the tension rising.

The day after the 2001–02 season ended with a first-round playoff loss, Billy King, the Sixers' general manager, was a few yards away from his franchise player, regretting that he had ever suggested holding a damn press conference. Aaron McKie, Iverson's teammate and friend, stood in the media room, not far from the team's practice court, forcing himself to laugh. And Pat Croce, the team's former president, watched the coverage live on Comcast SportsNet, suspecting that Iverson was drunk—and, after a few minutes of seeing a tattered soul on full, agonizing display, asked his wife to change the channel. The twenty or so reporters scribbled notes, checked their stopwatches, and questioned whether the bizarre things they were hearing and seeing were real. Iverson had been asked about a sore subject, and he was now going on and on about it.

"What are we talking about? Practice?" Iverson said, his arms folded and wearing a white T-shirt and white Boston Red Sox cap, whose red outlines vaguely matched his slightly bloodshot eyes. "We talkin' about *practice,* man."

Iverson had disappeared for a while earlier, tipsy when he returned and eager to share his news with Philadelphia. King, standing next to the team's public relations director not far from the television cameras' view, searched his brain for any way to end this disaster. He had no idea Iverson's rant would become iconic, played thousands of times and eventually becoming a fixture in the sports vernacular. King wondered if he should step in front of the camera, causing a bigger scene, sure, but at least ending this sideshow.

When it was over, reporters and team officials rolled their eyes, gathered their notebooks, and began breaking down their cameras and tripods. One of them was Phil Jasner, the longtime *Philadelphia Daily News* beat man and a reporter with whom Iverson had clashed frequently, including a few minutes earlier.

When Jasner reached his car, he took out his phone and dialed his son, Andy. "Did you see that?" he asked.

THE DAY AFTER the draft, news conferences are usually artificial, predictable affairs with ready-made story lines of hope and salvation. Teams who make top picks are usually in that position because their previous seasons were terrible, and these gatherings are meant to curb the narrative of past losing and replace it with a new face who will surely bring on better days. They represent, if nothing else, boosts to the team's ticket office and an easy day of coverage for the reporters on the beat.

The top pick usually sits at a table or stands at a lectern, smiling and eager to meet the men and women who will chronicle his rise to stardom. For reporters, these are also opportunities to connect with a new face and a potential source; days like this are fertile chances to find common ground with the new player. Players welcome the attention, long before the act inevitably becomes tiring, media obligations becoming a repetitive, thankless part of the job.

The day after the 1996 NBA draft, Iverson said little and was suspicious of the reporters in the room. Who were they, and what right did they have to question him? A reporter for the *News Journal* in

Wilmington, Delaware, approached the Sixers' twenty-one-year-old top pick, and Iverson barely made eye contact. Tom Moore, a veteran reporter for the *Bucks County Courier Times,* shook Iverson's limp hand and asked about his love of art, hoping to lower the youngster's guard by talking about a comfortable subject. Instead Iverson just mumbled, apparently not understanding why he was being asked about a topic other than basketball.

As the months and years passed, Iverson developed an erratic and occasionally stormy relationship with the media. He was just as likely after games to sulk and be defensive as he was to offer heartfelt, thoughtful insight that stopped even the most cynical reporter in his pen stroke. Iverson might slap his knee within earshot of Larry Brown, asking his coach to come sit on his lap as reporters laughed, or he might lash out—nobody ever knew. But whether Iverson was angry or introspective, it made for good copy, great sound, interesting days.

"You wanted to hear what Allen had to say, and you didn't know what Allen *would* say," longtime Comcast reporter and anchor Neil Hartman said. "A lot of times when you ask a player what they're thinking, you know half the time what they're going to say. But with Allen, you had no idea, and that's what made it great television."

Phil Jasner was seen in the late 1990s as the dean of Philadelphia media. He had covered Charles Barkley and Maurice Cheeks, legends who were interesting even on their most boring days. Nothing, though, compared with the young guard out of Georgetown. "It just kept him working day and night," Andy Jasner, also a reporter, recalled of his late dad. "And he would always tell me: 'Andy, this guy is incredible to cover. He is also exhausting.'"

Jasner preferred typewriters and tape cassettes, even when laptops and digital recorders pushed out the old technology. He filled entire notebook pages with great loops and pen strikes, the pages flying violently past after he had scribbled five or ten words. He was an aging, white reporter with few basketball bona fides, other than a keen eye on how to dissect the game and analyze a team's most essential needs. And

Iverson was a young, black world-class athlete, destined, it seemed, to forever butt heads with the likes of Jasner.

McKie arrived at the practice facility most days unaware of what had been written and said about himself or the team. Sometimes a columnist had teed off on Iverson's practice habits, his relationship with Larry Brown, or the tenuous game the Sixers were playing by enabling such an unpredictable personality. Other times an opposing player had been quoted making promises about stopping Iverson, maybe vowing to embarrass the little man on national television. In the late 1990s, the Philadelphia media was a battleground, even locally. Iverson saw himself as an unfair target, forever misunderstood by those who saw the world through a far different lens.

"The worst thing is, just reading, looking at the newspapers, you see terrorism on the front page, then you see all the deaths in Philadelphia on the local page and all that negativity," he would tell reporters in 2006. "Then you get to the sports page, and when there's supposed to be something gratifying, you see even more negativity."

It became common for Brown to send public jabs at Iverson, thinly veiled challenges he knew his best player would read—and could not help reacting to. Reporters came to understand Brown's codes for calling out Iverson. If the coach said publicly that he needed Iverson to "be more engaged," that meant he wanted him to attend practices more frequently—and, ideally, not be drunk or hungover. If Brown said he wanted Iverson to be a "total basketball player," that meant he was tired of how many shots his shooting guard was taking. Reporters had cracked the Larry Brown code, and so had Iverson, one of the more creative—albeit passive-aggressive—ways for Brown to motivate his star player.

Iverson was just as willing to work his own agenda through the media, though he rarely bothered with tact. Reporters came to see Iverson as high-maintenance but an undoubted godsend: a pain in the ass sometimes, sure, but they would never hurt for quotes or color, making even the most common group interview an unpredictable event.

"I believe in my heart I'm the best player in the world," he said in 2002, showing his confident side.

"You honestly don't really feel it when the shots are going down. You don't ever get the goose bumps until the fans start to appreciate what you're doing," he said in 2005, showing the kind of vulnerability that made him so beloved.

"If your kid goes out and blows somebody's head off because Allen Iverson has said he was going to blow somebody's head off on wax, then you're doing a bad job as a parent," he told the *Philadelphia Inquirer* in 2000, discussing his rap album and showing how defiant he could be.

Iverson at one point announced his wife's pregnancy during a nationally televised interview, rankling Tawanna because he never considered himself in the business of keeping secrets. She had asked Iverson to keep the pregnancy quiet, considering it had been unplanned and that Tawanna had been hoping to return to school. She asked Iverson for time to "process" the news, as she would later describe it during a court appearance, but instead of maintaining discretion and allowing his wife to whisper their news to family and friends, those people heard about it for the first time on television. The point was, nothing was out of bounds, no topic too banal; no question that was not loaded with nitroglycerin.

"We hated it when Larry and Allen left," *Philadelphia Daily News* columnist John Smallwood said, "because then it felt like work again."

Iverson became a fascination for the men and women who chronicled him, and how they interpreted and transmitted his words and actions supplied equal entertainment for him, a match made in heaven—or maybe in hell. He forged alliances with friendly reporters, the deepest relationship built between Iverson and Stephen A. Smith, the former *Philadelphia Inquirer* beat writer and columnist, each of them finding ways to push their own agendas through one another and becoming friends in the process. On the other side of the spectrum was television and radio personality Howard Eskin, who feuded with Iverson and the player's entourage; many Philadelphia reporters believed Eskin simply hated Iverson, who refused to appear on Eskin's show. For his part, Eskin would later say that he resented how Iverson was enabled by the Sixers and protected by reporters who would dance at Iverson's whim in exchange for a nibble of access.

Phil Jasner was somewhere in the middle, more of a curiosity for Iverson than anything. He wrote honestly about the players he covered, coming to see accountability and transparency as his hallmarks rather than using cheap ways to advance his career—including babying or attacking Iverson. Jasner, like Iverson, was fearless. If he ripped a player, there he was in the locker room the next day, hackles up, if necessary, to defend his position. He cared about his craft and, even during a period of significant change in American journalism and the reporter's role in the sports context, Jasner stayed true to what he believed was right. Iverson kind of liked that.

"Iverson might perceive the same old, wary eyes watching him," Jasner wrote in the *Daily News* in 2000, "but he clearly has put a dent in some of those discerning faces who saw only the wrapping and not the man inside."

Not that Iverson, never comfortable inside a journalist's crosshairs—even if the bullets were deserved—always saw it that way. After McKie dressed each day into his practice gear, he would find Iverson locked in a bathroom stall, the sound of angrily turned newspaper pages echoing off the tile. Each day Iverson instructed his bodyguard, Terry Royster, to pick up a copy of the *Daily News* so he could do what so many Philadelphians did each morning: read what Jasner had written.

Not everyone had the same reaction as Iverson, though: "Them motherfuckers," McKie would hear his teammate grousing to himself in the stall, shortly before the door flew open and Iverson thundered out.

BROWN HAD WAITED long enough, so he checked his watch and headed for the parking lot. Four nights earlier, the Boston Celtics had thrashed the

Sixers, 120–87, eliminating them in the first round of the Eastern Conference playoffs, a disappointing and sudden finish a year after Philadelphia had reached the NBA Finals. Brown told his players that night in the visitors' locker room that over the next few days, he would meet with each of them. After that, they were free to clear their lockers and leave.

One by one, players dropped by Brown's office—McKie and George Lynch, Raja Bell and Eric Snow—to talk about what was needed from them during the summer, and if their contracts were expiring or they were potential trade chips, the factors involved in whether they would return to Philadelphia. But one, of course, had never shown up. Iverson had not just blown off a scheduled media availability, reporters' final opportunity to interview players before they spread across the country for the off-season. Now he was standing up his coach.

Again.

"I admire him, I love him personally. I love the way he competes and tries to win. But I've had issues with him as far as coming to practice and being on time and becoming a better player," Brown had said during a news conference late in the season. "I've got a young kid on my hands that's looking for direction."

The last of the exit interviews was supposed to have been completed in the morning, and here it was afternoon when Brown's phone finally rang. Iverson apologized, saying he had run late, promising that he would be there at three o'clock. Brown had heard the reasons before: why he was late or would be a no-show, so sure, Allen, see you at three.

When the hand hit the three on Brown's wristwatch, Iverson still nowhere to be found, Brown got up, left his office, and headed for his car. He had just pulled out of his parking space when Iverson pulled in, a friend in his passenger seat.

"What are you doing, Coach? I'm here!" Iverson shouted toward Brown through the lowered window.

"You weren't here at three o'clock," Brown told him, his patience long since having run dry. "You weren't there this morning. My time is just as valuable as yours, and I'm not waiting for your ass."

"Ah, Coach," Iverson said with a smile, and sure enough, Brown put his car back in gear and returned to his space.

They stood outside the team facility, Brown telling Iverson that his tardiness on this day was just the latest in a series of disappointments. People counted on Iverson, the coach reminded him, and it was clear he respected no one's schedule but his own. Iverson grew defensive, and soon they were both raising their voices, pointing their fingers. King, the general manager, found his way outside and tried to referee the latest bout between his legendary head coach and his future Hall of Fame shooting guard.

Brown told Iverson that he was no longer certain he possessed the energy and patience to coach him, and Iverson said he was no longer sure he could continue to play for Brown—same song as always, just a different verse. On and on it went, their voices bouncing off the facility's walls. And as it always seemed to be, these strong-willed men needed a brief war to find peace. "There was nothing held back," King said. "But by the end, I think they both had a better understanding of, all right, we can make this work. I think Allen understood, and Larry understood."

With their voices now lowered, Iverson looked his coach in the eye. "So are you gonna trade my ass?" he asked.

Brown shook his head, promising Iverson that he would be back in Philadelphia in the fall, back in the starting lineup, back on a team that, Brown hated to admit, needed him badly, pain in the ass that he was. And, yes, Brown would return, too, keeping the two most important pieces in Philadelphia.

That was all Iverson needed to hear. He wrapped his arms around Brown, who slapped his star player's back. Brown was relieved but drained, the same as he always was after NBA seasons, but King and Iverson were excited. This was a crossroads moment, and with the latest bit of drama behind them, the tension released, next season was going to be epic.

King reminded Iverson that, unlike his teammates, he had never spoken to Philadelphia media. The only way to make up for it was to hold a press conference, even though many of the reporters had already left. Iverson agreed, eager to tell the media and Sixers fans that, yes, he would be back in Philly and that he and Brown had forged their latest peace accord, and watch out, Eastern Conference, because the Sixers were coming back stronger. "He wants to let everybody know Coach and I have worked this shit out," Brown said. " 'And I'm staying. Coach told me I'm staying. He's staying. Everything is all right.' "

They agreed on a press conference early in the evening, and with a few hours to kill, Iverson left with his friend. "I assume he went and fooled around somewhere," Brown said, tipping his hand upward like a bottle.

When Iverson returned to the facility, King greeted him, noticing that something was different from a couple of hours earlier. His energy was higher, and he was much more talkative. His words were less sharp, and his eyes raced. "If we had thought that he was drinking or whatever," King said, "we'd have never done it."

But the fuse had already been lit. The reporters were in their seats, the lighting had been checked and white balances corrected. King took his place near a wall, McKie stood in the back to watch the show, and Iverson glided toward the table with the black cloth and microphone. Hartman, the Comcast reporter, relayed to a studio anchor, Michael Barkann, that Iverson had arrived. "He's starting right now, Michael. Let's go," Hartman said into his microphone.

Hearing the words, Iverson dropped his voice into a newsman's baritone, mocking Hartman—"*He's starting now, Michael, llllet's go!*"—and taking the first swing during what was about to be an unforgettable main event.

MORE THAN ANYTHING, Jasner told people, he enjoyed the routine nature of the Sixers beat. Late-morning practices, watching from the balcony, group interviews and one-on-ones with coaches and players, and then time to write and file—repeating the process tomorrow.

If a new reporter joined the beat, he would advise them to join a hotel's loyalty program, make the extra call to one more source, and always show up in the locker room the day after you rip someone. Forget everything else; that part came first: Do not write and run; if you have balls enough to write big, better come back to the facility the next day, face the music, hold your ground. No room for pussies and hacks on this grind, no time for bullshit.

Jasner loved trips to Toronto and walking around the Eaton Centre and staying in the same hotels he always stayed in. If a new arena had opened or, God forbid, he could not get into one of his preferred hotels or restaurants, he would drive to the arena the day before the game just to make sure, before the clock was actually running, that he knew the way. He did not like change, and he never cared much for the Internet, because it seemed not to care much for him. Social media confused him, and the insta-journalism movement felt cheap and forgettable. "He had his way," said Smallwood, a longtime *Daily News* colleague, "and he never got comfortable with the supposed new generation. He thought the way it used to be done, was better."

The years passed and the seasons ended, the beat of the drum, just the way Jasner seemed to like it. Which is why everything changed when Iverson arrived in Philadelphia, as much Jasner's turf as anyone's because he had been around longer than most anyone. Julius Erving, Barkley, and Moses Malone had all come and gone, but Jasner and his wasted, half-filled notebook pages remained. But there was nothing routine about covering Iverson: News conferences could erupt into explosive affairs, and a night's sleep might be interrupted by a police source or hotel clerk, telling the middle-aged *Daily News* reporter it was time to suit up and go.

Iverson would come staggering in sometimes, Brown already hinting to the media horde about where he believed his shooting guard had been the night before, and Jasner would ask some of the first questions, no matter the backlash or bad breath.

It was common for Iverson to roll his eyes at Jasner, telling him he did not understand the game or any young black man. And it was no rarity for Jasner to fire back at the young star, wondering aloud how good Iverson might be if he did not so often get in his own way.

Then, when the nerves calmed and the questions eased, the people around them sometimes noticed something odd: Two of the strongest-willed sons of bitches in the building, one who dribbled a basketball and the other who pushed a pen, seemed to enjoy their little run-ins. Sometimes they were even seen over by Iverson's locker, a day after their latest blowup, standing there smiling.

WHAT THE HELL, Hartman thought, and asked the question on most everyone's mind: "Could you be clear about your practicing habits since we can't see you practice?"

Iverson adjusted himself, chomping a cheek packed with gum. He wanted to announce that he would return the next season, and so would Brown. But no one was asking about that. Like always, Iverson preferred to play offense, but these questions were putting him in a defensive posture.

"If Coach tells you that I missed practice, then that's that," he said, his words slightly slurred. "I may have missed one practice this year, but if somebody says he missed one practice of all the practices this year, then that's enough to get a whole lot started."

He went on, touching on the subject of the Sixers potentially trading him. Maybe now someone would ask about the renewed vows between him and Brown. Instead . . .

"So you and Coach Brown got caught up on Saturday about practice?" another reporter asked.

Iverson, his arms folded, looked irritated.

"If I can't practice, I can't practice, man. If I'm hurt, I'm hurt," he said, pausing. "I mean, simple as that."

He looked downward, then his eyes lifted. His voice was louder now.

"It ain't about that. It's not about that at all. You know what I'm saying? But it's easy to talk about it. It's easy to sum it up when you just talk about practice. We sitting in here—I'm supposed to be the franchise player, and we in here talking about practice. I mean, listen: We talking about *practice*. Not a game. Not a game. Not a *game*. We talking about *practice*. Not a game. Not the game that I go out there and die for and play every game like it's my last. Not the game. We talking about practice, man. I mean, how silly is that? And we're talking about practice.

"I know I'm supposed to be the—I know I'm supposed to lead by example. I know that. And I'm not, I'm not shoving it aside like it don't mean anything. I know it's important. I do. I honestly do. But we talking about practice, man. What are we talking about? Practice? We talking about practice, man."

A group of reporters laughed, and even Iverson chuckled. They were deep into the rabbit hole together now.

"We talking about practice. We talking about practice. We ain't talking about the game. We're talking about practice, man. When you come in the arena and you see me play, you see me play, don't you? You see me give everything I got, right? But we talking about practice right now. We talking about prac—"

He shook his head as Hartman tried to ask a follow-up question.

"Man, look, I hear you. It's funny to me, too. It's strange to me, too. But we talking about practice, man. We're not even talking about the game, the actual game, when it matters. We talking about practice."

Twenty-two times he said it, and although reporters tried to lighten the mood, those who knew Iverson and had an investment in Iverson or the franchise were incredulous. King wondered how the hell to put a stop to this. Croce, who had come across the Comcast broadcast while he was flipping channels, was disgusted. *Get him off the stage,* Croce thought to himself, feeling not amusement but pity because he knew about Rahsaan Langford, who had been gunned down months earlier, and how it had affected Iverson. These were not the musings of a man attempting to be funny or make a point, Croce thought; this was the stream-of-consciousness rambling of a man in pain. "Someone, grab him off there," Croce recalled thinking. "Stop him."

Croce changed the channel, but a few miles away, the show continued. Some were entertained, and others watched the train wreck unfold—knowing from experience that Iverson was drunk. "He was lit," said Smallwood, who attended the conference. "If he had been sober, he would have been able to get himself out of that. He never would've gone down that path. Maybe you had to have been around him all the time to know the difference, but we all knew." Karen Frascona, the Sixers' public relations director, tried several times to throw Iverson a lifeline, either end the gathering or at least get the team's best player back on point. But Iverson was revved up now, fueled by irritation and alcohol, and he kept waving Frascona off. He was ready to fight, and there was a man sitting in front of him who, if Iverson wanted it, was not afraid of a confrontation.

Jasner, who had not been amused by the rant, had serious questions to ask Iverson, who now was in no mood to be accommodating. "What are some of the things you can do during the summer that can help you?" Jasner asked.

Iverson cracked wise.

"I'm going to come back and be the biggest, strongest bodybuilder in the world. That will make me the best player in the world. If I come back next year and look like Arnold Schwarzenegger, will y'all give me the MVP automatically? Please do that. If I come back and be huge and big, y'all will give me the award."

"You have to earn it," Jasner said.

"Why not? I've earned the MVP small as hell. Y'all tell me what y'all want me to do."

"May I respond to that?" Jasner said, the conference becoming a full-on showdown.

"Yeah."

"There are people that have suggested, myself included, that instead of shooting forty percent, you . . ."

"What do you know about basketball?" Iverson asked Jasner. "Have you ever played?"

"Yes."

"I don't know, Phil, I don't know you as a basketball player. I know you as a columnist, but I have never heard of you as a player, though."

"Why is that an issue?"

"Why is that an issue? Because we're talking about basketball."

"Let me ask my question."

"Go ahead, *Philip*."

Among Sixers and media insiders, this was almost as memorable as the *Practice* response. Iverson was trying to embarrass Jasner, talking down to him by calling him by his full name. "For him to take it on such a personal level, mocking him for his name—because no one called Phil 'Philip'—now he was hitting below the belt," former *Philadelphia Inquirer* reporter Ashley Fox said. But Jasner would not let Iverson off easily. He was the veteran in this room, not Iverson. Jasner asked his question, and Iverson submitted by answering. This was, after all, Jasner's turf, and a moment later Iverson seemed to accept that he could not win. Iverson lowered his voice. It would be largely forgotten, Iverson's vulnerability after the most disappointing series of months since Iverson's childhood—and less than a year after he had reached the professional mountaintop, winning the MVP and pushing the Sixers to the Finals.

"Look at me. Look at what I'm going through," he said. "I have to listen to Phil talk to me about this shit. For what? It's summertime. I'm supposed to be with my family, chillin'. But this is my life. This is what I have to go through.

"I know that I don't do everything right. I do a lot of shit that ain't right. I know I do. I'm just like y'all, though. I'm just like you. I might be better or I might not be, but I am human just like you."

SHORTLY BEFORE THE NBA All-Star Game in 2009, Jasner's appendix burst. He asked his son for a ride home from the hospital, and when

Andy arrived, the elder Jasner just stared at his boy. Looked him in the eyes, said nothing for a long time.

Then, when his lips moved, Andy heard the words: It was stage-four cancer that had caused his appendix to rupture.

The disease spread, but Jasner kept working. He kept making the calls, kept staying in his hotels, and, because it was what he always impressed upon the youngsters, he kept showing up, because this is what you do.

He and Andy would take car rides sometimes, and Jasner would tell his only son about why he loved the job; why outsiders could never understand this life. He told him about covering the Sixers in the NBA Finals in 1982–83, about Malone predicting a championship and then delivering it to Philadelphia. About how Dr. J and Bobby Jones and Billy Cunningham called *him* to talk basketball, and about how, no, Andy, it was not the routine he loved all these years, as the others suggested; if the ordinary made a writer comfortable, it was the astonishing that made the memories and kept him eager to work each day. It was watching young men born with superhuman ability flying through the air and defying the odds, standing so close to greatness and wondering what a player such as Iverson could have been if he had taken better care of himself. Wondering about never-ending questions, such as what if Iverson had set aside the anger and the alcohol? What if he had listened to his coaches and teammates rather than following his own rules?

"My dad mentioned this to me a lot, especially as Allen got older and the Sixers got better, is that Allen's biggest enemy was really Allen," Andy Jasner said. "With all the success that he had, my dad would always say: 'Gosh, I just would have loved to have seen had he really put the work in [during] the off-season and really stayed fit and took care of his body like Grant Hill and had done all those things.'

"And he would always say Allen just—there were just some things you couldn't get through to him. And it frustrated him so much. Until the day he passed, it frustrated him."

Andy listened, and his sixty-eight-year-old dad told him about how, oddly enough, Iverson might have been his favorite one of all. He was so talented, so mysterious, so passionate—and, different as they were, at its core this job is about the pursuit of understanding the men and women you cover, and Iverson and Jasner somehow had come to understand each other.

On December 3, 2010, three weeks after his induction into the Philadelphia Sports Hall of Fame, Jasner's cancer defeated him. His pen stopped, and so did the questions, and tributes would pour in from around the sports and journalism universes. One of the first came from Iverson, posted over several installments on his Twitter account before a game in Istanbul, Turkey:

> My teammates and I are about to go into war, in a very important game. I am dedicating tonights [*sic*] game to the memory of Phil Jasner. If I considered by some to be one of best to have played the game. He clearly was the best to have ever covered one. This one is for you Phil. God Bless!

More than three years later, when Iverson's number three was retired in Philadelphia, he thanked Phil Jasner and, later, spoke to Andy Jasner as he sat in the front row of Iverson's news conference. Andy Jasner was almost moved to tears at the idea that this larger-than-life superstar, on one of his most important days, had thanked so many giants for being part of his unbelievable journey—placing his dad alongside them.

"Me and your father had wars, but I know he loved me, and I loved him," Iverson told the younger Jasner. "We would see each other, and we would talk to each other like we were best friends. And then tomorrow, I would be like, 'Can you believe this . . . that Phil wrote about me?' And I couldn't wait to get to practice the next day to confront him about it.

" 'Well, Allen, you know I had to. You know I'm not trying to hurt you,' and such and such. All right, well, hug and then it may happen again a month later."

Iverson smiled, and so did Andy Jasner. "But that's how we were," Iverson said. "We always had that respect for each other and the love for each other. Always."

CHAPTER 17

ALL THAT GLITTERS

Larry Brown stared at the hardwood as he walked off the court, his mind wandering. A moment earlier, he had been gesturing at his Sixers players, trying to conjure the perfect play against the Detroit Pistons, hoping there was some magic left in his plucky team now that it had pushed the Pistons to overtime in Game Six of the 2003 Eastern Conference semifinals. The Sixers trailed by three points in the final seconds, and then there it was, and Brown just stood and watched: Iverson had the ball, flying past him like he had so many times, running toward the basket with twelve, eleven, ten seconds to go, and then—*what?*—Iverson missed the layup.

Game over. Series over. Another long summer ahead, this one full of responsibilities and little time for rest, and anyway, Brown walked toward the locker room with his head down. Another speech directed at his heartbroken team lay ahead, along with another news conference that would undoubtedly fixate on his relationship with Iverson and what had happened hours earlier, another walk to his car and drive into the night, no idea whether, at age sixty-two, he had another long-ass, grueling season like this in him. It was too much. All of it. Three months earlier, Brown narrated a one-hour film session, then skipped his own practice to meet with general manager Billy King, who seemed to talk the Sixers coach off the ledge once or twice a year. Brown had stepped away during the 2000–2001 season, thinking of quitting, but then he returned and coached one of the best seasons of his life. This time, though, was different. The Sixers had struggled during the regular season, falling into fifth place, and Brown did not even feel like coaching, his first love. All the time, the battles, the bullshit—it was usually worth it only if the team was winning.

On this night in late May, with the Pistons moving on to face the New Jersey Nets and the Sixers gathering the next day for final meetings before scattering, the anxiety hung on Brown's shoulders. He could deal with Iverson's missed layup. It happens, even to one of the game's best players in one of the series' most important moments. Shitty, but it happens. Brown, who had drawn a technical foul late in regulation of Game Six, knew that was not what he would spend the next three months obsessing over, though, and it would not be what the reporters would ask him about, again and again. No, it would be about how Iverson, before an elimination game at the Sixers' home arena, had arrived thirty-two minutes before tip-off. Thirty-two minutes. Everyone else was in the locker room hours earlier, stretching and heading to the floor to shoot, and Iverson was, well, God only knew.

When Brown confronted him about it, asking *What the fuck, Allen?* Iverson first said he had been stuck in traffic. Then he said he had a flat tire. *Fuck it,* Brown thought. For six years now he had heard the reasons—these inconvenient little horrors that seemed to pop up so often to the same person—one too many times.

HE FOUGHT BACK tears and explained himself, sitting at that table for forty-five minutes, remembering the good times. Brown had spent the past few weeks in Florida, thinking it over and finally coming to the answer that felt right: He was finished. Brown had committed six years, the longest the vagabond coach had spent at any one place, to rebuilding the Sixers and finding ways to make it work with Iverson. Now the lump in his throat grew as he suggested that he and the team needed "a fresh look."

He had no idea what lay ahead, but he was certain of two things: He wanted to coach, and he did *not* want to coach in Philadelphia. In fact, he wanted out so badly that he vacated the remaining $12 million on his Sixers contract, forfeiting the money in exchange for the team waiving a contract clause ruling that, if he left the Sixers before his deal expired, he could not coach another NBA team. When it was finished, Brown met with most of the Sixers' players. They streamed into his office at the team facility, telling stories and turning handshakes into hugs. So many familiar faces came to say goodbye, though the most famous one of all—and a prime reason Brown had made this decision in the first place—never came through, instead passing the time poolside in Miami. Iverson never called, never asked for a reason why, never told the coach—even for old times' sake—to go fuck himself. They were finished, and that was that, Iverson and his homeboys draining bottles and peeling hundreds amid the neon lights of South Beach.

Brown tried not to take it personally. He never saw Iverson during the summer anyway; why would this be different? Gary Moore, Iverson's personal manager, took on his usual role of defusing blame directed toward the superstar, telling the *Philadelphia Inquirer* that Iverson "and Coach Brown were just fine. He told Al how proud he was of him, how far he'd come, and their relationship had improved by leaps and bounds." Brown knew the score, though, pausing years later when asked if the idea of another year babysitting Iverson, looking the other way when his selfish behavior jeopardized the team, was the reason he left. "Not entirely," he said before smiling.

What Brown had not factored into his decision, having been burned so many times by Iverson's broken promises, was that Iverson had actually committed to condensing his fun in Miami to a few days, maybe a week, and then getting back to work. Off-season work had pushed Iverson toward the MVP award and elevated the Sixers into the NBA Finals three years earlier, and he wanted another taste. He swore off Doritos and Snickers bars, cornerstones of the Iverson diet, and began lifting weights for the first time in years. Iverson wanted to resume his place atop the NBA mountain, but it had not been just to chase another MVP or push the Sixers toward the Finals or to somehow placate Brown. No, Iverson was and always would be an incentive-based life-form, inspired not by the hunt but by the idea of the kill, and now there was this: He wanted to be an Olympian. Wanted it bad. He had been snubbed four years earlier, Sixers general manager King among the committee members who had left him off the roster despite Iverson finishing second in the league in scoring in 1998–99. His play had apparently not been enough to offset the ink and the braids, the bad moods and the foul language, and so he watched as Team USA brought home gold from Sydney, Australia. Two years later, in the shadow of his MVP season, he was again left off the national team when the International Basketball Federation invited players to compete in the world championship. "Talent-wise," Iverson told reporters in 2003, "people look at it as though I'm supposed to be here. But personality-wise and who I am, people don't think so."

But this time Iverson was determined to scratch an itch that had nagged at him since watching the Dream Team, the iconic 1992 Olympic team built for the first time with NBA stars—Michael Jordan, Magic Johnson, and Larry Bird among them—and so he began publicly selling himself, walking that fine line between promoting his maturity and that deadly sin: selling out. "I'm not at the point where I'll stop dressing the way I dress or where I'm ready to cut my hair," Iverson would tell reporters in August 2003. "But I'm ready to become a real man. I don't want people to look at me like, 'Oh, there he goes again.' I don't want to be the young guy no more. I want to be the older guy. I don't want to do the things I've done in the past. I want to be sharp in my lifestyle like I am on the basketball court."

Tawanna had given birth that month to Isaiah, their third child, and Iverson said that was enough to settle him. He was no longer interested, or at least he was less interested, in slamming Coronas and hitting the titty bars. He no longer needed to torch the speed limit in one of his cars, throwing it into park and walking in to a scowling Tawanna. "I used to be able to stay out until three o'clock in the morning and give somebody forty points the next day," he said during that same meeting with reporters. "But that's not healthy, and my wife has a problem with that. She's like: 'Get in the house!' "

The months passed, and in March 2003 Iverson called Stu Jackson, the former NBA coach and executive who was assembling the 2004 Olympic team. Iverson begged Jackson for consideration, and Jackson said he would think it over. But Iverson never did call Brown, even for an endorsement. The old coach had dialed Iverson's number a few times, but he had never answered or called back. Brown had become the biggest free agent of the 2003 class, fielding overtures from the Los Angeles Clippers, Houston Rockets, and Washington Wizards before signing on to lead the Pistons, the very team that had eliminated the Sixers and hastened this move, tipping the scales, ending an era.

Brown had taken a shot at Iverson during his introductory news conference in Auburn Hills: "I was there at practice on time," he said, "and even for the games." Detroit was solidly built, packed with reliable veterans, and had a chance at a playoff run the next spring. Brown was eager and reenergized, but like always, regret weighed him down. He hated how he had left things with Iverson, and he thought of a way to make it right.

Brown called Jackson, assuring him that Iverson was a perfect fit for the national team's roster. He *was* USA basketball now, the attitude and the game spawned from the playground style Iverson helped usher into the league; did Jackson not realize that? Besides, Brown told him, Jackson would never have to deal with Iverson on a day-to-day basis. That burden would fall on the head coach, who had been put in place months earlier and would have to manage Iverson's ups and downs, weighing the talent against his mood swings.

Iverson took the call, the third round of selections now complete, and heard the news: He was in. The new roster included his name, and

Jackson invited him to join the team for a qualifying tournament at John Jay College in New York City. Iverson was so excited that he had American flags stitched onto the tongues of his Reeboks, and when he met with reporters before the Tournament of the Americas, Iverson wore a red, white, and blue do-rag as he spoke about his opportunity. "I have flaws just like people in any country," he said that day. "There's a lot of people in all different countries that have flaws and have made mistakes, and I just want to represent that." He said he could not wait to remove his shirt and show his coach his bulging muscles, at least by a skinny man's standards.

When Iverson headed off to practice, from behind he heard a familiar voice: "Take off your shirt," the Team USA coach called toward him. Iverson spun around to see Brown, his coach once again, standing there smiling.

THE CROWDS PACKED into the tiny Puerto Rican field house in the inland town of Caguas, and all around Iverson were reminders of his influence. Rappers had come for a glimpse of America's hip-hop basketball star, and kids wore do-rags and Sixers jerseys, more than five hundred fans waiting two hours—Iverson was, naturally, very late—to see and mingle with him at his three-on-three youth tournament.

Iverson was focused and determined, but the tardiness proved that at least in some ways, he was still the same Iverson. He had called a news conference in Philadelphia three weeks earlier to announce the tournament, and after thirty or so reporters waited two hours at the Philadelphia Hilton, a spokesman walked in and told the group that Iverson was not coming. He would later rile his Team USA coaches by arriving at training camp in Jacksonville, Florida, in a stretch limousine, then showing up late for a team meeting. But like always, if Iverson played well, all was forgiven, and Brown believed that during the qualifying tournament the kid was at the height of his powers. Team USA had stomped the Puerto Rican national team in New York before heading to San Juan to begin the march to Athens. Iverson scored twenty-eight points in a second-round game against Canada, including an astonishing seven three-pointers in a single quarter, breaking a United States qualifying record. "I never saw him do anything like he did tonight," Brown told reporters afterward, adding that Iverson was playing better than he ever had.

Brown installed Isiah Thomas, the NBA coach and former superstar point guard, as Iverson's personal adviser during the tournament. Not that he seemed to need much advising. Iverson was a dependable leader, and regardless of the star power the national team had, each of the famous faces seemed to look toward him for guidance. "They're coming to me, asking for advice, because I'm a hundred miles ahead of everyone else," Iverson told reporters during the tournament. "It's like I'm Eric Snow, like I'm the point guard, the father figure. And none of them mind, either. That's what happens when you've got a coach who knows what he's doing."

Iverson and Brown, brothers in regret, were now committed to pleasing each other, impressing each other, winning alongside each other. Where had this been all those years in Philadelphia? Why had it never been consistent? Men like Iverson and Brown needed to tear down a house, see its bricks strewn across the lawn, to know the best way the pieces fit together.

Team USA dismantled its first four opponents in the Tournament of the Americas, winning the games by an average margin of nearly forty points. Iverson sprained his right thumb, forcing him to miss the tournament's final two contests against Puerto Rico and Argentina—although, with the veritable all-star team of Vince Carter, Tracy McGrady, Jason Kidd, Jermaine O'Neal, and Tim Duncan in the lineup, the United States cruised. This was another Dream Team in the making, unbeaten in ten qualifying games, headed in a few months to pursue gold in the Greek capital.

After a quick break, it was time for Iverson to return to Philadelphia, where the Sixers were undergoing a transition. Team officials had closely watched their superstar guard during the qualifying tournament, and his behavior in Puerto Rico was enough to convince the front office that, finally, Iverson had grown up. Whatever it had taken—losing Brown, Tawanna giving birth for the third time, or just the passage of time—Iverson was a man now, and the team offered him a four-year contract extension worth $76.7 million. Iverson saw it as a chance to complete his career in Philadelphia, and the Sixers saw it as a chance for Iverson, his days as the sinister Mr. Hyde finally chased away for good, to cement his status as a legend in eastern Pennsylvania, the same as Wilt Chamberlain, Mike Schmidt, and Charles Barkley. When the team elevated Randy Ayers, one of Brown's top assistant coaches, into the vacant head coaching job, Iverson was thrilled—and he requested a meeting.

In mid-September 2003, Iverson and the forty-seven-year-old Ayers sat across from each other at a table. They talked philosophy and exchanged hopes for the upcoming season, promising themselves that they would communicate better than Iverson and Brown ever had. Toward the end, Iverson offered a simple message to his team's new leader: Avoid overthinking things, which can occasionally create drama, and instead take things at face value. Iverson looked into Ayers's eyes: "Just coach," he told him.

AFTER FIVE MONTHS of hope and occasional peace, Iverson stood in late February surveying the destruction he had engineered as much as anyone. The Sixers were getting worse as the months passed, Ayers losing control, Iverson breaking promises he made in that initial meeting. He had duped the organization yet again into thinking he had changed, that he cared about something besides himself.

The Ayers promotion, in hindsight, had been uncreative; Iverson saw his new coach less as a colleague on the climb back toward the NBA's peak and more as a man whom Iverson could control; he knew Ayers needed Iverson far more than Iverson needed the inexperienced coach. And Ayers had made a strategic mistake: Iverson asked to be moved back to point guard, years after Brown wisely shifted him to the two-guard slot and allowed him to just play, and Ayers went for it. To make matters worse, Ayers had terrible luck: His intended starting five played only ten games together, injuries decimating the Sixers' core and eliminating any chance of developing chemistry. "When Larry left," former Sixers general manager King said, "all hell broke loose."

King fired Ayers after 31 losses in 52 games, infuriating Iverson because he had lost his pet, and the experience seemed to sour Ayers on ever pursuing another head coaching position. In the following decade after the disastrous run in Philadelphia, he never accepted another job atop a coaching staff, preferring to remain in the shadows—as he had for years under Brown—as an assistant. This time King temporarily elevated another assistant, the edgier Chris Ford, who immediately clashed with Iverson. Ford had never coached under Brown, but like most everyone in the profession, he had heard stories about dealing with Iverson. Now he was seeing them unfold up close.

A week after Ford's promotion to interim head coach, Iverson returned from the All-Star Game in Los Angeles and missed a Monday evening practice, the team's first gathering after the break. Ford had heard about how, months earlier during the NBA playoffs, Iverson had flip-flopped his excuses—was it traffic or a flat tire?—before arriving thirty-two minutes before tip-off of the deciding Game Six against the Pistons. This time, Iverson told his coach that the plane he had chartered from Southern California had undergone engine trouble, making his on-time return impossible. Ford did not buy it, pulling Iverson aside at shootaround the next day and telling him flatly that he would not start that evening against the Denver Nuggets. Iverson was also fined. And, not surprisingly, he was irate. "The relationship between us goes out the window," he told reporters, still angry at his new coach. "I told him why I couldn't make it, and it wasn't good enough."

He went on, throwing down the gauntlet. "I can play for him, though. I can play hard for him, and I can do exactly what he wants me to do," he said. ". . . But as far as having a relationship with him outside of basketball, that's done from day one."

Iverson, whom months earlier Brown believed to be at the height of his abilities, responded to Ford's hard-nosed coaching during the following weeks by revealing the depths of his petulance. After Ford benched Iverson during a game because his injured knee had supposedly prevented him from practicing, Iverson changed into a retro Kareem Abdul-Jabbar jersey, paying a Sixers ball boy to bring him a plate of nachos, which he snacked on while sitting on the bench. Ford, who won only a dozen games during his brief audition, would not be retained; in his place King hired Jim O'Brien, the Sixers' fourth coach in the past twelve months.

Brown, meanwhile, had apparently been the missing piece to the Pistons' machine. With Brown's instruction sharpening the talents of Tayshaun Prince, Chauncey Billups, and Ben Wallace, Detroit finished second in the Central Division but charged through the playoffs, dispatching Milwaukee, New Jersey, and Indiana before toppling the heavily favored Lakers in five games in the NBA Finals. Three years after Brown's Sixers had been walloped four consecutive times by Los Angeles after winning Game One, and Brown had forced himself to shake hands with Lakers coach Phil Jackson—"the fish," as Brown would remember Jackson's weak handshake—this time Brown shook and patted the Lakers coach's hand, becoming the only coach to win both an NCAA and NBA title and cementing his place among basketball's best coaches ever.

That night, Brown's phone rang. Iverson finally called his old coach, this time offering congratulations.

But Brown, of course, could not bask in his achievement. In the churning emotional reservoir contained in that sixty-three-year-old body, joy had no chance against regret. Besides, even from afar he could see the wreckage his departure had in part brought to the Sixers, a team he had fallen in love with. The day after winning the championship, Brown fiddled with his glasses, shook his head, and pushed back tears. "I wish we could have done it in Philadelphia," he said.

IVERSON AND BROWN met once again in Athens, Greece, looking around and realizing it was once again mostly up to them. Vince Carter had scheduled his wedding during the Olympics and eventually withdrew, which was at least better than Tracy McGrady *forgetting* that his wedding date had also been scheduled for late August. Jason Kidd was rehabilitating an injured left knee and Pistons stars Rip Hamilton and Wallace stayed home because they were afraid of a terrorist attack during the first summer Olympics to take place since the attacks on New York City and Washington, D.C., on September 11, 2001.

In all, three members of the qualifying team that won all ten of its games in San Juan made it to Athens. Nine others, for one reason or another, had left Iverson, Tim Duncan, and Richard Jefferson to lead a pack of rookies and youngsters. LeBron James and Carmelo Anthony were the most famous and talented of them, but they lacked the experience that Brown wanted when imagining his own dream team. Once again, no matter the drama he had left behind in Philadelphia, Iverson stepped up, showing a perhaps surprising patriotic side. "I stayed here for my country," said Iverson, whom the coaching staff named a captain before the Games.

He was again taking his spot on the national team seriously, or at least as seriously as he was capable of doing. Iverson, James, and Amar'e Stoudemire missed an eleven o'clock team meeting the morning before an exhibition contest against Puerto Rico, and Brown quickly remembered the bullshit that drove him out of Philadelphia. Iverson, motivated as he was, just could not do it: could not show up on time, could not be the man off the court that he showed so many promising glimpses of, could not give his coach—whoever that was, whatever the circumstances—a headache-free existence. James apologized, but Iverson was defiant; Brown *still* sweated the small stuff:

Iverson claimed that he "couldn't have been more than five minutes late."

"I'm the captain on the team and to be suspended just for being a couple minutes late just doesn't sit well for me," he told reporters in Athens. "I'm supposed to be one of the leaders of the team, and this is not a good look." Brown, for his part, shook his head; Iverson never did get it: No, it was *not* a good image to project on a global stage, but if he had not been late, there would have been no suspension.

But this look was worse: During Team USA's opening game, against the Puerto Rican national team it had drubbed five times over the previous eight months, the Americans simply could not make open shots, losing a stunner, 92–73, as fans from the tiny nation joined arms inside Hellinikon Indoor Arena and waved their own red, white, and blue flags, that single star on the left side. Iverson, despite his star power and decent behavior, had become the unfortunate face of the state of United States basketball. The national team had not lost an Olympic basketball game since 1988, four years before NBA players were allowed to represent their homelands, and now its reputation was that all American players could do was fly toward the basket, looking for dunks and highlight plays—refusing to play a team game amid the nearly extinct art of the jump shot.

To make matters worse, Iverson fractured his thumb against Puerto Rico, but he strapped a Band-Aid on it, vowed to keep playing, promising to keep his teammates motivated. He was first to address reporters who were thirsty for blood, first to suggest a sharper mind-set, first to admit that this was not the 1992 team that started the American tradition of bringing home gold. "The Dream Team is already dead," Iverson said then. "We ain't the Dream Team. If we make it to the gold medal and win, it's not going to say 'Dream Team' on the trophy case. It's going to say all of our names. That's what we had to get over. We had to get over ourselves."

Team USA defeated Greece and Australia, but then it lost to Lithuania; six days later, another loss, this time to Argentina, ended the

Americans' hopes of a fourth consecutive gold medal. Iverson led the team to a win against Lithuania in the bronze medal game, and as the Argentine national anthem played, Iverson stood next to Stephon Marbury, letting the bouquet of blue amaranths and olive tree leaves dangle near his waist. Iverson and Brown had been given one last ride, a chance to correct the wrongs of the past, but as they now stood there, a frustrated look on Iverson's face, all they could think about was yet another failure.

CHAPTER 18

TIME LONG PAST

He slid on a dark gray suit with pinstripes, tucking in a black pocket square to match his black tie. Iverson clipped a boutonniere on his left lapel and finished the look with sunglasses, two gleaming chains, and tightly braided cornrows. Then it was time to pick up his date.

When she walked out to join him, the young lady was wearing a black dress with spaghetti straps, offset with a white silk shawl. Her smile, which she would flash so often during the next few hours, was unmistakable. Then they rode together to York High School, just north of Newport News, Virginia, and when they walked in the lights were low and the music blared and the students rushed to show off their outfits and prom dates.

Iiesha Iverson, by 2010 an eighteen-year-old high school senior, had the only international superstar by her side at the York High prom. Her older brother, back on the Peninsula for part of the summer, had agreed to be Iiesha's date. They danced and posed for pictures, and for one night the cameras caught a glimpse of Iverson's famous tenderness. Iiesha, though separated from her famous brother in distance and age—she is sixteen years younger and spent most of her youth in the Tidewater region of Virginia—had never been far from Iverson's mind. Ann, their mother, had given birth to Iiesha more than a week late, and following complications during the delivery, Iiesha would spend a childhood suffering frequent seizures.

As a baby she was among those squeezed into the Hampton city courthouse in September 1993, squealing to break the silence and wrapping her tiny fingers around Ann's to soothe an anxious time, just before Judge Nelson Overton announced that Iverson's role in the brawl at Circle Lanes was worth five years in prison. Later, after Iverson was freed and allowed to enroll at Georgetown, he cradled her and made her laugh, making high-pitched sounds that squeaked from the back of his throat and through his lips, Iiesha smiling as her brother entertained her. Iverson witnessed the fear and the struggle: that she could suffer an episode at any moment, along with the reality that Ann's government checks, meant to offset Iiesha's medical costs, just didn't cover everything—not the specialist she needed and certainly not proper housing, rather than the one-story brick home in Hampton next to a barbecue store. It was because of her, along with his own daughter, Tiaura, that he entered the NBA draft after two seasons at Georgetown. "My baby sister was having some medical problems," he told reporters in 1996. "And I think that really pushed me out the door." He later formed a youth foundation in Iiesha's name, hosting an annual benefit with basketball and gospel music, watching as she grew from toddler to teenager to young woman.

Now at her senior prom, Iiesha's medical problems mostly behind her, Iverson wanted to be there when she walked through the doors. A tiara held the curls from her face, and with her classmates' eyes turning toward her, that smile lit up the darkened room.

NOT LONG AFTER Iverson walked off an NBA floor for the last time as a player, so much history behind him and all the uncertainty ahead, he began trying to make amends. Whether he admitted it to himself or not, in the back of his mind he had come to realize that things would never be the same. He no longer needed to play the bad boy, and so he made an effort to let his goodness shine through.

It had been there all along, buried so often by the reputation and the entourage, and so many who had grown close to him wanted to believe this was more representative of the real Iverson than the drinking, philandering, gambling, absentee father and husband. No one, they told themselves, would say the things he said, do the things he did, think the things he clearly thought, if he was the son of a bitch the headlines sometimes made him out to be.

Years later, when his old Bethel High teammate Tony Rutland's mother died, Iverson called Rutland's father, Larry, and told him how much, when he knew only turbulence at home, their family had meant to him. "If Larry was living today," said Mike Bailey, who coached Iverson and Rutland at Bethel, "he would be telling you this part of this conversation with tears. That's who Allen is. That's what family means to him, and when times are tough, the survival skill in him as a man comes out." When Larry Rutland died in June 2014, there was Iverson sitting in the back row during the funeral. "That's the man that I know and love," Bailey said.

Years earlier he had heard that Sue Lambiotte, the tireless woman who tutored him before and after he was released from prison, had been diagnosed with cancer. Iverson had, when he played at Georgetown, provided tickets to Hoyas games, Lambiotte as responsible as anyone for his opportunity, and when he became a young star with the Sixers, her family would occasionally drive to Philadelphia and watch the game; then afterward in the locker room—no matter the result—Iverson would stand and wrap his arms around his former teacher, greeting anyone who had made the trip with them. But that part of his life was, in many ways, finished—the last of the embers from the bowling alley incident long since having turned to ash.

It would have been understandable for Iverson to have moved on, even after word reached him in 2003 that Sue Lambiotte was dying. He could have spent a quiet moment reflecting or simply put the bad news behind him. Instead, a man whose life had been defined in part by commotion and rampant undependability sat down and began writing. A few days later, Art Lambiotte fished through the mail. There was a note from Iverson, in his own handwriting, including his own memories and thoughts. "I was just appreciative of the fact that he really did understand that she had been a great influence in his life," Art Lambiotte would say eleven years after Sue's death, their four kids all grown and Iverson's name still cherished in their home. "And he showed me that he had that appreciation of her and for that reason. And I mean, that was—I was just happy about that."

For years Iverson had supported friends and family members, Tawanna cutting checks for car payments and light bills and mortgages. Even after much of his fortune was gone, he still found ways to help those he loved: One of the terms of the divorce between Iverson and Tawanna—one of the few things they actually agreed on during such an explosive time—was that Rahsaan Langford's three sons would still be taken care of. If there was a basketball camp to attend or tuition bills to pay, the Iversons would find a way. A promise is a promise.

Iverson, sometimes through Gary Moore, reached out to the Sixers and asked for forgiveness. He spoke occasionally with Larry Brown, who had pushed Iverson to the brink of detonation many times, and just like so many others, Brown just could not turn his back on him. Iverson was not a bad person, many of them said; he had just never grown up. They could no more harbor long-term dislike for Iverson than they could a child who knocks over a precious heirloom. He was an adult, fully in charge of his own decisions, but they believed the innocence remained—of this they were certain, and if not certain then terribly hopeful, and as much as they worried about him, wishing he would change, they just kept hoping more of this part of him would be revealed. "He never turned down anybody," Brown said. "He was there to help everybody. He didn't think about the future. He just thought about taking care of people that he felt were loyal to him and important to him."

Iverson made peace with friends who had wronged him, or who he felt had wronged him. David Falk, Iverson's first NBA agent, occasionally would see his former client, and Iverson made it a point to ask about Falk's family. He would again mention Phil Jasner, the late *Philadelphia Daily News* reporter, during his jersey retirement ceremony in March 2014, the same as he had when he announced months earlier that his NBA career was finished.

"I'm just appreciative of the kind of man that he became, loyal to his convictions," said Bill Tose, who was a coach on Iverson's youth teams on the Virginia Peninsula. "And that's the way he lived, and that's the way he is, whether you have to embrace that or not. And I choose to embrace that. He's not a bad person. I don't care what has happened. We've all had some things happen in our lifetime that we wish hadn't happened."

YEARS LATER, ANOTHER old friend had fallen on challenging times. When Iverson was a student at Georgetown, he became close with Lorry Michel, the Hoyas' longtime basketball trainer. She taped ankles and set broken fingers, and mostly she did it quietly. This was a job, the faces constantly changing, and it seemed pointless to get to know John Thompson's players on more than a cursory basis. Besides, most of them wanted only to receive their treatment and then to leave, rarely bothering to engage in conversation the private woman who put them on crutches or cinched a walking boot. "So many kids," Michel, now in her early sixties, would recall, "that you've forgotten about over thirty years."

Iverson, though, was different. She had an edge and did not bullshit him, and he liked that. Michel was too proud to idolize or fawn over athletes, a submissive and weak-minded approach that many sports fans never realize turns their heroes off. And in Michel's eyes, Iverson did not look for shortcuts or a chance to deflect blame, whether onto coaches or the lesser-known trainer, and she appreciated that. So they talked in the training room, in the practice gym, on the floor before games. He would poke his head into her office sometimes, just checking on Michel if he had not seen her. They were each guarded, with scars of the past that had never faded, and somehow they discovered they stood on common ground. "You go along life, you run into people," Michel said. "And some really intrigue you more, maybe, I don't know. Or they just treat you differently than others."

During a trip back to Washington for an all-star reunion at Georgetown, Iverson and Michel caught up, and Michel studied the tattoos on his arms and shoulders and neck, asking that he never get ink on his face—where she could look and still see his youth and innocence; that kid who wandered into McDonough Gymnasium still wounded from missing his senior year of high school. He agreed, laughing about it, and then he headed into the gym, where he was the star attraction. Amid the crowd, Iverson took a few steps and turned around, telling Michel that he would see to it that she would get in, offering to see her inside. No, no, she told him, she would be fine; remember, Michel told Iverson, she *works* at Georgetown. "It's just a mutual respect, I guess," she said. "That comes with just trusting people. That's probably a good way of putting it: He's tenderhearted, and he would do anything for you."

Michel, because she rarely read the reports of Iverson's distress or listened to the whispers about his marriage, felt no worry about whether Iverson was more bad than good. "I don't think there's a bad bone in his body," she said.

Then in June 2011, as Georgetown's basketball camp was beginning, Michel saw a doctor. She had a brain tumor, and less than a month later she underwent surgery to remove the mass. Afterward the doctor offered to share her prognosis, but, no, she stopped him; Michel had no interest in hearing it. She did not want to know how much longer she had, even if the news was good. After treatments, she would refuse to ask if the cancer was gone. "Put it this way: I'm recovering, I guess, and I'm doing well," she would say in spring 2013. "I don't know if they call that a survivor or what. I don't worry about it. I'm in God's hands. . . . I handled it a little bit differently than most, I guess. I wasn't into trying to fight anything. I just decided this is bigger than me."

Iverson checked in anyway, adding to the pile of text messages and emails. Then, when word reached Iverson that Michel would be inducted into Georgetown's hall of fame in February 2013, alongside athletes and more famous names, Iverson asked a friend to point a phone toward him and record a video. It would be played on the big screen during the ceremony, the blurry footage showing Iverson standing behind a lectern, mimicking his most famous moment.

"So Allen, man, tell us, man, you been practicing?" a voice called toward him from off screen.

"Practice?" Iverson responded, fully in character. "We talking about *practice*? Again?"

"Well, not necessarily the practice; we're talking about Ms. Michel. You know, Lorry Michel?"

"Oh," Iverson said, pausing. "We're talking about love. We talking about love? Not Coach Thompson. Not the baddest guard that ever played at Georgetown. Not Alonzo Mourning. Not Patrick Ewing. Not Dikembe Mutombo? But we talking about love? Oh, we talking about love."

It was the most authentic, heartfelt moment of the gathering—coming, perhaps, from an unexpected source.

"I'm supposed to be here talking about Georgetown," Iverson continued. "But we talking about love. We talking about love? Ms. Michel? Oh, we talking about love."

He paused for a beat, and Michel smiled. "I love you. I miss you," he went on. "Well-deserved congratulations. I love you. I can't put it in words how much I do love you. I truly love you. I love you, Ms. Michel. And congratulations."

CHAPTER 19

RIP CURRENT

It had been in the back of Billy King's mind for three years now, but he tried to suppress the voice in his head. *It's time,* King heard faintly. *The Iverson era is finished.* King heard it shortly after Larry Brown left the Sixers, leaving King the keys to the Philadelphia basketball kingdom—and a steering wheel to control Iverson—on his way out. Brown knew his protégé's history, and he was confident King could handle it. The general manager himself was not so sure.

Years earlier, King had impressed Brown with his strength, even during the strongest of storms. He was a prodigy of basketball and communication, and if King had not made up his mind to play basketball at Duke—he prepared and gave a ninety-minute presentation to the school's interim head of admissions—Brown wanted him to play for his Jayhawks at the University of Kansas. King was smart, eloquent, patient, and thoughtful, and even after his four seasons—and two Final Fours, including one semifinal victory against Kansas—at Duke, Brown wanted him close within his universe. He hired King as an assistant coach when Brown led the Indiana Pacers, then insisting to co-owners Pat Croce and Ed Snider in 1997 that any deal that brought him to Philadelphia must also include a place for King in the Sixers' front office. Snider balked, Brown threatened to walk away, and then

Snider offered King a one-year tryout as vice president of basketball administration. He wound up staying more than a decade, rising all the way to team president, and by age thirty-two King was the Sixers' general manager, one of the most powerful seats in professional sports. He signed off on contracts and trades—albeit with the experienced voice of Brown as a sounding board. But no job was bigger than brokering peace between the Sixers' legendary coach and the team's superstar guard. "Allen and Larry needed each other," King said much later.

But after the 2002–03 season, Brown was gone, and King wondered if he was strong enough to manage Iverson. If *anybody* was. The voice told him after Brown's departure, signing on to coach the Detroit Pistons, that the time had come for the Sixers to push Iverson out the door. King muffled it, watching Iverson's performance in the Olympics before three more coaches came and went—neither Randy Ayers, Chris Ford, nor Jim O'Brien could swim free of the Iverson vortex—and before the 2006–07 season, with former Brown assistant Maurice Cheeks now leading the Sixers, there was the voice again. Iverson refused to tell the Sixers about a knee injury that would end his season—team officials learned of their star player's injury by reading about it in the newspaper—and then the team found out Iverson was skipping rehab sessions. In April 2006, though, Iverson had crossed the line: On the evening of the Sixers' final home game, an event dubbed Fan Appreciation Night, Iverson arrived at the Wachovia Center at 7:07 in the evening, not bothering to show up on time for the seven o'clock tip-off, and then refused to dress in his game uniform.

Afterward, King blew a gasket. "I've got a lot of fucking work to do," the normally mild-mannered executive said of the coming offseason. "And this is some shit that is a distraction to me. Am I pissed off? You're goddamn right I am. Is that what you want to hear? You fucking heard it."

He reasserted his authority, vowing a remade roster and adjusted attitudes when the Sixers reconvened in the fall.

"Shit *will* change," King said.

It's time, King kept thinking, time to chase away a hero and cut out a cancer, one move that would be both the best and worst things for the Sixers and Philadelphia. *It's time,* the voice repeated even as a trade with the Denver Nuggets came together, neared completion, then fell apart. Another trade with the Boston Celtics before the NBA draft crumbled at the eleventh hour. King was stuck with Iverson, at least for a while longer.

A month into the new season, the Sixers played at Chicago's United Center, the young Bulls blasting Philadelphia by twenty-seven points. That was bad enough, but King sat near the bench and watched as Iverson, who had argued with Cheeks a few days earlier during practice, came out of the game late in the third quarter. He told his coach that his back was injured, and then he walked toward the locker room. Just walked away, leaving his teammates on the bench to endure the rest of their beating. Iverson missed the entire fourth quarter, and it was not Iverson's antics that gripped King's attention; it was the faces of the other Sixers players. Veterans who had understood Iverson, rolling their eyes at him but embracing his value, were gone; in the places of Aaron McKie, George Lynch, and Eric Snow were young, impressionable players such as Andre Iguodala, Samuel Dalembert, and Rodney Carney. "Just watching their eyes," King would recall years later. "And I just—you know. They didn't understand Allen as much as those other guys did. I saw in his teammates' eyes that we needed to trade him."

The voice had started as a whisper. Now it was screaming at him, and King no longer had the energy to fight it.

KING LOOKED HIM in the face, the time for pleasantries long since having passed. "You want to be traded?" he barked at Iverson.

The words caught the player off guard. He had wanted to finish his career in Philadelphia, a city that felt like home but would come to feel even more precious after his departure, but he was sick of being disrespected. By Cheeks, by King, by Snider, by every-damn-body. "Yeah," Iverson shot back, and that was all King needed to hear.

"Okay, I'm going to trade you," the GM said, knowing the fuse had been lit. After the game in Chicago, Cheeks told Iverson to stay away from the team and the arena. When Iverson arrived for a shootaround, Cheeks sent him away; after all, did he not have a back injury? The coach rubbed Iverson's nose in it, anger and frustration boiling over now, and Iverson called his agent, Leon Rose, and asked that Rose draft a statement, an attempt at controlling the message. "A change may be the best thing for everyone," the statement read in part, but the Sixers did not flinch. Cheeks told reporters that Iverson would not play against Orlando and would not even travel to central Florida with the team.

When the Sixers returned from their road trip, Iverson was nowhere to be found. The team had removed the nameplate above Iverson's locker stall in a far corner of the room, the familiar clothes and sneakers gone and leaving only a white bathrobe on a hanger. Footage of Iverson had been removed from a highlight video shown before the team's game against the Portland Trail Blazers, eleven years of history and highlights now forgotten and buried. It was as if Iverson had never existed—and, at least for the moment, he was still on the active roster.

On this night and those that followed, Iverson was placed on the inactive list, and eventually King and Cheeks refused to even speak his name. That was how bad they hated Iverson now, how much they wanted his ass gone.

Iverson was still a talented scorer, and franchises were inquiring each day on what it would take for Philadelphia to off-load him. Executives, knowing the Sixers were fed up, were looking to acquire Iverson for cheap. But there was a smart way to handle things, and King was too much of a pragmatist to simply accept another team's first offer. King, occasionally overwhelmed by the enormity of his feud with Iverson and the responsibility to collect as much in a trade as possible, dialed a familiar ally, Brown, who after the 2004–05 season had done what he so often had throughout his career: He left the Pistons and joined the New York Knicks, and after the Knicks lost fifty-nine games in Brown's only season, the old coach apparently having lost his fastball, he was fired. Brown moved back to Philadelphia, where he could have occupied most of his time by counting the $18.5 million the Knicks paid him to leave New York. Instead, he followed the NBA and answered calls in his home office.

His phone rang in December 2006, and a friendly but desperate voice was on the other end. King was asking his mentor what to do, afraid that no matter which decision he made, it would get him fired. Brown, no longer inside the vortex, told King to calm down; it would work out. Snider, the Sixers' owner, had contacted Brown earlier, asking if he would be interested in taking over the team's personnel matters, but Brown knew what that really meant: get rid of Iverson. Brown turned Snider down, knowing he would be undermining King's authority, and besides, he knew he could not be the one to push Allen Iverson out of Philadelphia. "I can't tell a kid I love him," Brown recalled, "and then say: 'By the way, you're worthless.' "

Brown did agree to come on as a consultant, seeing the Sixers—and, more specifically, King—through this pivotal phase. He helped sift through the offers, King continuing to run point on trade discussions and fielding so many queries that he eventually told other executives to send questions or throw long-shot ideas via text message; call only if there was a serious offer.

A week after Iverson was sent home from the practice facility, King's phone rang. The Denver Nuggets issued a final offer, take it or leave it, with a nonnegotiable noon deadline to accept or reject the proposal. In exchange for Iverson and Ivan McFarlin, Denver would part with Andre Miller, a talented young point guard, and forward Joe Smith, along with two first-round draft picks. King discussed the offer with Brown, the same way they had made so many franchise-altering decisions years earlier, during far more prosperous times. Brown told King that it would be a difficult move, one laced with occasional feelings of regret, but it was the right move. Years later, though, Iverson's former coach would remember his decision much differently: "A big-ass mistake," Brown said, believing the trade—and his role in it—played a major role in Iverson's downfall, to say nothing of the other careers that Iverson would help derail in the coming years.

But regardless of the dominoes that would fall, it was done. Late that afternoon, King called Iverson and delivered the news: For the first time in his NBA career, he did not play for the Philadelphia 76ers.

THE NUGGETS ANNOUNCED the trade on their website, and within a half hour the team had sold 340 season tickets; they expected thousands more to be sold on the promise of Iverson leading Denver to the NBA Finals for the first time. Iverson was big on promises, on and off the court, along with front-end optimism, and before heading toward his new home, he called Carmelo Anthony, the Nuggets' twenty-two-year-old franchise player, and made another: "We're going to make it work," Iverson told his new teammate.

Anthony was eager to cash in on his own potential, and so he believed Iverson. "People are saying we can't play together," Anthony told the *Denver Post* shortly after the trade was finalized. "He was saying he's tired of doing everything himself."

DerMarr Johnson, a veteran swingman, agreed to change his jersey number to eight, allowing Iverson to wear his trademark number three. And there it hung, that white jersey with the familiar name and number but a new logo and colors. The Nuggets, though, were tired of promises. They wanted a sure thing. George Karl, the team's head coach, had never won a championship despite leading the Seattle SuperSonics to the Finals in 1996. Karl knew that acquiring Iverson, adding one strong personality alongside Anthony, another superstar, could become volatile. But success at sports' highest level involves going for it, taking the chances that can either win you a championship or get your ass fired. The way Karl and the Nuggets saw it, their only chance of overtaking the Los Angeles Lakers and San Antonio Spurs was to add another scorer, just battering teams with warp speed. "We knew we were able to get to the playoffs, but how could we find the edge to try to win a playoff round?" said Chad Iske, a Nuggets assistant coach at the time. "We thought maybe there was too much weight on Melo's shoulders to score the ball, and if you bring in one of the top scorers of all time alongside him, how could you guard both sides of the court and both of them at the same time?"

Iverson was, of course, late arriving in Denver, caught in a snowstorm and arriving at the Pepsi Center with only five minutes left in shootaround. Anthony was among three Nuggets players suspended for their role in a brawl with the Knicks, leaving Karl with a depleted roster and a delay in seeing how all those promises would translate into reality. Would Anthony and Iverson, both possessing massive but justified egos, truly coexist? More than that, would Karl's high-risk experiment pay off with a championship? Iverson, as he had done before, made a strong early impression, addressing his new teammates and encouraging them to play hard and have fun. Iverson played well, scoring twenty-two points, but the Nuggets lost his debut.

Afterward, he found Deuce in the arena's tunnel, dropping an arm on his eldest son's shoulders. "Good game, Dad," the boy told his father, according to the *Philadelphia Inquirer*, and then Iverson saw Tawanna, smiling when he noticed her. She was already in Denver, looking for new schools for the kids and moving the massive Iverson family operation to a new city. By late 2006, Tawanna was in full control of the family's finances, setting up trust funds and enterprise accounts. She employed a chef, a personal assistant, and two nannies—one of whom was made full-time shortly after the trade, driving the cost of in-home child care to between $8,000 and $10,000 per month—but she retained some domestic responsibilities to stay in touch with a simpler time. She laundered Iverson's clothing herself, refusing to let household staff handle his things, and occasionally prepared meals for Iverson. "Depending on whether he got up in the morning and wanted breakfast, if he wanted it, I fixed it," Tawanna would say later during deposition testimony. "If not, he had a meal when he came home from practice. . . . He only ate certain things, where sometimes I'd be fixing two different dinners."

She selected schools herself, believing it was an important job, and although her assistant, Candis Rosier, offered insight, it was Tawanna who surfed the Internet late at night and visited the facilities before her children enrolled. She learned that Iverson had no interest in such matters, so she usually did not bother even telling him where their kids would study. She handled the rental of a condominium, then the purchase of a sprawling estate in nearby Englewood, customizing the more than ten-thousand-square-foot home—a grand walk-in closet, downstairs game room, and home theater—and going to unusual means to keep their address confidential. After the high-profile incident in 2002, Iverson chasing Tawanna around Philadelphia with a pistol tucked in his waistband, reporters and fans had camped out in front of their home in Gladwyne. This was a side effect Tawanna hoped never to repeat, and so she purchased the Englewood home using a trust fund, Rosier the personal assistant as the trustee—one more layer of cover.

With all the touches, and no detail or luxury spared in the sprawling Mediterranean-inspired mansion, the price came to $3.8 million, later becoming an early casualty of Iverson's financial ruin. But for now, maybe life would not be so bad in Colorado; maybe this change was exactly what Iverson and his family needed.

Iverson, his mind clear of all thoughts beyond basketball, partied with Anthony during his new teammate's suspension, and when Anthony's thirty-seven-day exile ended in late January, Karl and Denver finally saw their earliest returns on a risky venture—but one with a potentially enormous payoff. During a home game against the Memphis Grizzlies, Anthony returned to a standing ovation, rewarding the crowd with twenty-eight points compared with Iverson's twenty-three, pushing the Nuggets to a seventeen-point win. Nothing, though, would make a statement more than a play in the fourth quarter, when Iverson ran up the court, tossing an alley-oop pass toward Anthony, who threw it through the basket with one hand. The cheers rattled the arena, and Iverson looked toward his new audience, a hand cupped around his ear the way he used to do in Philadelphia.

IVERSON REGALED HIS new teammates with impressions, jokes, and war stories, but nothing cracked up the men on the bus like Iverson's impersonation of himself. "*Practice?!*" he shouted, delighting his audience. "We talkin' about *practice*?!" He earned his teammates' respect with his play, winning their friendship with his lighthearted personality and postpractice challenges. Sometimes another player would dare Iverson to compete in a three-point contest after the morning workout, sweetening the offer with a few hundred dollars in it for the winner, and that was enough not only to pique Iverson's interest—but also to get him serious. Even against Earl Boykins and J. R. Smith, the team's best long-range shooters, Iverson drained basket after basket, taking their money with him.

Karl was pleasantly surprised by his new star's attitude, and the reality was, Iverson brought little of the drama with him that had soured the Sixers on him and would later push him out of the NBA. "A.I. never was a problem from that standpoint," Karl would recall. Iverson respected his new coach because he let his best players do their thing, rarely urging wholesale changes or personality shifts. Nothing held more value to Iverson than being allowed to be himself, and it did not hurt that Karl rarely implemented the old-school drills that Brown loved, and players were rarely subjected to marathon film sessions and microcoaching. In exchange, Karl would not remember Iverson skipping even one practice or missing one curfew. Where the team struggled, though, was in managing the egos and playing-time expectations for so many top-shelf players. Anthony and Iverson were not the Nuggets' only famous names: Kenyon Martin, Marcus Camby, and Smith also wanted their share of touches. "Just throwing him on top of it just made it that much harder," former Nuggets assistant Iske would say of Iverson, "which we knew always was a challenge around there. What are you going to get every day, on just a practice day or a game day? Who's going to be in the mood today? Who's not going to be in the mood today? That's our jobs, but it was definitely as extreme as it could get."

Denver's stars brought their handlers with them on road trips, and the team's public relations man, Eric Sebastian, could count on Gary Moore calling before a trip to Los Angeles or New York or Miami, asking Sebastian for two courtside tickets—roughly $1,000 per ticket, Sebastian estimated. The cost was simply deducted from Iverson's paycheck, one of the million tiny cuts that would eventually bleed his accounts to death. It was common on road trips for coaches to be in a car when a radio ad touted one nightclub hosting an Iverson party and another hosting Anthony's high-dollar get-together, and the next morning the coaches' phones would ring. Tawanna was sick, Iverson or Moore would fib, making it so Iverson had to watch the kids and could not attend shootaround. The Nuggets knew that Iverson kept vampire hours, his life unfolding at night in bars and then sleep when the sun was out; knowing what he had gotten himself into, Karl looked the other way. "We didn't have a bunch of perfect citizens," Iske said, "so it wasn't something that was exactly new to us. George had a way of getting through without blowing it up and making it a big issue and going to war with the guy. We knew it wasn't a perfect world, but we found a way to navigate it, basically."

The Nuggets finished in second place and lost in the first round to the Spurs, and the next season the team began to notice an erosion of Iverson's commitment. The calls came later in the morning and more often, the stories of Iverson's late-night exploits and blowups with Tawanna growing more common, the scouting report from Philadelphia looking more and more accurate. The team had, in some ways, sold its soul for a chance to pursue a championship, taking on the headaches as long as there was a payoff somewhere on the horizon. The team was better in Iverson's second season, winning fifty games but again losing in the playoffs' first round, this time swept by the Lakers. The Nuggets' poor effort, no matter that the Lakers would reach the NBA Finals, left a sour taste in team officials' mouths throughout the summer. When the team reconvened for training camp before the 2008–09 season, Iverson's attitude had deteriorated further, and it was clear that at age thirty-two he was no longer the explosive, lightning-quick player he had once been. The Nuggets had gone for it, taking on with eyes wide open this experiment in highlighting two electric shooters. Now, with Iverson becoming more of a distraction, the feeling was that the attempt had, if not failed, then certainly run its course. As one former Nuggets official put it, Iverson's presence "just kind of lost its luster."

After three games, two of them losses and with Iverson failing to reach twenty points, Karl's phone rang. This time it was Joe Dumars, the Detroit Pistons' president of basketball operations. His team needed a change, and it wanted Iverson. Dumars was offering a trade involving Antonio McDyess, Cheikh Samb, and, the topper, Chauncey Billups, a smart point guard and well-known leader who happened to be from Denver. Billups was not the scorer Iverson was, but he was also not the pain in the ass that Iverson was. Karl thought about it for a moment. Then he said yes.

BY THE TIME he reached Detroit in November 2008, Iverson was well versed in how to say the right things. It was part of his charm. It was also a big reason why teams were so excited about bringing him into the fold and believing that any stories of the past must surely have been exaggerated. "You know, I think it's all about being a basketball player and being willing to sacrifice whatever I have to sacrifice for the betterment of the team," he said, cornrows tight and wearing an oversized white dress shirt while seated next to Dumars at a table. "I haven't accomplished my number-one goal, and that's to win a championship.

Like I was telling Joe earlier today, I'm willing to sacrifice whatever I have to sacrifice to get it done."

Dumars interjected, surprising even Iverson. "Even practice?"

Iverson did not miss a beat. "Practice?!" he said, falling into character and reciting a word he made famous. "We talkin' about *practice*?"

The Pistons' top basketball executive laughed alongside his new guard, and an instant later the assembled reporters joined in on the jocularity. "I knew I set myself up for that one," Iverson said. All was right in the world, Dumars—the architect of the team Brown led to the 2004 NBA championship—having pulled off a clever trade that loosened the salary-cap noose around the Pistons' neck, all while bringing in one of the world's greatest basketball players. Iverson had behaved himself in Denver, and that gave Dumars hope that Iverson would take it easy on head coach Michael Curry, a longtime NBA player now in his first year at the Pistons' helm. "One thing is for sure," Iverson said during that news conference. "I'm going to do whatever the coach wants me to do."

Those words would echo through the Palace of Auburn Hills and onto the streets of Detroit. The NBA would hear them, again and again, as the months passed and the goodwill of that day and the sincerity of Iverson's promise lost steam and crashed to earth. Relationships within pro sports are dependent on everyone offering everyone else a blank slate, the sins of the past behind them, and within the NBA, team chemistry is possible only if the players forget their coach's bona fides and allow him to do his job. Early on, it was clear the new-look Pistons had little respect for Curry, a journeyman player who had spent only one previous season in Detroit as Flip Saunders's assistant coach. Players denied Curry even the most basic show of respect, calling him "M.C." rather than "Coach," and occasionally rolling their eyes when a reporter asked about him. Three weeks after Iverson's introduction and soon-to-be-laughable vow to follow his rookie coach's instructions, Curry assigned his team to practice on Thanksgiving Day. The decision was unpopular, but Curry's reasoning made sense: Billups had been the Pistons' team leader, and now he was gone; Iverson, now filling Billups's place in the lineup, had not been with the team during training camp and needed to learn the scheme. There were no days to waste. Not even holidays. "The price," Curry told reporters, "to get to where we need to be."

Players arrived that Thursday morning, their families gathering and eating turkey without them, and practiced. That is, everyone except Iverson, who did not bother to show up. Or call. Or offer a reason or even one of his trademark excuses. Nothing. He just stayed home. He did apologize a day later, calling his absence a "personal matter" and insisting such a problem would never happen again. Curry, seeing it as a blatant challenge to his authority, fined Iverson anyway, refusing to start him in a game against the Milwaukee Bucks.

The men put it behind them, at least for the time being, but soon Iverson had his next foe: Rip Hamilton, the Pistons veteran whom Iverson was now pushing out of his natural point guard role. The vortex was spinning again, new personalities and careers to consume. Although Iverson and Hamilton coexisted, they did so only at the expense of Curry, who indeed made a mistake by telling the team that Hamilton would take on a reserve role—before telling Hamilton face-to-face. Curry moved Hamilton, a three-time All-Star, to small forward, but by then the dark cloud of doubt hung over Curry's head, justifying those reservations about Curry's competence and essentially allowing players to tune him out. The Pistons saw weaknesses in Iverson's game, in particular a hesitance toward pushing the ball inside the way he once had. He was less willing to take on the big men inside and risk getting knocked on his ass. Besides, his speed was deteriorating, and his attitude stunk.

Still, he played well enough on a mediocre team that he was named to his tenth All-Star team. He averaged less than twenty points per game for the first time in his career, but he cruised into All-Star weekend in Phoenix, Arizona, on his reputation and popularity. He was still a marquee attraction, the memories of that cornrowed youngster still sealed in memories across America. But Iverson had decided that that weekend was time for a change. At thirty-four, his hair, like his legs, was not responding the way it used to, the rows not staying tight as long as they once had. After ten o'clock one evening in Phoenix, Iverson sat in a hotel room and unfurled his hair into a straggly Afro. "Getting ready to cut it off," he said into his phone, and in his mind, this was a decision worthy of an announcement. "Man, I'm dead serious!"

The barber pulled a pick through Iverson's hair, prepping it for its first major cut since 1996, when Iverson and Que Gaskins received weekly haircuts during Iverson's rookie year. "All right, this is thirteen years," Iverson said over the sound of a blow-dryer, the occasion captured on a video sponsored by Reebok. A moment later, Iverson smiled as the clippers vibrated and touched his hair. "That's a wrap, Jack!" he said, watching as the clumps fell to his shoulders, a few unfortunate realizations coming along with the new look. "I've got gray hairs?"

He joked throughout the session, saying Tawanna was going to like him again; after all, he looked like the sixteen-year-old she had met when they were both juniors in high school. Three days later, in the US Airways Center, Iverson hid his new style under a white do-rag, and when he removed it in the locker room, a cluster of NBA stars—including a few who had grown up watching Iverson—howled and took pictures. LeBron James teased Iverson about how long it had been since Iverson's last haircut, and Kevin Garnett lamented the passage of time. "Man, we getting old, dog!" Garnett said as Iverson stood there saying nothing, only rubbing the unfamiliar contours of his head and staring in a mirror at a face he barely recognized.

IVERSON CHASED HIS youth into bars and casinos, some things never changing as his age advanced. His new environs—and Curry's lack of authority—allowed him to indulge his favorite pastimes other than basketball. He came to know the insides of Detroit's finest gambling halls, though his luck hardly seemed to come with him. He ran up $25,000 in markers at Caesars Palace and just refused to pay his debt (Tawanna would later testify in divorce proceedings that she covered it) and, according to a blog item published—although later deleted—on the *Detroit News*' website, he lost so often at his beloved blackjack that he was warned for "throwing his chips or cards at the dealer"; the blog added that Iverson was rude to dealers and waitstaff and—although the casinos would later deny this—was banned from the MGM Grand and Greektown Casino. He found the north-side bar districts to be delightful, and he spent many of his nights pounding his favorite beers alongside a few friends, fueling the Pistons' fears about Iverson's commitment and whether his bad habits were pushing him toward the dark side.

"Iverson and his cronies are continuing the antisocial behavior that was part of his decade in Philadelphia," wrote *Philadelphia Daily News* columnist John Smallwood, who had observed and criticized Iverson for years. "They are not kids anymore. They are grown men. It would appear that the decline of Allen Iverson is heading toward free fall."

By February 2009, though, his lifestyle seemed to be catching up with him. A back injury seemed unwilling to heal, and rather than allow the Pistons' medical staff to care for him, Iverson preferred to return to Georgetown University, where he was advised to sit out two weeks. Curry allowed it, despite that an MRI showed no structural damage to Iverson's back. But when he returned a month later, Iverson learned that he had lost his starting job. Hamilton was the starter now, round-and-round once again, and Iverson would be the team's sixth man. Although he released a statement in March saying he would happily come off the bench, all the right words once again, Iverson had no intention of giving up his starting job—at least not quietly.

He would later tell a *Detroit Free Press* reporter that Curry begged him to accept the bench role or else the coach would lose control of the team. Hamilton also would claim that Curry "lied to us a million times" about playing time and assignments. Although the statement accepting the bench role seemed to support his coach, Iverson quickly applied pressure to regain his starting job. He told reporters that the Pistons "rushed" him back, and after three games as a bench player, he erupted: "I'd rather retire before I do this again," he told reporters after a loss to the New Jersey Nets.

He refused to play at all in the team's final seven regular season games, declaring a cold war on the team, which responded by ruling him out for the season with the back injury—a passive-aggressive but effective way to get its point across. Dumars met with Iverson and his agent, Leon Rose, in early April, and the sides agreed that it was simply time to move on from this hellish experiment; the Pistons, tired of Iverson's bad attitude and nighttime extracurriculars, released him.

Iverson, who averaged a career-low 17.4 points in his unmemorable, fifty-four-game stint in Detroit, celebrated his early vacation—the Pistons would go on to make the playoffs but be swept in the first round by the Cleveland Cavaliers—by going to a bar. While he and several friends drank in the VIP section of Detroit's South Beach Pizza Bar on April 11, watching as the Pistons lost to the Indiana Pacers, Iverson's crew jawed with a group that included a man named Guy Walker. Eventually the confrontation turned into a full-on brawl, and Antwuan Clisby, a friend of Iverson and one of his security guards, allegedly "sucker punched" Walker, according to a court summary, and Iverson was rushed out of the bar by another member of his security detail, Ralph Godbee, who would later become Detroit's police chief before resigning amid a sex scandal.

Walker sued Iverson for $2.5 million, alleging that Iverson conspired with Clisby to attack him. But the suit was eventually dismissed, though not before a deposition in which Iverson tried to intimidate Walker's attorney, with whom Iverson had history, with profanity and odd basketball metaphors: "This is the line, and we got a ball in here. This is my court. I know I'm gonna win this one. I gonna move in front of you," Iverson said, according to a transcript published by the *Detroit News*. Gregory L. Lattimer, based in Washington, D.C., had been involved with two other lawsuits against Iverson. The player was outspoken and defiant, convinced Lattimer was among those targeting him. "I die before I let you get me this time," Iverson told Lattimer. "I'm as clean as the Board of Health, man."

The months passed, and Iverson kept passing the time, emerging into free agency and watching from afar as the dominoes fell. The Sixers fired Billy King in December 2007, a year after he traded Iverson, and Cheeks was let go a year later. Philadelphia searched in the summer of 2009 for a sixth head coach since Brown left, and the franchise lay in ruin. The Nuggets never reached the NBA Finals with or without Iverson, and although Curry was publicly assured of a second season as Detroit's head coach, Dumars changed his mind and fired Curry anyway. Along Iverson's path lay nothing but wreckage, of franchises and team officials believing his words and, by doing so, watching as the Iverson machine devoured them. Not that he felt remorse. That July, Iverson waited for his children to finish summer school so the family could move on to whatever waited in the future. They were looking at a house in Atlanta, eager to move into an estate on West Paces Ferry Road in the northwest part of the city.

In the meantime, he blamed others for this latest drama-filled chapter of his career, in particular the men who had been sacrificed in the name of Iverson, and this was convenient reasoning, as always, focusing only on his own next destination. A predator will always be hungry again, no matter how much he eats in one sitting, little thought given to the decaying remains behind.

One summer evening, he invited a *Detroit Free Press* reporter to join him as he dined on chicken wings. Iverson called his experience with the Pistons "the most miserable of my career." But he was jovial, confident that better days lay ahead, and, hell, maybe they were already here now that he sat, naturally, at T.G.I. Friday's in nearby Southfield, smiling as he pitilessly sucked the meat off the bones.

CHAPTER 20

"IRRETRIEVABLY BROKEN"

Tawanna moved out in 2010, certain this time that her marriage was finished, nearly two decades of history with Iverson—a family built and a long, winding story arcing from Virginia to Philadelphia to Atlanta, from poverty to riches—now seemingly gone.

She rented the same apartment they had lived in during less turbulent times, the final touches being completed before they moved into the mansion on West Paces Ferry Road in northwest Atlanta. It would be their home, where their five children would grow toward adulthood, and Iverson and Tawanna would enter the next phases of their lives—no matter how that looked. It needed to be perfect before they moved in.

But now the house was a war zone, the arguments turning violent more often, Iverson's drinking becoming a problem Tawanna could no longer control. Two weeks after Iverson left yet another NBA team in tatters, dealing now with legitimate personal problems after years of faking them to get out of minor responsibilities, Tawanna filed for divorce, signing a legal document stating her marriage was "irretrievably broken."

"I couldn't deal with Allen anymore," she would testify later, "and living like that."

Then, with some distance between them, the days turning to weeks, Tawanna would look back on that history together and all they had accomplished. Was he really the monster she occasionally convinced herself he was? Could he truly not change? Her conscience sometimes ate at her: In many ways, she had created this, feeding Iverson's darker tendencies by never following through with her threats. Iverson never performed household duties or made important decisions because, in reality, Tawanna never made him do those things. Her anger loosened its bite; she told herself that if she made changes in the way she behaved toward Iverson, he would have no choice but to change as well.

Besides, most everyone else in Iverson's life talked constantly about how inspiring he was, the good he had done, how he might have problems but was easily more good than bad. Like clockwork, Iverson would send her a message at the perfect moment, tender words during an instant of vulnerability, changing everything. "I miss u so much I hope u won't hate me 4ever," he wrote to her during one tense time.

She would, against her better judgment, text back. Then they would talk. Then she would move back in, in the back of her mind knowing it was temporary, but unwilling to throw away eighteen years because of impulse and anger. In 2010 she rejoined the family, leaving some of her things in the apartment a few miles away. "A test run," Tawanna would describe it later in a court proceeding. "Basically I was giving him another chance. His history is that he'll say what he needs to say to reel me back in and not follow through."

This was the same thing Iverson had forever done with NBA teams: He made promises, usually believing that things would be different, before he grew too comfortable and paranoid and destructive, leading to yet another explosion—then, when the smoke cleared, he was regretful and motivated again, eager to make it work.

The divorce filing was dismissed after Iverson convinced a judge that he and Tawanna had had sex within the previous thirty days—a lie, Tawanna would later testify. But in a show of stability for the kids, Tawanna did her best to resume the old routine. She continued doing

Iverson's laundry and helping the children with their schoolwork, and when Iverson was ready to sleep, he expected Tawanna to interrupt or end her day, too. "He wanted me to lay when he laid," she testified. "I mean, if he was home and he wanted to just chill and watch TV, that's what I did during the day and he had no problem with that."

Then, when Iverson was again comfortable with the state of his marriage, Tawanna laying down none of the law as she had planned during their most recent separation, the wars would resume. He and Tawanna attended one counseling session before Iverson decided that was enough. They went home and shouted at each other or threw punches or champagne bottles, the children sometimes within earshot, and one day during a quieter time Tawanna noticed something disturbing—an observation that would finally act as the tipping point after all this time.

Deuce was always late, relying on his mother to drive him to school after missing the school bus, a lack of punctuality that had become an Iverson hallmark. Tawanna had moved out of her mother's home as a teenager, refusing to listen to instructions; now Tiaura had a similar relationship with Tawanna. Another time, Deuce punched Isaiah in the stomach and called him a faggot, one of their father's favorite slurs. "Leave him alone. Don't bother him," Tawanna recalled snapping at her eldest son, and it was at that moment she saw in Deuce an image of a young Allen Iverson, so short with his temper and quick to turn to violence. The kids had seen it all, absorbing some of their parents' worst traits, a kick to Tawanna's gut. "It just flashed back to me," she testified, "that it's all repeating itself."

Thinking of her children, she had reconciled with Iverson. Now, as she again filed divorce paperwork in June 2011, she told herself she was thinking of them again.

AT THE END of 2011, the possibility of one more reconciliation on her mind, Tawanna arranged for the family to spend Christmas with Iverson, who was playing for a professional basketball team in Istanbul, Turkey. Iverson's hairstylist and the stylist's two daughters would travel to Turkey along with Tawanna and the kids. They could enjoy the peace of the holidays and maybe try one last time to work out the deep knots in the marriage.

Then, unsurprisingly, Iverson picked a fight over the phone with Tawanna the night before the trip, and she opted to stay in Atlanta. The kids and the hairstylist could still go, but Tawanna decided not to ruin Christmas with one more knock-down, drag-out fight in front of God and everyone. When the children arrived in Turkey, Iverson had not stocked his pantry with any food, and there were no bedsheets, soap, or towels for the kids. When Tawanna Skyped with her children, they passed along reports that Iverson was always out, leaving and not coming back until the next day, even after the stylist had left Turkey and returned home. Tawanna allowed the latest reminder to sink in: Iverson had not changed, even in the face of desperation, and she was now certain he never would change—no matter how much she and all the others wanted it. He was who he was, by God, and nothing ever made him prouder.

What came next was either deviously Machiavellian or naively hopeful, depending on who was most believable during the final divorce proceedings. After he returned from Istanbul, Iverson offered one more peace accord, begging his wife to salvage the marriage, unwilling to end the story of his relationship with Tawanna in such an ugly way. He would do anything, he told Tawanna, who also suspected Iverson was cheating on her. But he was willing to bet it all on making things right—including transferring to her 100 percent of the $32 million trust that, years earlier, Reebok had set aside when Iverson was blowing through money and saving almost nothing for the future. This, Iverson told her, was how serious he was: If he did something that ruined the marriage, he would be forfeiting his rainy-day fund.

She told him she would think about it. Afraid for her children's financial future in February 2012, Tawanna visited her attorney, John

Mayoue, the Atlanta lawyer who had represented Usher, Chris Rock, and the wife of Big Boi during their own divorces. More than a decade after Tawanna braced herself to sign the prenuptial agreement she assumed Iverson's people would insist upon, when he approached her before their wedding but then lit the document on fire, attorney Aaron Thomas drafted a four-page postnuptial agreement.

"Mrs. Iverson would like to stay married to Mr. Iverson and it is her fervent hope that this family can be put back together," the document began. It went on to list four "triggering events," or indiscretions that Iverson had been guilty of many times before, along with fifteen provisions and five more bullet points that could cripple what was left of Iverson's finances. Iverson was to remain faithful to Tawanna, refrain from physical and verbal abuse, and avoid fathering children outside the marriage. The provisions outlined the transfer of the Reebok trust, marriage counseling between Iverson and Tawanna, Iverson meeting regularly with a therapist to address his problems with alcohol and gambling, Iverson agreeing to never gamble again and to be home each night by midnight, discussing all purchases of more than $5,000, the execution of a last will and testament for both Iverson and Tawanna, and putting a stop to supporting Iverson's friends and family. The list went on and on, more than a dozen extreme behavioral modifications for Iverson and outlining what would constitute a cold-turkey personality change.

And, if he violated one of the triggering events, it would cost him more than the Reebok trust, which he had dangled in front of Tawanna if she would just come home. He would be ordered to immediately place an additional $100,000 into a separate trust for each of the five children, any remaining property would be transferred into Tawanna's name—though Iverson would retain responsibility for the debt—and Tawanna would waive alimony rights (he was mostly broke anyway) in exchange for fifty cents, split between Tawanna and the children, of every dollar Iverson made in the future from books, movies, or any other media deal. Considering Iverson's basketball career was all but finished, this represented the majority of the earning power for the rest of his life—and, if he screwed up even once, this document was asking him to potentially hand over half of it.

Tawanna offered to withdraw her divorce filing if Iverson agreed to the list of demands. If Iverson could not stay true to his word, making wholesale changes and eliminating the flaws that had shadowed him for years, this was Tawanna's knockout punch—a lopsided agreement only a desperate man would agree to. But going all-in, which his wife was asking him to do, was the only way he could save the marriage, preserving the history between them and the future that he hoped would follow.

The document was finalized and sent to both Tawanna and Iverson. Not long after, it came back with Iverson's signature.

LESS THAN TWO weeks after the postnup was drafted, Tawanna was back in the family home, preparing for Valentine's Day. She had not exactly moved back in full-time but was rather inching her way back, giving the impression of a happy family under one roof.

Some nights, she would stay with Iverson; occasionally they would have sex and other times they would argue. Many evenings, after feeding the children and putting the younger ones to bed, she would retreat to the quiet solitude of her apartment. One night around ten, when Iverson for some reason was convinced that Tawanna was out on the town without him, he knocked on her door again and again. "Me going out was not cool with him," she would testify later. He kept knocking, even as Tawanna looked out the peephole and refused to answer it for fear he was drunk. Iverson had apparently not noticed Tawanna's car in the driveway, and when he grew tired of knocking, he kicked the door hard enough that the hinges separated from the frame; he later left a message on Tawanna's voice mail, wondering aloud where she had gone.

On another occasion, Iverson dropped off Deuce at the apartment, and when Tawanna tried closing the door, Iverson stuck his foot into the doorway, preventing Tawanna from closing it and then forcing his way inside to air a few grievances and to call Tawanna a whore. "He just talked about me like a dog in front of the two big kids," Tawanna said, referring to Deuce and Tiaura, who unbeknownst to Iverson had a friend upstairs. Tawanna, seemingly becoming a master at passive-aggressive warfare, dialed 911 with one hand, setting the phone down so that the dispatcher could hear and record Iverson screaming at his wife.

Another time Tawanna picked the kids up from the house, and Iverson, alcohol still on his breath from the night before, jumped in, saying he wanted to ride with them to school. When they returned, Tawanna dropping off her husband at home, he called her all manner of insult: "piece of shit, you dirty dog, bitch, whore," Tawanna would later describe, and again she would call the police. "The difference between Mr. Iverson and I," she testified, "is that I learn from my mistakes, and he continues to repeat his."

As usual, though, she was not fully without fault. She often screamed back at Iverson, inciting her husband by suggesting he and Gary Moore were lovers and writing in lipstick on a mirror that Ann Iverson was a crackhead. Iverson responded by threatening to expose their children's secrets to America, telling Tawanna that he would inform TMZ, the celebrity gossip website, about every problem their family had ever endured, along with his suspicion that Tawanna had been infected with a sexually transmitted disease—part of Iverson's paranoia that she was having an affair, she would later testify. "TMZ & the courts will know everything about her & Deuce 2day! I'm letting it all out!" he texted to Tawanna in March 2012, going on to specify what he would reveal about two of his children. "My need shit 2 b taken care of so my lawyer will b contacting yours 2day. Our kids will have 2 deal with it & I hate it but I tried!"

Later, a series of stories involving Iverson and Tawanna indeed appeared on TMZ, though none mentioned the kids. Tawanna would tell the court later that she was contacted by the website but never spoke to a reporter, and although Iverson denied it, too, she saw him shaking hands with a reporter with a camera, who she assumed was from TMZ, outside the Fulton County Superior Courthouse.

As 2012 drew to a close, with Tawanna's chess pieces now where she wanted them, she was confident Iverson had given her plenty of ammunition for a judge to grant her a divorce. Iverson would later admit under oath to having cheated on Tawanna, violating at least one of the triggering events in the postnuptial agreement, and Tawanna believed his behavior had breached others. On November 16, 2012, a video camera was pointed toward her at the office of her attorney. "Miss Iverson, can you state your name, please?" she was asked.

"Tawanna Iverson," she said as the deposition began. Iverson sat nearby and listened as their relationship entered its final stage—though not before reliving it from the start.

"When did you meet Mr. Iverson?" Tawanna was asked.

"Nineteen ninety-two," she said, telling the story from the beginning.

CHAPTER 21

HOME AND AWAY

Iverson waited in the tunnel, ready to hear those familiar sounds, to once again feel Philadelphia teammates slapping his back and hear Sixers fans chanting for him. The past three years, and in particular the previous six months, had seemed like a lifetime. The journey had begun in December 2006, when Iverson left Philadelphia—a place he maybe had not realized was in many ways its own kind of kindred spirit—and moved to Denver to Detroit to Memphis to Philadelphia, to hell and back.

Six days earlier in December 2009, word came that the meetings were over and a contract was ready. He was, thank heavens, still an NBA player. The Sixers were taking a chance on him, whatever their mutual sins of the past now behind them, that glorious blank slate. The Sixers needed Iverson, and Iverson, God knew, needed the Sixers.

Iverson arrived at Wachovia Center at 5:55, a little more than an hour before game time, hurrying through the players' entrance and into a corridor. He wore a black leather jacket over an untucked white button-up, a beanie tying the outfit together and protecting him from the harsh cold of the air beyond these walls. Months earlier, he had said he would rather retire from the NBA than become a bench player. But that was bullshit, and it took him retreating home to Atlanta, surrounded by personal drama, to realize that. On this night he hurried through the corridor, running late as always, and cameras captured his approach to a locker room that three years earlier had been stripped of any indication that Iverson ever played for the Sixers. He touched the hand of a smiling arena worker, hugging a woman he recognized from his previous life. Then it was time to go to work. Iverson slid on his number-three Sixers jersey, pulling the trademark sleeve over his right arm, and wrapped a headband around his cornrows. He jogged toward the floor, so many in the crowd wearing Iverson jerseys and chanting "MVP! MVP!" and suddenly it was 2001 again. Only in his mind, Iverson was wiser now. Different. Ready, at age thirty-four, to be a leader. He told himself this was destiny. That this was where he belonged. That this time he would not fuck it up.

As Iverson stood in the tunnel wearing warm-ups, the arena lights went low and public address announcer Matt Cord started belting the names into his press row microphone, the final syllables bouncing with an echo effect.

Thaddeus Young-oung-oung!

Elton Brand-and-and-and!

Sammy Dalembert-embert!

Then Cord's voice rose an octave. The crowd grew louder. "A six-foot guard from Georgetown!"

Iverson pressed his lips together, holding back tears and running onto the floor. "Number three," Cord said as Iverson jogged from the darkness toward the light, "Allen *Iversoooooooon-son-son*!" Iverson slapped the hands of his teammates and kept walking, past them, stopping finally at half-court and falling to his knees. He mumbled something to himself, and before he stood, he kissed the Sixers logo. He was home.

THE HOTEL RESTAURANT was closed for Labor Day, so they met with Iverson in the fourth-floor conference room at the Westin in Buckhead, the tony uptown district in northern Atlanta. Iverson walked in alone, wearing his business attire: an oversized white T-shirt, jean shorts, and a New York Mets cap—promising himself that, yes, he would leave with a contract offer.

But first he had to sell the three representatives from the Memphis Grizzlies—owner Michael Heisley, general manager Chris Wallace, and coach Lionel Hollins—that he was not the pain in the ass he was made out to be in Detroit. Yes, he was unhappy there, and yes, he felt betrayed by Pistons coach Michael Curry, who Iverson felt was a liar. Iverson was a starter, not a damn bench player, and those three games standing and clapping while the other starters were announced just killed him inside. He had been in starting lineups since he was a kid in the Aberdeen youth leagues, and now this punk-ass, first-time head coach, not even seven years older than Iverson, thought he belonged in a rocking chair? Why did Detroit even trade for him, then, only to bench him? Sitting him was so disrespectful in Iverson's eyes that, when he was to return to the lineup, he instead benched *himself*, refusing to play. It was all on his mind as he scanned the Westin lobby, but no, now was not the time for that kind of talk.

The group sat at an oval table, sipping water from bottles. Heisley went first. He was a Georgetown man, class of 1960, and he sure did enjoy watching Iverson play for the Hoyas so long ago. Had it really been fifteen years? Wow, time flies, and even before Heisley addressed Iverson, the other men with him, Wallace and Hollins, knew this was a done deal. The owner wanted Iverson, a star who could sell jerseys and tickets and maybe elevate the Grizzlies to the playoffs for the first time in franchise history. Now the coach and GM were the ones who would have to make it work. Heisley had, in previous days, talked big: He would instruct Hollins to make it clear in their meeting with Iverson that he would not be a full-time starter. He was in his mid-thirties, and besides, the Grizzlies had a set backcourt, Michael Conley at the point and presumptive young star O. J. Mayo at shooting guard. But on the way to Atlanta, Heisley softened, fearing such a stance would scare Iverson away. So instead he asked Hollins to avoid the topic altogether.

The truth was, Iverson was desperate, too. The Pistons made no effort to re-sign him after the 2008–09 season, his worst as a pro and fuel for the notion that the once-electric Iverson had lost a step. For the first time he would be a free agent. He had actually been looking forward to it. Other than Reebok, no one had ever *recruited* Iverson. Georgetown took a chance on him while he was still an inmate at the Newport News City Farm, serving time for the brawl at Circle Lanes, and the 1996 NBA draft led him to Philadelphia. Trades sent him to Denver and then Detroit, and when his contract expired, he was ready to be wooed. "I'm a Free Agent, healthy again, and capable of signing with any team," Iverson wrote on Twitter in July 2009.

He waited, the summer months passing, and his phone rarely rang. Iverson's agent, Leon Rose, was working the phones, right? And Gary Moore was out spreading the good news, telling teams how eager Iverson was to be a leader now, ready to help young players. Iverson spent the summer shooting hoops with Eric Snow, the former Sixers point guard who now lived in Atlanta with his estranged wife, DeShawn, spending the slow hours at the Hawks' practice facility. When the Grizzlies called in early September, asking for a meeting in Buckhead, Iverson was relieved. He would talk about wanting to win, the most important thing, and even if they brought up a bench role, he would accept it just for the chance to walk through the door, collect a few million dollars, and then prove himself as he had done so many times before.

Two hours passed at that oval table, no gauntlets thrown down or cross words shared, a risk but one Heisley hoped a fellow Georgetown man would not exploit. Even if united at the altar of desperation, this was a marriage with potential. The Grizzlies offered Iverson $3.1 million, a pay cut of nearly $18 million from the year before. But this was the offer, and Iverson stood and shook their hands, telling them he was ready to come to Memphis.

Three days later, hundreds of fans packed FedExForum, the Grizzlies' home arena, welcoming the team's new star to southwestern Tennessee. It felt about as far away as he could get from Detroit, and maybe that was a good thing. Someone handed Iverson a blue Gibson guitar, and a fan gave Iverson a book. Another fan, apparently overcome and seeing Iverson as balm to all things, told the player about a son who had committed suicide. The Grizzlies team store hung Beale Street blue number-three jerseys and marked them for sale, and a drum corps introduced Iverson to his new home.

When he stood at a lectern and spoke into the microphone, the cheers finally weakening, he told the crowd how personal this was for him. He promised to dazzle them at the Forum. Then, the deal done, Heisley and Wallace and Hollins having made their decision and listening along with so many others, Iverson used his platform to, even if in a lighthearted way, finally throw down a gauntlet: "Everyone wants to start," Iverson told the crowd. "I've been starting since I was eight years old."

FIVE DAYS AFTER the news-conference-turned-celebration, another pimple emerged. Iverson departed on an eight-day, three-nation tour of Europe as part of a Reebok promotion that brought him back to Memphis three days before training camp began in Richmond, Virginia, not far from where he grew up on the Peninsula. The trip had been planned before Iverson signed with the Grizzlies, and although Moore took on his familiar role as public reassurance officer—"It'll work out fine," he told the *Memphis Commercial-Appeal*, adding that Iverson's international appeal was "mind boggling"—Hollins was put off by Iverson's nonchalance.

The coach tried to overlook it, though, amid the excitement elsewhere within team headquarters: The first shipment of Iverson jerseys had already sold out, and the team was managing increasing demand for season tickets. But not long after Iverson returned, he suffered a partially torn left hamstring, an injury that suggested he had not bothered to train during his European tour or maybe even the months preceding it. Hollins, a no-nonsense former NBA point guard, was growing increasingly suspicious that Iverson had, during their meeting two months earlier in Buckhead, sold them on a lie. He also noticed that Iverson's knees were slower to heal, his legs far less powerful than they had once been.

To make matters worse, Iverson was growing increasingly doubtful that Tawanna would move the family to Memphis. After three moves in as many years, settling now in Atlanta four years after buying a summer house in nearby Alpharetta and later purchasing a permanent home less than a mile from the Georgia Governor's Mansion, Tawanna had little desire to uproot yet again. It made Iverson anxious, because as often as he had taken his family for granted, his happiness depended on them being at his side.

Iverson tried to gut it out alone, but he never did like being by himself—and he pleaded with Tawanna to join him. When she hedged, Iverson tried to occupy himself with basketball and his new team. By November 2, Iverson was healthy enough to dress in a Memphis uniform for the first time, coming off the bench against Sacramento. He played seventeen minutes and scored eleven points in the overtime loss to the Kings, feeling like an afterthought. He told his teammates after regulation ended that they must not have realized he was even in the game; none of them so much as looked in his direction. Afterward, a reporter asked Iverson about his hamstring. It was fine, he replied, but "I had a problem with my butt from sitting on the bench so long. That's the only thing I had a problem with." He was not joking. Iverson did not smile. And, raising his voice so that his teammates could hear, Iverson went on—his words beginning to sound like an ultimatum.

"I'm not a reserve basketball player," he said. "I've never been a reserve all my life, and I'm not going to start looking at myself as a reserve. That's something for the media to talk about. It's only a big issue when the media talks about it. The subject never came up in my career until everything happened in Detroit. No one talked about me being a sub or anything like that until last year.

"In all the other years of my career, it's never come up. I've been a starter on All-Star teams, Olympic teams, and NBA Finals teams. It's just a big deal now. I think it is something people should let go. To answer your question, no, I'm not a bench player or the sixth man. Go look at my resume, it will show you that I'm not a sixth man."

The next day, Wallace called Iverson's comments "inappropriate," and Heisley publicly backed Hollins's judgment. Iverson again came off the bench on November 4 against Golden State, and again Iverson chirped about playing time. Friends and personal colleagues still saw Iverson as a superstar, and because he trusted their opinions, never seeing them as sycophants, he saw it this way, too. "It was boiling," Hollins would later tell the *Commercial-Appeal*, "under the surface." So the next day, Hollins asked visitors, including basketball legend Jerry West, to leave the gym in Los Angeles where the team was practicing. He stood in front of his players, looking Iverson in the eye and telling him that he had *better* conform to Hollins's way, or else he needed to leave the team. Get with the program—one team, one goal—or get the hell out. It was a move that earned the respect of Hollins's other players, but Iverson, predictably, was livid—his frustration with his personal life pulling his emotional strings so tight they nearly snapped. How dare this coach disrespect him in front of his teammates, a cardinal sin even during his earliest days on a basketball court? Who did Hollins think he was? He told reporters after his third game, another loss in which he did not start, that Hollins "makes all the decisions around here" and that because Hollins had not confronted Iverson in private, it would "always be hard for me and him to see eye-to-eye."

Heisley, the team owner, flew to Los Angeles the next morning for another meeting. The situation was indeed boiling over now, Heisley's experiment failing miserably, and Iverson and Gary Moore asked for a sit-down. After a walk-through at the team hotel, Moore and Iverson met with Heisley, Moore doing most of the talking. Iverson's marriage was failing, and Iverson's youngest daughter, Messiah, had been sick with a persistent illness—something the doctors back home in Atlanta had been unable to diagnose. Iverson was stressed, Moore explained, which is why he said what he had said, and now it was best for Iverson to go to Atlanta and be with his family. The excuses were actually true this time, but in part because of Iverson's history, the team was puzzled by the timing. It was so early in the season, and there had been no previous mention of marital strife or a daughter's health problem; these problems had come to the team's attention only after Iverson voiced his displeasure with Hollins. Heisley, his hands tied, granted Iverson permission to leave the team, and he flew back east while the Grizzlies, whose coach already had mentally moved on from this disaster, prepared for their next game.

A week later, another ultimatum came from Atlanta—Iverson, through an anonymous source, was threatening to retire if he was not named a starter—and that was the final straw. After Iverson had promised big things to the crowd two months earlier at FedExForum, the Grizzlies cut him after three games, sixty-seven minutes, and thirty-seven points. He never so much as played a home game.

BASKETBALL MEN HEARD the news, and across the nation they gathered, wondering if the risk was worth it. Hubris is part of any championship formula, and the great coaches and executives see themselves as reformers. It is as arrogant as it is necessary, though in reality, major gambles are far more likely to bring on firings than a championship. Still they try, because of that remote chance: Elsewhere it failed, but here it could represent the missing piece of the championship puzzle.

The New York Knicks mulled over signing Iverson, after someone leaked from Iverson's camp that he dreamed of playing in coach Mike D'Antoni's up-tempo offense. It had not succeeded in Memphis, but could it work in New York? No, the risk was too great, and so the Knicks passed. In Charlotte, North Carolina, Larry Brown pleaded with Bobcats owner Michael Jordan, who had taken an interest in Iverson early in the young player's career, but even with two planetary egos—no shortage of hubris there—leading the young team, deep down they both knew bringing in Iverson would be a bad idea.

But Brown kept fighting, kept telling his boss that it would work in Charlotte, no matter what had happened elsewhere. Had Jordan forgotten the magic Brown and Iverson conjured in Philadelphia? Yes, Jordan said, but had Brown forgotten the explosions they caused, too? "A big fight," Brown said. "Michael loved Allen. Michael admired the shit out of Allen." But the legendary former player made a good point: Brown, that old soft spot flaring up, would not be able to help himself: He would force Iverson into the lineup, giving him the minutes instead of young guards D. J. Augustin and Gerald Henderson. "And he was right," Brown would admit later. "Because I would have."

In late November, as teams across the league decided that Iverson just was not worth the headache, Iverson tapped out. It was finished, apparently, and so he contacted Stephen A. Smith, the former *Philadelphia Inquirer* columnist who had grown close with Iverson years earlier, and on the day before Thanksgiving, Smith posted a message from Iverson on his website:

> *I would like to announce my plans to retire from the National Basketball Association. I always thought that when I left the game, it would be because I couldn't help my team the way that I was accustomed to. However, that is not the case.*
>
> *I still have tremendous love for the game, the desire to play, and a whole lot left in my tank. I feel strongly that I can still compete at the highest level. Stepping away from the game will allow me to spend quality time with my wife and kids. This is a reward that far exceeds anything that I've ever achieved on the basketball court. I have prayed for this day and I see it as my greatest gift. I want to*

> *thank the people of Reebok International Ltd., for always allowing me to be me and for supporting me my whole career through all the ups and downs. I have enjoyed 13 wonderful seasons in the NBA, and I am grateful.*

He went on to thank the fans, former Bethel High coach Mike Bailey, Georgetown coach John Thompson, Brown, Jordan, Heisley, and many others. He closed with a final message.

> *And finally, to the city of Philadelphia: I have wonderful memories of my days in a Sixers' uniform. To Philly fans, thank you. Your voice will always be music to my ears.*

That last part brought a lump to Brown's throat. Jordan might not let Brown sign Iverson, but that would not stop him from flinging Iverson a life vest. He called his friends in the NBA, lobbying Adam Silver, the league's deputy commissioner, and begging friends in Philadelphia to overlook the past and give Iverson one last chance. Just let him come back for the rest of the season and say goodbye. Surely Iverson realized now, after the shit show in Memphis, that he was no starter; that his days of superstardom had passed. Brown knew Iverson, and he believed the kid just wanted closure. Just wanted to come home to Philly for one last ride before the sun truly went down. "Somehow, some way," Brown recalled imploring them, "we've got to get this kid a job in the NBA, at least to have people show their respect to him in every arena."

That was the way Brown saw it: Iverson parading from Orlando to Chicago to Phoenix to Sacramento, fans rising and bidding Iverson farewell. It would not matter how much Iverson played or how many points he scored. He had made his point, been the face of his generation. Now, the old coach thought from afar, this would be goodbye. The Sixers were terrible, losers of seven consecutive games and headed for last place. Where exactly was the harm? Executives brought the idea to Ed Snider, the team's majority owner, and he called Grizzlies owner Heisley, the old Georgetown man, who despite the embarrassment he had overseen in Memphis encouraged Snider to go for it: Give Iverson a victory lap in Philadelphia, where he had changed the game.

Iverson heard the whispers. He wanted this. Badly. He had taken for granted the comfort he once felt in Philadelphia, the mutual understanding that came from city to player, even after his departure. More than a year after the Sixers traded Iverson to Denver, the Nuggets played at the Wachovia Center. The Philadelphia crowd gave Iverson a standing ovation, in his first game in a different uniform, and he acknowledged the moment by instructing his team at Reebok to design a tribute sneaker for the occasion. On the evening of March 18, 2008, Iverson jogged onto the familiar court wearing a pair of P.E. Question III shoes, the Denver powder blue and gold colors familiar but including a nod to the Sixers fans—THXPHILA, embroidered in blue—near his ankle. Once again, he had been unable to appreciate a good thing until it was gone—but now a chance to return, a chance to finish his career where it began, dangled in front of him.

In late November 2009, Snider and team president Ed Stefanski approached Eddie Jordan, the coach who would have to deal with the fallout if the experiment went sideways. Iverson did not so much play for coaches as he did consume them, but at this point Jordan knew something was missing on his team. He was willing to give it a shot. "This talk came up that, 'Hey, there's nobody out there that we like. Let's try to bring Allen back. What do you think?' " Jordan recalled. "And I said: 'I would love to coach Allen.' And I knew. I knew everything. I knew about his knees. I knew about his habits. I knew he didn't like to practice, on and on. But I wanted his spirit on that team."

Fuck it, the Sixers thought, and on the first day of December, Stefanski met with Iverson, Rose, and Moore, and Iverson said many of the same things he had said to the Memphis contingent. Only this time he had felt the cold slice of being unwanted, of writing that retirement memo and seeing his career flashing before his eyes. Whatever he said, the Sixers liked it enough to offer Iverson, this face from the team's past, a nonguaranteed contract worth the league's minimum salary, less than $650,000. It was a fraction of what he had made throughout his career—but, considering what was going on at home, Tawanna threatening divorce and the couple long since having lost control of finances, these were dollars Iverson badly needed. "He was like a drowning man reaching for some help," Jordan would recall of the meeting. "And they were all reaching. Sometimes people say a drowning man will reach for razor blades. You could see it: He was sad that it had come to this."

Iverson arrived at the arena and hurried through the corridor, seeing some of the same faces in the locker room, where like many superstars he had once been assigned two or three stalls, space to spread out. Now his locker was wedged between two other lockers, and if he thought about it long enough maybe that would have pissed him off. But who cared, here was Aaron McKie, his old running buddy, now in a suit and tie, an assistant coach. "A.I.," McKie told him after throwing Iverson a few warm-up passes, "I don't know nobody in this city who is more beloved than you are."

Iverson signed autographs, smiled at the greetings, and later waited as the lights went low and the other starters were introduced, standing in the tunnel and feeling the bumps rise on his skin as he heard the echo and the cheers, hearing his name called in Philadelphia one more time.

EARLY IN THE fourth quarter on February 20, 2010, in what would be a meaningless, blowout loss to the Chicago Bulls at the United Center, Iverson pulled up near the wing and shot a nineteen-footer that bounced off the iron and into Bulls forward Taj Gibson's hands. It was a routine, forgettable play, lost in a game not worth holding on to, but although no one realized it at the time, it happened to be the last shot of Allen Iverson's NBA career.

Forty-seven seconds later, Jordan called for Iverson to take a seat, sending in Jason Kapono. Iverson had been a model citizen in Philadelphia, a promise fulfilled that he would mentor the Sixers' youngsters and cause no locker-room drama. During that first game against Denver, Jordan had drawn up a special half-court play, finishing with Iverson driving through the lane for a layup. It was executed perfectly—the blocks, the space, the drive—but then Iverson missed the easy shot. His legs lacked the strength to drive his body and the ball upward, and he would later admit to Jordan that the only training he had done during his brief retirement was shoot hoops in his driveway. "He didn't have his legs," Jordan recalled. "He didn't have his moves. He couldn't lose people off the dribble like he did before. He couldn't break free. He couldn't create as well as he did in the past. But he was good enough to get by."

The coach overlooked it, chalking the miss up to jitters, and for more than two months his career was back on track, a chance to end things the right way. Iverson never no-showed practices, never kept the team plane grounded as team officials scrambled to find him, never was absent on the bus to the next arena. The Sixers were losing, but he was playing, and that was enough for him. "He just kept saying: 'Come on, we'll break through,'" Jordan said. "And I loved every bit of it."

Iverson felt as if his life was finally steadying, even if things were still rocky at home with Tawanna, who had again stayed with their children in Atlanta. He had no idea what the future held, but for now, the situation seemed tolerable. His knees ached, he walked off the practice floor with an occasional limp, and he lacked any shred of the dominance he had once known. This is what Allen Iverson, that face of perpetual youth and rebellion, looked like when the sun was going down: His legs hurt, his face was puffy, his hair was graying. Even Iverson, who had forever swatted away normal realities, was unable to outrun or cross over the ticking clock. He tried to ignore it, same as he always did, but others could not. "Like a wounded antelope in the jungle," Jordan said. "He's going to survive a little bit. He knows how to get around. But eventually, the lion's going to get him. Father Time's going to get you."

When the game ended in Chicago, the Bulls winning by thirty-two points, Iverson conducted a brief interview in the locker room and then called his wife. How was Messiah? Was she feeling okay? Their four-year-old daughter had been in and out of doctors' offices, mysterious symptoms receding for months and then returning with a vengeance. Iverson, who had left the Memphis Grizzlies months earlier during an especially tense time on and off the court, had also stepped away from the Sixers here and there in the early part of 2010, with Jordan's permission missing a road trip and then excusing himself from a practice. He sat out the All-Star Game for personal reasons before finally telling reporters that, of his five children, "none of them have ever been this sick."

"All I do is just pray on it, because that's all that can be done right now," he said, adding that he assumed his daughter had pneumonia. Tawanna had shuttled Messiah to hospitals in Atlanta, but there were rarely answers. Then, while Iverson tried to rekindle his NBA career with the Sixers, Tawanna brought their daughter to Philadelphia, familiar territory, and Children's Hospital, where Messiah was admitted and stayed seven days. She was diagnosed with Kawasaki disease, a rare infection that strikes children and causes the inflammation of blood vessels. Doctors would get it under control, but it would take time.

Iverson stepped away again, and Jordan approached team officials. The requests to leave the team were coming more frequently now. The sad thing was that, maybe for the first time, Iverson was doing everything right. Desperation will do that to a man. But, Jordan said, he could not have an absentee shooting guard, not with so many young players watching how things were done. Jordan's bosses asked him what he wanted to do. The coach, his voice low, told them that if it happened again, he wanted Iverson off the team. No other choice, and for a veteran coach like Jordan, it was an easy trade: one career sacrificed to save the soul of the organization.

Tawanna, although she was still contemplating divorce, kept Iverson posted on their daughter's health after games and while he was away on road trips. When Messiah was released, she asked to go see her daddy play. Tawanna made a drive she had made so often, though it seemed so long ago, merging onto South Broad Street and pulling into the sprawling arena parking lot. She and her young daughter sat in the stands, hearing the cheers, watching Daddy do what he does, or at least a version of what he used to do. Then, when the worry subsided, Tawanna and Messiah returned to Atlanta.

On that evening in late February, Iverson spoke for a few minutes with Tawanna. He knew by then that another leave of absence would end his homecoming with the Sixers, maybe finish his career. But in the moment, his heart heavy, Tawanna put Messiah on the phone. Iverson heard his little girl's voice. She asked him to come home.

CHAPTER 22

TWENTY-ONE YEARS

The deposition went on, hour after agonizing hour, as Tawanna described in detail how she met and fell in love with Iverson, gave birth to their children and accepted her role as the head of the household, and how his increasingly disruptive behavior slowly ate away at their relationship and marriage like acid. She had filed for divorce the first time a week after Iverson left the Sixers in 2010, rejoining his family but unable to save his broken marriage.

More than two years later, Tawanna now outlined, in painful detail, the alcohol-fueled confrontations and his violent temper, how he had gone from poor to rich to poor again, and how he became increasingly desperate to regain control of a life that had long since gotten away from him. There were important other forces in his life, some of them destructive, but Iverson could not bear to part ways with them, even when so many people were, for the sake of his family and future, begging him to. He had goodness still inside him, of this Tawanna was certain, but it was now buried under layer upon layer of anger, denial, and booze. Iverson, known for so long for making the big play when his team needed it most, just could not perform in the clutch in his personal life. He never could, really, and with the bright lights of professional basketball no longer keeping his problems in the dark, his many shortcomings were on full, public display.

"Do you still love him?" Iverson's attorney, Melanie Fenwick Thompson, asked Tawanna as the deposition was ending, the memories and stories of two decades compressed into four hours.

"I love him and respect him," she said, "just off the strength of him being my kids' father."

"And you no longer desire to reconcile with him?"

"Not at all."

Iverson just sat there, barely reacting.

TWO MONTHS LATER, their divorce advanced to trial, Iverson on one side of Judge Bensonetta Tipton Lane's courtroom and Tawanna on the other. Iverson, his paranoia intensifying, believed he had little chance of victory in Lane's court, at one point entering what would be an unsuccessful request for a new judge. Fenwick Thompson, his attorney, had little to build a defense on except Iverson's belief that Tawanna had set him up with the postnuptial agreement, a suspicion that she had successfully concealed her own indiscretions, and a notion that Tawanna had spent twenty years building a relationship with Iverson for this reason—a former high school groupie pulling the ultimate con and now hauling him into court to drain the last of his money. It was not much, especially considering Iverson's reputation, along with the high-powered case Tawanna's team had assembled. And to make matters worse, when court representative Dawn Smith reached out to a list of people who could vouch for Iverson's character—some of whom Iverson had supported financially during better times—most never responded.

The witnesses on Tawanna's side painted a picture of a man with a weakening, if nonexistent, grip on reality, a celebrity who thought he could manipulate people and situations for the right amount of money, and the truth was, for a long time that was true. LeRoy Reese, the substance abuse evaluator and NBA fan who admired Iverson, had interviewed Iverson as part of a haphazard assessment and would testify that he had no drinking problem and was an upstanding father, husband, and citizen of the world, and that he, Reese, saw no reason why Tawanna or anyone else would suggest anything different. Gary Moore, who now had his own doubts about Iverson's stability, told Smith that Iverson could be saved.

More impartial observers saw something much different. Michael Fishman, the court-appointed substance abuse doctor, provided a stark report that outlined how Iverson completed his repeatedly rescheduled evaluation still drunk from the night before, alcohol still coursing through his veins at four in the afternoon. Fishman diagnosed Iverson as an alcohol abuser, stopping short of calling him an alcoholic. Smith had, when Iverson had not blown off their scheduled appointments, occasionally encountered Iverson with alcohol on his breath from the evening prior; she had struggled to even contact Iverson during a closely watched period in which it would be determined how often he would see his kids. She recommended to Judge Lane that Tawanna be granted full custody, simply because Iverson could not be trusted with the simplest of tasks and because, she testified, Iverson "has some really fundamental roadblocks to get over."

"I will tell you," Smith went on, "I have never, short of a domestic violence situation, I have never recommended this. And I thought long and hard. But I believe some decisions need to be made about these children, and they need to be made quickly. And all that Mr. Iverson has done is delay or either be nonresponsive or attacking."

Tawanna again went through her side of the story. She testified about the progression from the innocence of teenage love and Iverson's inspiring climb to the sports mountaintop, followed by the troubling details of a restless man who, once he reached his goals, had to find other ways to fill the hours—doing so with habits that became increasingly sinister and corrosive. When it came time for Iverson to take the stand and defend himself, he simply declined. The kid who once had refused to quit, the young star who would never back down, the international superstar who had stood up to even the tallest and most powerful of opponents—he was gone, and in his place was a small, beaten-down man who, after listening to others describe how they now saw him, just could not bring himself to leave his courtroom chair.

"There have been a lot of realities hitting everybody," Fenwick Thompson, Iverson's attorney, said during her closing argument, "hitting this family, hitting the children, hitting their families. It's a reality check for everybody. We've all got to make some changes here now."

Fenwick Thompson tried leaving the court with the image of Iverson eager to take on a new role, simple as it might seem, as an ordinary man with ordinary responsibilities. He was weak now, humbled, his attorney argued—but he could be better. And, with help, he *would* be better. When she was finished, John Mayoue, Tawanna's representative, began a summation that went for Iverson's jugular. It was the kind of attack against a weakened opponent that, years earlier on a basketball court, Iverson might have even admired. Mayoue recounted how Iverson frequently stayed out all night, came home and passed out, pissed on the floor, and then showed up drunk to his substance abuse evaluation; how he refused to follow the court-ordered visitation guidelines for seeing his children; and how this supposed warrior kept taking body shots during the deposition and hearings, refusing to so much as put his gloves up.

"I believe, your honor, that Mr. Iverson has thumbed his nose at every opportunity given to him," Mayoue said, "not just during this case but during the period of eighteen years that he's been permitted the blessing and the privilege of being a parent to these children."

He went on, telegraphing his knockout punch.

"I am startled almost beyond description," Tawanna's attorney said, "that this father chooses not to even take the witness stand to say, 'Man, y'all lying about me; all that stuff is junk. None of it is true. Let me tell you the real me and the real evidence in this case.' He chooses to call one witness and one witness only, when the future of his children [is] at stake."

• • •

JUDGE LANE COMPLETED her ten-page decision on January 21, 2013, sending the document to the attorneys on both sides. Tawanna was awarded sole legal custody, and if anything, Iverson had his nose rubbed in the darkest points of his life—one of the first times his achievements had not overruled his personal shortcomings. He would be guaranteed to see his kids no more often than every other weekend and rotating holidays, unless he and Tawanna could quiet their grudges long enough to discuss other options.

"Testimony at trial established that he does not know how to manage the children; has little interest in learning to manage the children and has actually, at times, been a hindrance to their spiritual and emotional growth and development," Lane's final ruling stated. "For example, he has refused to attend to an obvious and serious alcohol problem, which has caused him to do inappropriate things in the presence of the children while impaired."

Lane ordered Iverson to abstain from alcohol for eighteen months, likely constituting the longest he had gone without a drink since he was a teenager, and never drink within twenty-four hours of visiting his kids. He was to submit to two random and supervised urine tests for the following eighteen months and complete a year's worth of weekly therapy sessions, Lane wrote, "for the purpose of exploring healthy coping mechanisms, stress management, substance abuse and anger."

Iverson was to attend weekly Alcoholics Anonymous meetings for a year, allowing Tawanna to withhold visitation if she suspected he had been drinking; he would not be granted visitation again before passing another alcohol evaluation. Lane also ordered Iverson and Tawanna to attend monthly meetings with a "parenting coordinator," with the idea that the counselor find a way to help Iverson become more involved in his kids' lives. Planning for Iverson's well-known aversion to punctuality, she allowed Tawanna to terminate the sessions if Iverson missed three or more scheduled meetings. Iverson was made to pay for the counselors, the attorneys' fees, for so many of his sins of the past twenty-one years—the most expensive of which were the terms of the postnuptial agreement and control of the Reebok trust.

Someone close to Iverson and his financial situation said two months after the divorce went final that, before the final decree, Iverson and Tawanna had agreed to split the $32 million waiting in the Reebok trust, a sympathetic move by a woman who had once loved Iverson, trying so hard to see only the good in him. A short time later, Iverson would instruct Reebok to release Tawanna's share to the court registry, which then would turn it over to her.

Shortly after the ruling, though, Iverson released a statement through Gary Moore's office suggesting Lane's ruling was biased and calling it "one-sided." He appealed to the Supreme Court of Georgia, though the appeal was submitted improperly and was eventually dismissed on a technicality.

At any rate, it was over. The divorce was final, the ugliest period of Iverson's life now seemingly behind him. He tried looking at the bright side: At least now his mind was free to focus on resuming his NBA career, more than two years after his final game. And like supporters who refer to an aging, broken-down boxer as "Champ" long after the sun has set on his career, Iverson's band of enablers and coattail riders kept assuring him he still had something to give the NBA. He was Allen fucking Iverson, and the league was where he belonged. Eight days after Lane issued her final decree, Iverson posted on Twitter that he was declining an invitation to join the Dallas Mavericks' Development League team.

No, Iverson was aiming much, much higher—at age thirty-seven, there was perhaps a little fight left in him: "Should God provide me another opportunity I will give it my all," Iverson tweeted. "My dream has always been to complete my legacy in the NBA."

CHAPTER 23

FADED

He wore diamonds and a black New York Yankees cap, and members of the Turkish basketball franchise Beşiktaş Cola sat in the St. Regis hotel alongside Iverson at a table in midtown Manhattan. It was October 2010, and he was thirty-five now. His mysterious departure from the Sixers eight months earlier had galvanized what NBA executives and coaches already suspected about him: He was not just a pain in the ass; he was a broken-down pain in the ass with baggage, and when millions of dollars and team chemistry are involved, that becomes a toxic combination. The truth was that other than Larry Brown there were few respected NBA men willing to give Iverson a positive scouting report. Even Eddie Jordan, the Sixers coach who brought Iverson back to Philadelphia, lost contact with Iverson after the team released him in March 2010, eventually going years without speaking with the fallen star. "It was just kind of like smoke," Jordan said. "It just kind of blew away."

Gary Moore and Leon Rose kept working the phones at Iverson's insistence, but this time there were no nibbles, no curiosity about what Iverson had left. He was finished, at least in the eyes of those who ran NBA teams. But yet again, Iverson would not hear of it. "He started believing," Moore said, "that he was defined as a basketball player."

So they kept calling, finding no luck within the borders of North America, eventually extending their outreach and connecting with a man named Seref Yalcin, who worked on the executive board for Beşiktaş. Yalcin sent a contract across the Atlantic Ocean, offering two years and $4 million, and although Moore told reporters that Iverson was slow-playing it, considering his options, the truth was that there were no other options. This was it: If Iverson wanted to play, he had to play in Turkey, that historic and diverse land where Europe meets Asia.

Iverson signed the deal, and Yalcin and team owner Yildirim Demirören flew to New York to formally welcome their new star, telling him about the excitement that awaited. Though it might not have quite been the same level of exhilaration Iverson had come to know. The men enthusiastically told Iverson about the team's home arena, BJK Akatlar, which could hold 3,200 maniacal fans. And they would pack the house every night he was playing—as long as there was no soccer game on television. There would be a light and music show in Istanbul to welcome Iverson to the ancient city, and when the time came, team officials would assist in finding schools for Iverson's five children.

There would be adjustments, though, including one they pointed out as Iverson held a black Beşiktaş jersey, emblazoned with the loud red and white logo of the team's sponsor, the snack manufacturer Krispi, and its motto—*"Çıtını Çıkar!"*—translated roughly as a call to break down barriers. There was a number three pasted onto the jersey, but some things made a better photo opportunity for the dozens of Turkish reporters and photographers who had traveled to America. No, the truth was, European rules forbid players to wear jersey numbers lower than four, and so Iverson was now holding nothing more than a media creation.

Iverson told himself it was okay, the price of doing business, and he explained to the reporters that it felt good once again to be wanted. He insisted that this was not the act of a man desperate for money or attention. Then, the questions finished, the men stood, and Iverson unfurled the white jersey. With the red and white Turkish flag behind them and Turkish popular music blaring on the ballroom speakers, Iverson looked into the audience and forced himself to smile.

THERE WERE REALITIES that Beşiktaş would have to accept, too, beginning with Iverson arriving at the airport without his passport before his flight to Istanbul. He was sent home and would not board another jet for two days, which sadly forced the light and music show to be postponed.

American media debated how Iverson would fit into the European basketball culture. Many Turkish Basketball League teams—Beşiktaş was not even in the more prestigious Euroleague—practiced twice a day, and in Iverson's new home nation, gambling was illegal. Iverson was forever restless, addicted to stimulation, so how would he pass the time? Iverson was no icon here, and basketball was mostly an afterthought. It was a fleeting activity to dissolve the hours, a curiosity that gave Turks a taste of America, but nothing more. A few thousand fans welcomed Iverson to the arena, but there were no police escorts and live feeds like those he had once known in Philadelphia. The games were so insignificant that NBA TV aired only one, as much a novelty as anything, to the late-night audience back in the United States, and viewers saw one of their former superstars playing in what looked like a high school gymnasium.

As always, the games ended, and Iverson tried to answer the questions of how he would fill the hours. He told himself that Tawanna and the kids were coming soon, and then it would feel normal here. They would like the walks along the Bosphorus, the visits along the cobblestones to the Blue Mosque and the Hagia Sophia, and maybe they would all make a family activity out of learning Turkish. Iverson sat in his room at the Swiss Hotel, a half hour's drive from the practice facility, and initialized Skype calls back to Atlanta. He looked into the laptop's small camera, smiling when he saw Messiah, her health problems cleared now, and her four brothers and sisters.

Tawanna sat there, too, updating Iverson on how the kids were doing in school and how Deuce and Tiaura were growing up, just as restless as their father, occasionally sneaking out of the house or breaking windows or getting into altercations at school. Iverson laughed about it, looking forward to the family's reunion. "They were coming. That's what he said," recalled Robert Huber, a writer for *Philadelphia* magazine who traveled to Istanbul to profile Iverson. "The tenor of it was that things were on the upswing. He seemed sunny about that."

But on occasion the distance or the time change or the frustration led to friction and short tempers, and a taste of home came in the arguments with Tawanna. She changed her mind about spending Christmas 2010 in Istanbul, allowing the children to visit Iverson and see the sights but refusing to board the plane herself. "I wasn't going to go and be arguing and ruin Christmas arguing with him," Tawanna would say during her divorce deposition, "ruin Christmas for my kids."

The weeks passed, and eventually Iverson's denial washed away: She would not be joining him in Istanbul, and neither would the kids. He was here by himself, basketball or his family once again in the balance, and even he had no idea which one would win out. His fantasy of chasing happiness to a faraway land, satisfied by the proximity to his family no matter the modesty of the basketball, was fading and almost gone. Now he sat here alone, both of these powerful forces in his life fractured and barely resembling the images that lived in his mind. Perhaps predictably, not long after he realized his family would never move to Turkey, Iverson developed a leg injury that conveniently would allow him to return to America for treatment.

While he waited, though, for a flight that took him away, there were still hours to kill. He spent time with Moore, who moved with Iverson to Istanbul, along with several other old friends. The Iverson entourage, once dozens strong, was being kept alive by three or four men. They spent some nights at Club Reina, a nightspot overlooking the waterway that separates two continents, but that barely soothed his homesickness. Iverson found solace only in the place on Nispetiye Caddesi, a little more than two kilometers from BJK Akatlar Arena, where the bar lights danced off liquor bottles and the music was familiar and a man could get a proper plate of chicken fingers and, praise God, a cold Corona.

There he sat, so many nights, waiting for his next chapter—sitting at a booth or at the bar at Istanbul's one and only T.G.I. Friday's, ordering home on a plate and, while the bartender was at it, one more round.

THE LAST YEAR of Iverson's basketball life was hurried and sad, like the final months of a life. Supporters lamented the fact that Iverson, who opted out of his Beşiktaş contract after thirty-two games, would never have a proper goodbye in the NBA, and realists pointed out that, really, that's what the Philadelphia experiment in 2010 was supposed to be. Iverson just had not realized it, telling himself he could still be a contributor, and others beyond his innermost circle waited for Iverson to accept reality. "He should've ended it in Philly," Brown would say early in 2014.

But in Iverson's mind, the dream was still out there somewhere. "Just give me a training camp," he told reporters in June 2011. "Maybe I've rubbed people the wrong way as far as saying the things I've said in my life and in my career. But if any team needs me to help try and win a championship in any capacity, I'm waiting."

He had convinced himself he would rediscover stardom, rebuild his fortune, maybe win back Tawanna. There were more highlights waiting, he just knew it, like so many that had forever masked all else. The details of Iverson's life never mattered because it was so much fun to watch the memories on repeat. "I don't want to not play basketball," he said. "I don't have any more years to be wasting."

Iverson traveled to China in 2012, a basketball and attention junkie chasing one last fix. He appeared in an exhibition game, an audition of sorts for the Beijing Shougang Ducks, and crossed over Stephon Marbury, his old Big East and NBA foe, before missing the shot—an image that would have been understandable during an old-timers' game, but not when Iverson's representatives were demanding a $1 million salary. His legs were still tired and weak, his focus was still circling the drain, his explosiveness and speed gone but not forgotten. Hope brought him to Beijing, same as always, but once he was on the ground, he showed his true self: poor training habits, an inability to run the floor without becoming exhausted, a vow to improve his conditioning, but a broken-down body that showed otherwise. He left China without a contract, and put more simply: Allen Iverson was not even skilled enough to play in the China Basketball Association. "He's not that good right now," said Brendan Suhr, a former NBA assistant coach who was leading the visiting United States team in China.

Iverson returned to the States, begging teams to take one last chance on him. His divorce had gone final, and the stories of Iverson's incredible fall had made their way into the mainstream. Although he continued denying that he was beaten and broke, everyone around him knew the truth. "I know he's not good with how it ended," said Que Gaskins, who was Iverson's point man at Reebok in what now seemed like a past life. "I definitely wish he could have went out on his terms. That's how he did everything else."

He showed up at college basketball games and insisted that Moore hound the Sixers into a position of some kind. Iverson did not care what he did, as long as he was around basketball. Moore told Iverson that it was close, Allen; if he stayed on his best behavior, putting down the bottle and saying the right things, there would be a place for him. The appearance at the Sixers game in March 2013 was laced with drama—he arrived one minute before he was to be introduced—and that did Iverson no favors. More than a year later, a Sixers official said, no serious discussions had taken place about offering Iverson a full-time staff position. "I know the people that have been here for years and years, a lot of office people and equipment managers and trainers and stuff like that," the Sixers official said. "Everybody loves Allen. The people who have been here forever, they love him to death, but they obviously know all of his demons."

What was left of his good name took a beating. Invite Iverson to an event all you want, but understand that his appearance is never as simple as an agreement, signed or not. In late 2012, Quincy Simpson, a basketball promoter in Ohio, paid $6,000 after receiving a signed contract calling for Iverson to attend a street ball contest. More than fifteen hundred people showed up at a high school in Lima, Ohio, paying ten dollars each and waiting for Iverson to walk in, and then Simpson received a call saying that Iverson made it only as far as the Dayton airport. Simpson, who blasted Iverson in the local media, later claimed that he had fallen victim to a scam—by a man in Atlanta who supposedly did not know Iverson. "I'm trying to erase the whole memory, to be honest," said Simpson, who said he lost more than $10,000 in event planning and ticket reimbursements.

Iverson, meanwhile, passed the months by waiting for the phone to ring. Sure, he thought, there was one more opportunity out there, one more team in need of a scorer. Right? Wasn't there?

WHILE HE WAITED, reaching for a dream that no longer existed, Iverson missed out on chances to see his true legacy taking shape. On a warm day in Hampton, Virginia, a car pulled into a 7-Eleven parking lot, former Bethel coach Mike Bailey behind the wheel. The boys had gotten hungry, and so they were not at home. Bailey, who once had gone looking for Iverson, had now been dispatched to find Deuce and take him for a workout at the Boo Williams Sportsplex, a massive basketball facility that launched the careers of many young players on the Virginia coast.

This time, rather than have Bailey drive from here to there, Tawanna called and made this an easy hunt. Deuce wanted a snack before the workout, she told her ex-husband's old high school coach. Bailey had teased Deuce about being "Iverson 2.0," and although the young man was confused by the dated reference, it made Bailey smile anyway. Deuce was taller, around six-three, and still possessed that signature Iverson quickness. Deuce had traveled here from Atlanta, and Bailey would work with the young man and help him gain entry into the Elev8 Sports Institute, a high-level academy in Del Ray Beach, Florida, where Bailey had once tutored young athletes, telling them about the young man he had once gone to war with, the kid he had won games with, the man he came to love like a son. Now Bailey would be teaching Iverson's own son about the "Iverson cut," a horizontal move off a screen that Larry Brown had invented but Deuce's dad had made famous.

When Bailey pulled into the lot and Deuce walked out, he had a familiar face with him. Rahji Langford was Rahsaan Langford's middle son, one of the children Langford had left behind in 2001 after a joke turned to an argument turned to a murder. Iverson and Tawanna had continued supporting the Langford family, and even after their bitter divorce, they agreed that Tawanna would continue looking after Ra's boys, providing them with the kinds of opportunities Iverson and Langford once dreamed of on these same Virginia streets. If Rahji, who attended nearby Warwick High, was accepted into Elev8, his tuition would be taken care of.

Deuce, carrying his snacks, opened Bailey's car door, climbing into the front seat. Rahji climbed into the back. Bailey could not help but stare at them and reminisce, an Iverson and a Langford sharing a car ride to the basketball court once again.

• • •

ON OCTOBER 30, 2013, a car idled in the players' parking lot, and Iverson climbed out surrounded by his entourage—albeit with a far different look than from a decade earlier. Moore was at his side, and so were three of his children: Tiaura, Isaiah, and Messiah. Iverson was, of course, late.

The convoy walked onto the court at the Wells Fargo Center in Philadelphia, surrounded by empty arena seats and silence, Iverson wearing a white and black jacket, a cluster of gold chains, and a black hat turned sideways. He sat in a leather desk chair, and reporters fiddled with their notebooks and checked their microphones. Josh Harris and David Blitzer, two of the Sixers' managing owners, introduced Iverson, whose lip quivered as he was introduced.

"Obviously, um . . ." Iverson said, leaning toward a microphone but fighting through a wall of emotion. "Everybody know . . . why we're here."

He pushed the words forward, his voice cracking as he slowly formed a sentence that, even a few months earlier, he could not have imagined speaking: "I'm formally . . . announcing my . . . retirement . . . from basketball."

There they were. He said it. It was out there. Iverson wiped at his mouth, pushing the tears back.

"You know, I thought that once this day came," he continued, "it would be, um, basically a tragic day. I never imagined the day coming, but I knew it would come. And, um, I feel proud and happy to say that, um . . ."

Another pause, his eyes glassy. ". . . I'm happy with my decision, and I feel great. I'm at a great mind-set making a decision."

He thanked God for giving him the chance, no matter his size and the odds, no matter that he came from the Virginia Peninsula, an area that had consumed and stifled so much talent. He referenced his mother, Ann, who encouraged him to fight, former Georgetown coach John Thompson for taking a chance on him and believing in him, mentioning Michael Jordan for giving Iverson a vision and a road map to success. He thanked his friends—"especially my day-one friends," he said—along with coaches, teammates, and family, and then the fans. "I'm always gonna be a Sixer till I die," he said. "I'm always gonna be a Hoya till I die. I'm always gonna be a Bruin till I die."

He went on, his lip trembling again.

"But most importantly," Iverson said, "I want to thank my kids. In this profession, you have no idea how hard it is, you know, trying to live up to all the expectations, trying to be a perfect man when you know you're not. Being in a fishbowl, everybody looking at every move you make and talking about everything you do, it's just a hard life to live."

He kept going, firmly in a reflective mood.

"I'm proud to be able to say that I changed a lot in this culture and in this game. It's not how you look on the outside. It's who you are on the inside. . . . I took an ass-kicking for me being me."

Messiah, sitting at her father's left, felt the tears coming, and so did Isaiah.

"I used my kids and [Tawanna] throughout my career as a crutch," Iverson went on. "When things were not going so [well] at work, I was able to come home and see their faces and forget all about it. And I love them for that. They helped me through just by loving me the way they loved me."

Iverson took a deep breath, turning the corner on his monologue.

"I promise you," he said, "it is a happy day for me. . . . It's just a game. It's real life, but it's a game that teaches you a lot about life and sacrifice and what you have to do to win in basketball and in life."

His voice cracked once again as he went on, staring directly ahead, looking at nothing.

EPILOGUE

The line snaked around Wells Fargo Center, fans pulling their red and blue number-three jerseys from their closets once again before they went to watch the Sixers. On the first day of March 2014, the arena sold out for the first time all season, the last-place Sixers the warm-up act to the main attraction: At halftime, Iverson would have his jersey retired, lifted into the rafters alongside the franchise's other greats.

Iverson and Gary Moore killed time at the downtown Ritz-Carlton a few miles away, waiting until Iverson was ready to leave. When the time came, Moore inspecting his man's outfit the same as he had done for the better part of three decades now, they were ready. Iverson wore all black for the special occasion, the darkness making his gold chains and jacket zippers pop, and he completed the look with a black porkpie hat and thick-rimmed glasses. As much as anyone, Moore wanted this night to go off without hitches. He had continued working with the Sixers behind the scenes to find Iverson a job—something disguised as a front-office position but more of an ambassadorship, something to keep Iverson focused and engaged. Something to pass the time, beyond the dark insides of restaurant and hotel bars, until his pension kicked in. Moore, for whatever people may have thought about his supposed opportunity-seeking, still cared about the kid.

They rode the elevator to the lobby, about ten minutes to five, more than two hours before tip-off—and long before Iverson would have left years earlier. Outside a car was waiting, and on the walk through the lobby Iverson did not say much. Then a couple in their early sixties passed, the woman's brown scarf falling to the floor without her noticing. Iverson saw it and turned. "Excuse me," he called toward the woman, picking up the scarf and extending it toward her. "You dropped this." She thanked him, seemingly unaware of whom she had just encountered, and boarded the elevator. Iverson and Moore walked toward the doors and climbed inside the idling car, heading toward the arena.

Before the game, there was a buzz surrounding the arena, inside and out. Interstate 95 was dotted with digital billboards showing a screaming Iverson, and inside the arena fans herded past iconic photos of Iverson, hung above section entryways and throughout the concourse, and pushed their way toward a display of Iverson's jerseys through the years, his classic number three flanking his ten All-Star jerseys: from his first appearance in 2000, the 2002 jersey when he honored Julius Erving by wearing number six, the final one he never wore from 2010. Famous faces from Philadelphia's past were in attendance, Erving and Moses Malone, and current players wore a red, white, and blue patch on their jerseys, Iverson's name and the number three stitched in blue thread, along with SIXER FOREVER.

As the first half wound down, Iverson made his way toward the tunnel. A single folding chair was placed at center court. Luminaries took their places on the floor, and public address announcer Matt Cord dusted off his old introduction for Iverson. The lights lowered, a video began showing highlights—the crossovers against Michael Jordan and Tyronn Lue, steals and lightning-quick fast breaks, smiling and celebrating with teammates after winning the Eastern Conference finals in 2001—the kinds of images that, on the surface, had come to define his very existence.

Then, as the video played and the arena hummed and the crowd waited, Skylar Grey's soft, somber voice traveled through the speakers, kicking off Diddy's "Dirty Money" and providing an eerily appropriate introduction.

I'm coming home
Tell the world I'm coming home
Let the rain wash away all the pain of yesterday
I know my kingdom awaits and they've forgiven my mistakes

He emerged, cord introducing him once more, and in that moment it made sense why this came to be such a place of comfort: Here, inside the arena, the cheers drowning the sound of all else, no one cared about what Iverson did off the court. The lights were too bright, the sounds too loud to notice anything else, and when it all stopped, whether for a day or season or his entire career, Iverson could not help but chase this high down much darker alleys. Here he could not be judged. Here he could not be disagreed with or told no. Here he was an innovator, an icon, a man in control.

Now he was a face from the past, a symbol of a bygone era like those he once ushered out. On this night they chanted—"MVP! MVP! MVP!"—and Iverson made his way down a receiving line, Ann Iverson wearing her trademark Sixers jersey and blinding red lipstick, Pat Croce smiling through that graying goatee, former teammates slapping Iverson's hand as the show was about to begin. He sat and listened to the tributes, a recording from Larry Brown and an address from NBA commissioner Adam Silver, and then it was his turn. Iverson stood behind a microphone, taking a moment to gather his thoughts, and spoke. He rambled, his lip quivering, and stepped away. "Let me see if I'm dreaming," he said, walking to a corner and cupping his hand around an ear like he used to, pausing so that the tears would not come. He began issuing more thanks: to fans, the late sportswriter Phil Jasner, to his high school and college coaches, Mike Bailey and John Thompson, to anyone who had been there for him.

Then, the flood of tears returning, he thanked Tawanna.

• • •

IVERSON STOOD WITH three of his children as the red Sixers banner was raised to the rafters. As the ceremony closed, he kept staring at it. The lights came up, and Iverson was presented with a fishing boat named *The Answer*, and then he was led to a news conference. He was thankful. He was reflective.

"It's basically bittersweet," he said. "It feels good, but some part of my heart hurts because I realize and understand that it's over. Those situations right when I'm coming into the arena, you know, I'm stepping out on the basketball court with street clothes on, and I know I'll never be in a uniform again.

"You know it brings it back, but it kind of hurts still. It's hard for me. I'm a basketball fan, but it's hard for me. I can watch basketball, but it's hard for me to watch the Sixers play. You know what I mean? I can watch another team, another organization, whatever. It's different when I walk in here because it feels like just yesterday that I was trying to entertain these fans."

Then he turned his attention toward the future.

"I have a story, you know what I mean?" he said. "And my story wasn't, 'Okay, you make it to the NBA, then everything is peaches and cream all the way through. No mistakes, nothing. A perfect life.' Well, I didn't have that, and I didn't have that before I reached the NBA. And I have a lot of stories and things that I've been through in my life to be able to share it with young kids."

When the questions stopped, Iverson gathered his three youngest children, holding Messiah in his arms as he climbed down from the platform. Then it was over. Iverson was gone, disappearing back into the night and away from the arena. Those who cared for him spoke occasionally with him during the subsequent months, and they liked what they heard. They told themselves he was staying away from alcohol, spending more time with his children, trying even to make peace—if not work things out one more time—with Tawanna. "He ain't going nowhere, and she ain't going nowhere. Let's put it like that," said Aaron McKie, Iverson's friend and former Sixers teammate. Iverson told friends that he vowed to work things out with his ex-wife, but like his promise to resume his basketball career, many of those friends wrote it off as a futile effort. Tawanna, they knew, was never coming back, the same as Iverson would never again play in the NBA. They wanted to tell him to get over it, move on, but they knew that that was never how it was with Iverson. He would be the last to accept reality, for better or worse.

Iverson was a man who reveled in familiarity, and Tawanna had been at his side since they were both sixteen, just two kids with hopes and dreams and curious hands, making promises about forever. She grew up, and he never did; Tawanna raised their children and paid the bills, and Iverson concerned himself with only his next game, his next drink, the next roll of the dice on his favorite Dallas Cowboys Monopoly board. For a while, Iverson stopped paying the court-ordered $8,000 in monthly child support, assuming he and Tawanna would reconcile. She saw it much differently, though, eventually taking Iverson back to court, where Iverson was threatened with jail time if he did not hand over $40,000 in overdue payments.

"The things he'll say right now are that I want my wife back," Que Gaskins, the Reebok liaison who came to know Iverson as well as anyone, said. " 'I want to get Tawanna back. She's the most important thing to me,' blah blah. Being with the kids and having the family back is, in his mind, the most important. He'll say that he's good with not being able to play ball, but I know."

REGARDLESS, FOR THE first time in months, maybe even years, people close with Iverson smiled when they spoke of him. Brown walked through airports and struck up conversations with young players. Some of them wore cornrows or an elbow sleeve. Others asked Brown how to perform the crossover. Regardless, it made Brown happy to talk about a player who, years earlier, had driven him so crazy.

Brown spoke occasionally with Iverson, who regardless of his motivations did appear at Southern Methodist University and did address Brown's team. That was a start, and it gave hope to those like Brown: Maybe the athlete who had for so many years electrified crowds, defying the odds and his own physical limits, had one more comeback in him yet—this time in his personal life. Iverson's name had not been in the news or on the gossip sites, and to them, that was a good thing. He attended the *Iverson* documentary premiere alongside Moore in New York City, scheduled events throughout the summer, and planned for a November 2014 trip to the Philippines to coach a celebrity team for charity. He left Atlanta after the house on West Paces Ferry Road fell into foreclosure and was sold at auction, and split most of his time between Hampton, Virginia, and Charlotte, North Carolina, where he spent months living in a hotel near a shopping district. He returned to Atlanta only to see his children, starting an Instagram account to keep tabs on his kids but then giving it up when Deuce made his account private. Iverson checked Twitter sometimes, retweeting photographs and a few fans' favorite memories. He seemed especially engaged in August 2014, when the St. Louis, Missouri, suburb of Ferguson was split racially after a white police officer shot and killed a young black man—a city divided against itself as Hampton had once been.

Moore, who also had access to Iverson's account, sent most of Iverson's tweets for him, usually to promote business ventures to the hundreds of thousands who followed Iverson and still hung on his every word. Iverson joked sometimes that Moore was now the rich one; look at his house in Suffolk, Virginia, compared with the way Iverson was living. He would not turn his back on Moore, though, because now the tables were turned: Iverson had once been Moore's greatest source of income; now Iverson leaned on Moore and his connections to get by.

He still struggled financially, but he found ways to make ends meet. Reebok releases an Iverson sneaker each year, now considered a "legacy" collection, and although most every dollar of his annual stipend is accounted for, Iverson is also paid to occasionally make appearances at nightclubs. He appeared the week of the jersey retirement at Mitchell & Ness, a sporting goods store in Philadelphia, posing for photographs in front of a banner advertising Moore Management & Entertainment. A friend started an eBay store called "Iverson Authentic," selling what was left of the game-used memorabilia—leftovers from the storage unit, after it auctioned Iverson's belongings after numerous unpaid bills. As far as friends heard, he was honoring his commitments, thinking about a future of public speaking or game analysis or art, going months between stops at P.F. Chang's.

Yes, they told themselves as they did so many times, Iverson had finally changed. He had outgrown his bad habits. He was better now, his demons chased away once and for all, closure coming on that cold night in early March. This made it easier to remember him the way they saw him then: on a basketball floor in Philadelphia, smiling and staring up at that banner with his kids surrounding him, his eyes open with wonder like a child watching the night sky.

It was a comforting image, and for the time being it allowed them to forget that, time and again with Iverson, one uplifting scene—no matter how positive—was usually followed soon after by a disappointing one.

IVERSON WALKED DOWN an access road on Georgetown's campus in early September 2014, the sun hitting his shoulders and a frail right arm wrapped around his back. He walked slowly. So did the group that trailed them.

Georgetown was breaking ground on a new $62 million basketball facility, and among those scheduled to lift a shovel would be Thompson, Iverson's old college coach and father figure, and the man the new building would be named for. High-powered donors and well-known luminaries crowded under a tent, and a little after ten that morning, there was Thompson himself, Iverson flanking him—and Lorry Michel, the program's longtime athletic trainer, holding on to Iverson for support.

Michel had been diagnosed three years earlier with a brain tumor, undergoing surgery and somehow fighting off the disease. Her refusal to give up despite the long odds—she continued to refuse doctors' offer for a prognosis—was one of the things Iverson loved about her, along with her penchant for honesty and tough love. Still, she was thin and weak, and on this morning, Iverson was her support beam.

They reached the tent's entryway, Iverson sipping bottled water and dressed neatly in a light blue dress shirt with the sleeves rolled up, dark jeans, and an ivy cap. He wore a thin do-rag beneath the cap, the tails of fresh braids peeking out from the bottom. It was a morning, a celebration, an optional activity that Iverson could easily have blown off—but he was here, and he looked good, no other way to put it. His eyes were clear, his speech was sharp, his posture strong. As the group made its way through the checkpoint, Thompson, still hulking at age seventy-three, dropped a hand on Iverson's shoulder and looked down into his eyes, the way he had done nearly two decades earlier, and smiled the way a father would.

Iverson moved forward, swallowed by a crowd eager to visit with him. Dikembe Mutombo was there, along with Patrick Ewing and Alonzo Mourning. David Falk, Iverson's first NBA agent, mingled and said hello to familiar faces. It was a reunion, and Iverson was once again in the spotlight, showing the caring and charming side that endeared him to so many. He would slap hands with the rich and famous, wrapping old friends in hugs, and then he would sit in the front row as Thompson and other university officials stood in a line and pierced the earth.

But for now, Iverson was a few steps ahead of Michel, the crowd enveloping her, and when Iverson realized she was gone, he stopped and turned around. "Where Miss Michel at?" he said, his eyes scanning the faces.

Then she raised her hand and smiled, getting Iverson's attention.

Looking relieved, he walked back toward her and wrapped an arm around her waist, and before they took another step, she leaned toward him and kissed him on the cheek.

THEY TRIED TO hold on to images like that. Iverson was caring and thoughtful, and this was enough to help them believe that, in the fight for Iverson's soul, good still had a chance. The point was not that he was one or the other: a friend or a headache, a caring family man or an overgrown child without regard for responsibility, an astonishing success or a man who lost it all. He was both, and images like the morning in Georgetown were the ones they wanted to remember, because those were the ones that pushed back loudly against the ones that reached them via whisper.

In the summer of 2014, Iverson and Moore repeatedly promoted "Camp Crossover," Iverson's youth basketball camp, on Twitter. The four-day event would be held in July, and the flier encouraged fans to pay $225 each to "learn from One of the Best NBA players EVER!" The event, which was moved a week earlier from one school in suburban Atlanta to another, would teach youngsters five to fourteen years old the finer points of the game. But more than that, Iverson would meet and interact with kids who still idolized him—a new generation of players who, with a little guidance, might be a college or pro superstar of tomorrow.

"AI along with other high quality coaches and counselors will work with your camper," said a document distributed to one parent who paid for his son to attend, "in regards to all aspects of basketball. Come learn the infamous, crossover dribble, which put legendary Michael Jordan on his heels many of times."

About a dozen youngsters signed up for the camp, their entry fees paid, and each morning at nine, the day began at Hopewell Middle School in Milton, Georgia. The kids underwent instruction and coaching, sure, but as the hours passed, there was no sign of Iverson. Each afternoon the counselors offered reasons why Iverson had not made it. Tomorrow, they told the kids, would be different; bring whatever you would like Iverson to autograph, because they had assurances that he would be there the following day. On the camp's final morning, the kids carried basketballs and hats and jerseys, their young faces eager to meet their hero. Morning turned to afternoon, no promise of another session tomorrow, and eventually it was time to go home. Iverson never stepped into the Hopewell gym, no-showing his own basketball camp and blowing off a group of young and hopeful children, their parents livid and demanding to know exactly what they had paid for. The instructors had no choice but to come clean now: They had not been able to find Iverson, the parents were told, and he had not returned their own calls in more than a week.

A day later, he was advertised to attend a charity basketball game at a small university outside Philadelphia. Iverson had been the top-billed celebrity scheduled to help raise money for Philadelphia Eagles running back LeSean McCoy's foundation, which channels funds toward research and awareness of amyotrophic lateral sclerosis, also known as Lou Gehrig's disease. The disease had taken the life of McCoy's grandmother, and during the days before, McCoy appeared on television and conducted interviews to discuss the importance of his charity basketball game. He promoted the names of several stars expected to attend, singling out Iverson because he hoped the day would include a showdown between McCoy and one of Philadelphia's most iconic athletes.

But the event, like the youth camp, came and went, no sign of Iverson, McCoy and the crowd left to wait for a ghost. Iverson had made it only as far as the Embassy Suites in Hampton, the city on the Virginia coast where it all started, and spent his Saturday afternoon at the bar.

ACKNOWLEDGMENTS

On that perfect September morning at Georgetown, Iverson snaked his way through the check-in line, careful to keep an eye on and an arm around Lorry Michel, the ailing former trainer for the Hoyas. As famous and powerful people milled about, Iverson took a seat in the front row next to Michel, who made small talk with a former colleague.

After more than a year of research, dozens upon dozens of interviews, this—maybe thirty feet away—was as close as I had physically been to Iverson. I had tracked him to Philadelphia and Atlanta, spending six hours one summer evening at the P.F. Chang's at Cumberland Mall that I knew he hung out at. To Hampton, to Dallas, even to Istanbul—trying, as I followed in Iverson's footsteps, to cross paths with him somewhere along the way. Gary Moore and others had, depending on their place along the orbit of Planet Iverson, either considered connecting us or promised to put me in touch with someone who pushed me one step closer to a man who, by all accounts, didn't want to be found. The leads eventually went cold, and Moore, the most promising of them, stopped responding to my emails and calls.

Even so deep into the process, I simply had no idea what Iverson really knew about a project that would show him at his most naked and vulnerable. I felt I owed it to him to offer the chance to explain his triumphs and shortcomings in his own words, unlikely as this was. For a man so at home inside a swell of people, Iverson is uncomfortable with strangers, particularly in a one-on-one setting—and above all with unfamiliar reporters. I assumed my chances for that long, introspective sit-down were doubtful. Still, failing a full-on interview, I wanted him to at least know from me that this was being written, to face him and allow him to say or do whatever he felt was appropriate.

So here he was, sitting as close to alone as a man can be inside a crowd. I stood at the edge of the outdoor tent and jotted my name and phone number on a sheet of notebook paper, ripping it from the coils. I knew this was my chance and that the clock was ticking.

I hurried over, taking the empty seat next to Iverson.

"Hello, Allen," I began. "I know this isn't the time . . ."

"*Definitely* isn't the time," Iverson said, seeing my notebook, cutting me off but doing it almost playfully. I figured he thought I hoped to interview him about Georgetown's new building.

"But I'm the one who's writing the book about you," I continued. "I don't know what you've heard, but I have spoken with Gary a number of times. I just wanted you to hear it from me."

I offered him the page from my notebook, telling him that I was writing about every part of his life. "Please call me any time, day or night, if you would like to share your version of anything. In the meantime, enjoy the day."

"Thanks, bro," Iverson said in the most sincere and appreciative way, pushing the paper into his pocket as another, more famous face greeted him. I saw, even in those brief moments, the best of Iverson: He was sharp, friendly, charming, and charismatic. A friend of Iverson's joked later that I was lucky to have caught him on a good day. But the days and weeks passed, and he never called. I told myself that was okay; that I had at least given him the opportunity and told him to his face. Some old acquaintances and friends, such as Que Gaskins, speculated that Iverson might not have been at a point in his life that he was comfortable discussing the things that built him into an icon or the factors that came to ruin him. The wound of losing so much of his identity remains open and raw. Anyway, I wish he had talked to me. As thorough as I tried to be, forming a portrait of Iverson through more than six hundred pages of court records, dozens of interviews, and hundreds of news accounts, Iverson's own voice and his version of these events—no matter what he might have said or how he might have said it—represent a hole in the story. It is necessary that I acknowledge that here.

Another is that there is just zero chance this book could have happened without a great many wonderful people offering big ideas, small favors, phone numbers or email addresses, their time or their gas or their spare bedroom, their creativity and patience, or just an ear to listen to me blather on yet again about Allen Iverson.

The first is my agent, the wonderful Dawn Michelle Hardy at Serendipity Literary Agency. She had a vision for this project long before I was able to see it. She read my *Washington Post* profile of Iverson in April 2013 and just refused to let me say no to her about expanding the story into a book, a kind of determination I came to admire a great deal. She always tells me not to say this, and I recognize that it is not this way with most projects, but Dawn and Regina Brooks, Serendipity's president, made this process so incredibly easy for me, which is about the best thing I could say about those shepherding a first-time author through the process.

Todd Hunter, the talented and eternally optimistic editor at Atria Books, allowed me a behind-the-scenes view for all parts of this surprisingly mysterious process of putting together a book. These were things that he didn't have to do, but I'm grateful that he did.

One of the most essential people to this process was Avery Wilks, a new friend and—by the time this is published—a graduate of the University of South Carolina's journalism program, my own alma mater. Avery has become a young man I trust a great deal, but in the earliest days of this project, he was a stranger whom Doug Fisher, a favorite former professor of mine, recommended to, of all dreadful tasks, transcribe the interviews I had conducted. For about nine months, this poor college student would listen to hours of my sniffing and stuttering, repetitive questions about the same damn subject, day after day, file after file. He balanced school and a part-time job, along with an internship for a few of those months, and never complained about it. He claimed to even enjoy it at times. Anyway, I eventually sent him early drafts of each chapter, and he proved himself as an editor beyond his years and experience level. I eventually found myself unable to move on to the next chapter until Avery had given the previous one his check mark, because the kid has some serious, real-world storytelling chops. If you are the type of person who works at a newspaper, magazine, or website and has the ability to hire or influence personnel decisions, you should hire Avery, or get in line to hire him, because he has an incredible mix of talent, thoroughness, and an unwillingness to allow an imperfect product to pass peacefully through his universe.

This book could have never happened, at least for me, if in early 2013 I had not been assigned a story that was frustrating and rewarding, sometimes on the same day. But it was the persistence of Matt Vita, my editor at the *Post*, and the idea of Kevin Merida, one of the managing editors at the greatest journalism newspaper in America, that made the piece happen. Matt also took an enormous leap of faith on me, still a relatively new hire on the sports department's enterprise team, and allowed me to chase this insane book project with equal parts of encouragement and the occasional reminder that I had better not forget who my daddy is.

Greg Schimmel, a colleague of mine at the *Post*, somehow conjured up the world's most perfect headline for a story about Allen Iverson—"Not a Game"—which, I confess, I did not even attempt to top when considering a book title. As long as Schimmel and I are in the same juke joint, his first Corona will forever go on my tab.

The number of on-the-record interviews for this book came to around a hundred, and I am grateful for the time that each of them spent with me, sometimes recounting the most mundane story or ridiculous detail—in a few cases multiple times. Some of them fielded several calls, at least never letting me hear their annoyance, and here is a special thank-you to folks like Aaron McKie, Larry Brown, Que Gaskins, Butch Harper, George Lynch, Mike Bailey, and Dennis Kozlowski.

In a strange way, I also appreciate those who refused to discuss Iverson with me. Through these mostly polite rejections, I came to understand how protective they are of Iverson and how they still care for him, even after he has mostly self-destructed over the past few years and, in a few cases, either deliberately or thoughtlessly burned some of them. They thought they were doing Iverson a solid by keeping their thoughts and opinions to themselves, and maybe they are correct. At any rate, I respected their decisions, and it enlightened me on Iverson's effect on people.

Tzvi Twersky, the ridiculously in-the-know writer and editor for *SLAM* magazine, among other publications, was of particular help. Again and again, I went to Tzvi for advice about sources and their credibility, running ideas past him and hitting him up for contacts and the best way to get a particular source to talk. Tzvi is so knowledgeable about all things hoop that talking with him made me feel like, no matter how deeply I felt I had dug, I was nowhere near the nerve of the thing. He was, probably without realizing it and considering how nice he is, like a personal trainer: Keep pushing, keep calling, keep chasing the story down alleys until you have it cornered. He did all this with nothing in it for him, other than the exposition of truth, and for this I am very thankful.

Gordie Jones, the veteran Philadelphia sportswriter, was a wonderful resource of institutional knowledge and strategy; the wonderful thing about journalists is that, if we believe in your cause, we offer assistance and ask few questions. It is, as a friend of mine has put it, our tribe, and Gordie exemplified this by checking in periodically and offering a laptop bag packed with Iverson-related information that he had collected over the years.

I am lucky to be surrounded on a regular basis by an amazing group of mega-talented friends who happen to be journalists, or are they journalists who happen to be friends? Regardless, thanks to those who offered phone numbers or read chapters, who made suggestions on how to make this process even the slightest bit easier, or those who just listened to me think out loud or whine or celebrate, including Jon Styf, Todd Adams, Baxter Holmes, Rick Maese, Sam Mellinger, Benjamin Hochman, Michael Lee, Barry Svrluga, Rustin Dodd, Alex Prewitt, Mark Giannotto, Dan Wetzel, Dave Sheinin, Sally Jenkins, Chris Jones, Jason Whitlock, Kevin Van Valkenburg, Eli Saslow, Keith McMillan, Chris Fickett, Zach Berman, Chris Richards, Matt Bonesteel, Brendan Prunty, Jeff Passan, Brett Dawson, Lindsay Jones, Greg Bishop, Gerry Ahern, James Wagner, Mike Szvetitz, Nick Mathews, Izzy Gould, Gene Wang, David Meeks, Joe Person, Mike Wise, Mike Fannin, Seth Wickersham, John Niyo, Mike Jones, Nathan Fenno, Josh du Lac, Isabelle Khurshudyan, and Peter Schrager.

David Teel, the venerable *Newport News Daily Press* sports columnist, offered advice and a model of fairness and objectivity that I tried like hell to emulate. Teel is what so many reporters hope to be: balanced and nonjudgmental, meticulous and thoughtful. The people of Hampton Roads are very lucky to read him in their local paper. I read so many stories about Iverson, and after a while they mostly began to run together. There were exceptions, and running across the lyrical, thorough reporting of Teel, David Nakamura, J. A. Adande, Gary Smith, and Bill Brubaker became milepost reminders during a long, difficult hike to stop every once in a while and enjoy the view.

Thanks to Jason Wolf, the talented Philadelphia-based writer, who chauffeured me around his city one May afternoon and offered a puzzled look but no resistance when I insisted that we eat lunch at the T.G.I. Friday's on City Line Avenue; to Todd Adams for keeping me company during those six hours at the P.F. Chang's bar in Atlanta and for at least pretending to share my frustration that, in 2014, the lack of wireless Internet—at a *fishing shack*—is as suitable a reason as any for a temper tantrum; to Herman Hudson at Southern Methodist University for the next-to-impossible task of keeping Larry Brown organized and on schedule; to Nicholas Cotten in the Fulton County Superior Court's office of the clerk; and to my great friends Cam and Amanda Haggerty, who offered their most posh guest room for my trips to Dallas. Further appreciation goes to Bailey and Artie, my four-legged writing partners, for their support and the occasionally necessary distraction, and for the surplus of encouragement from my family—love and thanks to those who know who they are.

We remember the endings of movies and the fourth-quarter shots that either fall through the net or bounce off the iron, because it's the end of things we hold most precious. Which is why, here at the end, I thank Whitney, my beautiful, patient, understanding wife, who was supportive even as the nights at the computer grew longer and the pile of highlighted papers in the dining room grew and spread.

There were times during this process that I identified with Iverson, who like me came from humble beginnings, pursued success and validation in his own way, and married his high school sweetheart. Like Iverson, I am often gruff/focused, impatient/determined, and stubborn/confident; I have my manner of doing things, and in my mind, that sometimes must be allowed to be that. But there were times that I simply could not make sense of him, and although I am certain that there is more to the story than even these hundreds of pages have described, how he took Tawanna for granted and ultimately pushed her away was the most disappointing thing to me. And if I had to guess, for him, too. It was a cautionary tale and forced me to take stock sometimes and appreciate that no matter where the road takes me, the best place in the world isn't in the spotlight or at the bar or out with the fellas; it's at home, a few inches away from the one person in the world who understands me, or is patient enough, anyway, to try.